The Chivalric World of *Don Quijote*

The Chivalric World of *Don Quijote*
Style, Structure, and Narrative Technique

Howard Mancing

University of Missouri Press
Columbia & London
1982

Library of Congress Cataloging in Publication Data

Mancing, Howard, 1941–
    The Chivalric World of *Don Quijote*.

    Bibliography: p. 226
    Includes index.
    1. Cervantes Saavedra, Miguel de, 1547–1616.
Don Quixote. 2. Cervantes Saavedra, Miguel de,
1547–1616—Knowledge—Manners and customs.
3. Chivalry in literature. I. Title.
PQ6358.C54M3   ·863′.3   81–10475
ISBN 0–8262–0350–7   AACR2

For Enrique and Celia Paternain

Imagino que no sin misterio nos
   ha juntado aquí la suerte, y
   pienso que habemos de ser, de
   éste hasta el último día de
   nuestra vida, verdaderos
   amigos (*Rinconete y Cortadillo*)

Preface

The direction of my academic and professional career was suddenly changed when as a graduate student at the University of Florida I took a course on *Don Quijote*. The class was, first of all, brilliantly taught by John J. Allen, whose presentation of that greatest of novels has served as a model for my own *Don Quijote* course given at the University of Missouri–Columbia. More important still was the intellectual and aesthetic experience of responding to great literary art with a depth of feeling I had never before known (which I credit to Cervantes more than to Allen). Finally, and most directly related to the work at hand, while in that class I wrote a research paper (long since mercifully lost) on the topic of the archaisms frequently characteristic of Don Quijote's speech. My doctoral dissertation, completed in 1970, was titled "Chivalric Language and Style in *Don Quijote*" and represented an effort to expand that original research paper into a larger format, still with an emphasis on archaism as a hallmark of Don Quijote's chivalric style.

Since 1970, I have attempted, both in my *Don Quijote* classes and in a series of short publications (some revised and expanded chapters of the dissertation), to move toward a more precise description of the nature and role of archaism and of other matters relating to chivalry and to Don Quijote's concept of his chivalric world. I am now prepared to offer an extended study of that chivalric world.

The first draft of most of this book was written during a sabbatical leave while I was living in Madrid. I gratefully acknowledge the financial assistance provided by the Research Council of the University of Missouri, which helped to defray expenses for travel and typing. I also wish to extend my most sincere thanks to all those who helped to make this book possible: Jay

Allen, who personally and through his published works has influenced me more than I can ever recognize, and who read and offered valuable advice on large parts of my manuscript; my colleague Harold Jones, one of the best and most demanding critical readers I know, who read with great patience and criticized with great insight drafts of the entire work both in Madrid and at home; my colleagues and friends Vern Williamsen, Ben Honeycutt, Ed Mullen, and Bernard Flam, who also read all or parts of the manuscript and made valuable recommendations at various stages; the many students whose skeptical reactions to my drawings on the blackboard and to discussions of strange-looking graphs of Don Quijote's archaic speeches forced me to be ever more precise in my presentations; various persons (particularly Helena Percas de Ponseti) who offered oral and written comments on papers based on various sections of this work that I read at the Fordham Cervantes conference, December 1977; the I Congreso Internacional sobre Cervantes, Madrid, 1978; and the VII Congreso de la Asociación Internacional de Hispanistas, Venice, 1980; Wayne Hines, my research assistant; and Barbara Blunt, who managed to read my frequently labyrinthine revised manuscript and to type the final version.

Finally, of course, I must thank my wife, Nancy, who has provided the love, inspiration, and stability without which I could not have gone on, and my daughters, Catherine and Christina, for whom "Not now; Daddy is in his study room" became a way of life for two years.

A note on the text: It has been my aim to make this book accessible to readers who do not know Spanish as well as to Hispanic scholars. Therefore, I have provided English versions of the many obligatory citations from Cervantes's Spanish text. The Spanish quotations are from Martín de Riquer's edition, published by Planeta in 1975. The English translation that I used is the recently published Norton Critical Edition, which presents the classic Ormsby translation, revised by Joseph R. Jones and Kenneth Douglas, together with some background and critical material useful to the nonspecialist. This approximation of the original text is no more inadequate than any other translation (see Chapter 1, note 35), but readers who cannot refer to the Spanish text must always be aware of allusions and subtleties that are lost.

On those occasions when I cite other literary works (*Amadís de Gaula*, Alonso Fernández de Avellaneda's apocryphal *Don Quijote*, *I promessi sposi*, and so on), I use the same procedure and include the English translation after the original text. Whenever possible, I have used essays and critical works (by Salvador de Madariaga, Miguel de Unamuno, Michel Foucault, and so on) in their English versions. I have attempted to keep direct citations from critics in languages other than English to a minimum; when I have felt it necessary to incorporate their words into my text or notes (for example, Juan Bautista Avalle-Arce, Martín de Riquer, Luis Rosales), I have also provided my own translation. I hope that no reader will be seriously inconvenienced by these procedures.

H. M.
Columbia, Mo.
12 May 1981

Contents

Preface, vii
Introduction, 1

Part I: *El Ingenioso Hidalgo*
    don Quijote de la Mancha, 7

Chapter 1: Knighthood Exalted, 9
    1.1. The Life of Alonso Quijano el Bueno, 9
    1.2. Chivalric Archaism, 13
    1.3. The Romances of Chivalry, 22
    1.4. The Rhetoric of Chivalry, 27
    1.5. Chapters 2–5: The First Sally, 37
    1.6. Chapters 7–10: The Second Sally, 45

Chapter 2: Knighthood Compromised, 49
    2.1. Sancho Panza: Reality, 49
    2.2. Chapters 11–14: A Pastoral Interlude, 54
    2.3. Rocinante, 57
    2.4. Chapters 15–22: Chivalric Adventures, 62
    2.5. Sancho Panza: Chivalry, 72
    2.6. Chapters 23–28: In the Sierra Morena, 81

Chapter 3: Knighthood Defeated, 85
    3.1. Chapters 29–31: Princess Micomicona, 85
    3.2. The Priest, the Barber, and Dorotea, 90

3.3. Chapters 32–46: At the Inn, 97
3.4. Chapters 47–52: The Return Home, 103
3.5. The Pattern of Adventure, 112
3.6. The Critics and Part I, 118

Part II: *Segunda Parte del Ingenioso Caballero
don Quijote de la Mancha,* 127

Chapter 4: Knighthood Imposed, 129
4.1. The Rhetoric of Pseudochivalry, 129
4.2. Chapters 1–7: The Third Sally, 133
4.3. Chapters 8–29: Pseudoadventures, 137
4.4. Chapters 30–57: With the Duke and Duchess, 154
4.5. Chapters 58–73: To Barcelona and Back, 160

Chapter 5: Knighthood Denied, 167
5.1. The Pattern of Pseudoadventure, 167
5.2. Sancho Panza: Triumph, 171
5.3. Sansón Carrasco et al., 182
5.4. Miguel de Cervantes versus
Cide Hamete Benengeli, 192
5.5. The Death of Alonso Quijano el Bueno, 210

Appendix A: Chivalric Archaism, 217
Appendix B: Chivalric Motifs, 220
Bibliography, 226
Index, 235

Introduction

In order to understand Don Quijote, it is necessary to appreciate his concept of himself as a knight-errant in imitation of the literary heroes of the sixteenth-century romances of chivalry, especially *Amadís de Gaula*. The reader of Cervantes's novel should bear in mind that the world in which Don Quijote lives is a world of chivalry. The purpose of this book is to examine the characters, style, themes, structure, and narrative technique of that chivalric world. I hope to show, among other things, that Don Quijote begins to retreat from his chivalric fantasy and to reach an accord with reality in part I of the novel rather than in part II as is generally believed; that Sancho Panza both undermines and sustains his master's fantasy from the start; that the priest and the barber are not, as first presented, Don Quijote's friends, but rather his greatest enemies; and that Cide Hamete Benengeli becomes increasingly unreliable as a narrator and increasingly comic as a character in the second part of the novel.

My first chapter, "Knighthood Exalted," consists of a close examination of the first ten chapters of part I of Cervantes's novel and of the literary and theoretical background for the protagonist's choice of chivalry as a career. I begin with a description of the life and times of Alonso Quijano el Bueno, who finds his existence so unacceptable that he makes the radical decision to sally forth in search of adventure as a knight-errant (section 1.1). As preparation for following the knight's career, the archaic style and the rhetoric of chivalry that play a prominent role throughout the novel are examined carefully (sections 1.2, 1.3, and 1.4). The series of lists, charts, and graphs and the quantitative methodology of these sections provide a detailed documentation of the nature and distribution of the chivalric literary style in the novel. Next, Don Quijote's first sally and the beginning of his second sally are examined in detail (sections 1.5 and 1.6). Everything that Don Quijote says, does, and perceives in these early chapters is in strict accord with his fantastic vision of a world governed by chivalry. Subsequent sections of the novel are later compared with the standards established by this crucial beginning of the work.

My second chapter, "Knighthood Compromised," presents a study of the remainder of the first half of part I of *Don Quijote*. In this segment of the novel, Don Quijote retreats from his chivalric vision in many subtle but important ways. He must now attempt to cope with the reality of physical pain and with a distractingly nonchivalric squire, Sancho Panza (section 2.1). During the pastoral interlude centered around the burial of Grisóstomo, Don Quijote's knighthood is cast into a comparatively bad light by the words and deeds of several other characters (section 2.2). Even his horse Rocinante parodies Don Quijote's style and clichés (section 2.3). Each of the chivalric adventures in chapters 15–22 is undercut by minor but nagging concessions that must be made to nonchivalric reality (section 2.4). Don Quijote's withdrawal to the Sierra Morena provides further important evidence of the corruption of his chivalric world (section 2.6). Meanwhile, Sancho Panza has begun to master the rhetoric of chivalry and to integrate himself into his master's sphere (section 2.5). Overall, this section of the novel chronicles Don Quijote's decline in knightly stature according to his own ideals and presents the transition between his original dedication to chivalry and his inevitable defeat.

In Chapter 3, "Knighthood Defeated," I analyze the remainder of the first part of the novel, from chapter 29 to the end. The scene is now dominated by Don Quijote's so-called friends—the village priest, Pero Pérez; the barber, Maese Nicolás; and the discreet Dorotea and her company. These clever schemers and manipulators usurp Don Quijote's rhetoric of chivalry and his creativity, turning him into a mere pawn. They deceive him, lie to him, shunt him aside, and dehumanize him (sections 3.1–3.4). Though calling themselves his friends and rescuers, Pero Pérez and the others are Don Quijote's most formidable enemies, the real enchanters in his chivalric world, who use and abuse him for self-aggrandizement and for entertainment. Chapter 52 is especially important for its establishment of these characters' personalities and for its presentation of the absolute chivalric defeat of Don Quijote in his significant battle with the penitents. His recognition and acceptance of this defeat signal the end of his voluntary career as a knight-errant. Part I of Cervantes's novel thus traces a steadily descending trajectory in Don Quijote's chivalric career (section 3.5). Contrary to prevailing critical opinion, Don Quijote evolves significantly in part I and reaches a total accommodation with reality in this part of the novel (section 3.6).

Chapter 4, "Knighthood Imposed," begins with a brief discussion of the absence of chivalric archaism and rhetoric in part II (section 4.1) and then traces Don Quijote's progress as a reluctant knight-errant throughout the second part of the novel. Don Quijote does not choose to act as a knight-errant after his defeat in I, 52, but he cannot withstand the pressure of the priest, the barber, Sancho Panza, Rocinante, Sansón Carrasco, and, above all, the existence of *Don Quijote, Part I*, written by Cide Hamete Benengeli (section 4.2). Don Quijote's adventures throughout part II are more accurately described as pseudoadventures: a series of nonevents, shams, deceits, and unresolved pseudoconflicts. Don Quijote is incapable of responding to events as he had early in his career when he believed in his chivalric construct (section 4.3). The knight's stay at the palace of the duke and duchess represents the nadir of his career: at the same time that he is scorned and ridiculed, scratched and pinched, and generally ignored, he suffers envy and nostalgia and pines for his absent friend, Sancho Panza (section 4.4). In Barcelona and on the return to his village, Don Quijote undergoes further humiliation and ridicule; his second chivalric defeat, this time at the hands of his rival Sansón Carrasco, is thus less significant than was the one at the end of part I (section 4.5).

My last chapter, "Knighthood Denied," presents further considerations of several aspects discussed earlier and ends with an examination of Don Quijote's ultimate renunciation of his chivalric world. A final look at the structure of Don Quijote's chivalric trajectory reemphasizes the lack of validity that any concept of knighthood has after I, 52 (section 5.1). But if part II is the chronicle of Don Quijote's failure, it is also the story of Sancho Panza's triumph. At the end of the novel, Sancho returns home a wiser man. His surrender of his governorship serves as the symbolic capstone of his own quest for self-knowledge (section 5.2). Don Quijote's antagonists in part II—Sansón Carrasco, the duke, Don Antonio Moreno, and others—are consistently negative figures, even more hypocritical, self-serving, and insensitive than were Pero Pérez and company (section 5.3). Throughout part II, Cervantes calls the reader's attention to the narrative structure of the novel as he engages in a brilliant and highly original dialectic with his pseudohistorian-narrator, Cide Hamete Benengeli. If Don Quijote becomes more serious and sympathetic to the reader in the second part of the novel, Cide Hamete is put forth as a central comic figure, so that part II remains a supremely comic text, but with a radically different focus (section 5.4). Finally, Don Quijote's chivalric career having run its course, it is necessary to witness Alonso Quijano el Bueno's deathbed recantation of all that he stood for and did as Don Quijote. Alonso Quijano renounces and apologizes for his chivalric career in order to die as the friend of Pero Pérez and Sansón Carrasco (section 5.5).

The structure of *Don Quijote* is circular. The life and death of the conventional Alonso Quijano el Bueno, presented briefly in the first chapter of part I and in the last chapter of part II, serves as the frame for the story of Don Quijote, knight-errant. Don Quijote's career is one of the exaltation of knighthood at the beginning, with a significant period of compromise and concession in the first half of part I, and a diminished role ending in abject defeat at the end of the first part. In part II, Don Quijote is a reluctant knight, forced to suffer existentially in a role imposed upon him. The role of a knight-errant is one he no longer chooses but cannot refuse, a role that he eventually denies in his final act. Sancho Panza, Rocinante, Pero Pérez, Dorotea, Sansón Carrasco, the duke, and others in the chivalric world of Don Quijote are important in their own right as well as in comparison with the protagonist. They represent assimilation, self-knowledge, success, animalistic parody, envy, manipulation, derision, and self-gratification. Many of the reader's initial reactions are reversed: from laughter and ridicule to sympathy and pity for Don Quijote, from laughter and derision to respect and admiration for Sancho Panza, from respect and identification to scorn and disdain for the priest and the other defenders of society's norms, and from confidence and reliance to laughter and ridicule for Cide Hamete Benengeli. The chivalric world of Don Quijote is rich in great themes and dynamic characters, as well as in stylistic subtlety, structural complexity, and narrative innovation. It is a genial portrayal of human beings in action and tells a timeless story of failure and triumph.

Part I

El Ingenioso Hidalgo don Quijote de la Mancha

> Todo él es una invectiva contra
>   los libros de caballerías
>   (I, Prólogo, 17)

> (It is, from beginning to end, an attack upon the
>   books of chivalry, p. 13)

1

Knighthood Exalted

Le pareció convenible y necesario, así para el
aumento de su honra como para el servicio de su
república, hacerse caballero andante (I, 1, 36)

(He fancied it was right and requisite, no less for his
own greater renown than in the service of his country,
that he should make a knight-errant of himself, p. 27)

1.1 The Life of Alonso Quijano el Bueno

As Alonso Quijano[1] approached the age of fifty, sometime
early in the seventeenth century, he was living a reasonably
comfortable, modest life as a fairly typical *hidalgo* (member of
the lesser nobility) in a small village of La Mancha. He seemed,
by definition, to be a man who lived in harmony with his sur-
roundings and adjusted to his times.[2] He was financially well
enough off to support himself and his niece who lived with him
and to pay for the services of a housekeeper and a servant lad.
His residence, by no means luxurious, seems to have been at
least adequate and, moreover, was large enough that one room

---

1. In the early chapters of the novel, the protagonist's surname is
given as Quijada, Quesada, Quejana, or Quijana, a confusion that in
itself has a certain comic value. The name Quijano is suggested in the
last chapter of part II and thus seems definitive. At any rate, I have
chosen to use this name throughout.
2. Helena Percas de Ponseti, *Cervantes y su concepto del arte*, 1:27. But
see also Vicente Lloréns who, in his essay "Don Quijote y la decadencia
del hidalgo," has shown how by the late sixteenth century the Spanish
hidalgos were largely anachronistic, useless remnants of the late medieval period when the books of chivalry had comparative relevance; *Aspectos sociales de la literatura española*, pp. 58–65.

9

could be set aside to house an extraordinary library containing over a hundred volumes.[3] His holdings in land were probably not extensive, but he could from time to time sell parcels of land in order to purchase new books without bankrupting himself. Though reading was by far his favorite pastime, he also enjoyed hunting and visiting with friends, especially Pero Pérez, the local priest, and Maese Nicolás, the village barber.

These three men, in fact, were probably the village's intellectual elite. The priest, by virtue of his profession and his university degree, was perhaps the town's most prominent figure. Although he was a graduate of Sigüenza, a university of low esteem, Pero Pérez was probably one of the few inhabitants, if not the only one, who could claim such a distinction (at least until later in the novel, when young Sansón Carrasco returns home from Salamanca having just completed his bachelor's degree). The barber too was literate and clearly possessed the training necessary to fulfill his duties as a man of some professional standing (barbers at that time were expected to perform minor surgery as well as cut hair). The uneducated niece and household servants—indeed, the remainder of the community, which consisted primarily of farmers—must have looked on with a combination of pride and incomprehension whenever these three relatively distinguished gentlemen gathered to discuss literary matters or to argue over the merits of various fictional knights-errant. Furthermore, as we learn at the end of the novel, Quijano was held in such esteem by his friends and fellow townspeople that he was generally known as Alonso Quijano *el Bueno* ("the Good"). Most men of his type would have been prepared to enter their second half-century of existence content with life, but this particular *hidalgo* was an exception.

Alonso Quijano had always been an avid reader; there is evidence that he had some familiarity with classical literature, that

3. Later, when talking with Cardenio, Don Quijote makes the exaggerated claim that he owns "más de trecientos libros" ("more than three hundred books"); *Don Quijote*, ed. Martín de Riquer (1975), I, 24, 251. All references in Spanish in the text are to this edition and refer to part, chapter, and page as required by context. The English translations are from *Don Quixote*, trans. John Ormsby, ed. Joseph R. Jones and Kenneth Douglas; here p. 174.

he was reasonably well versed in history, that he was very familiar with the works of many Renaissance lyric, epic, and dramatic poets as well as with popular poetry, and that he knew intimately all the forms of prose fiction—chivalric, sentimental, pastoral, picaresque, Moorish—that were published in his day. But he had become increasingly captivated, even obsessed, by the romances of chivalry that had been the most popular type of prose fiction in sixteenth-century Spain.[4] He often considered becoming an author and writing a sequel to one of his favorite works, *Belianís de Grecia*, but he always postponed the task. He was obviously attracted by these books' artificial chivalric world where a man of courage and ability could gain honor and fame by sustaining right in the face of injustice and evil and could thereby win the admiration of other men and the love of a beautiful woman. His own life, in contrast, seemed not only commonplace but even useless and wasted.[5]

According to Juan Bautista Avalle-Arce, Alonso Quijano rejected his monotonous existence as a village *hidalguete* ("impecunious noble") to convert his life into "una obra de arte" ("a work of art").[6] Furthermore, had the ill-humored and aging Alonso Quijano never left home, it is unlikely that he would ever have been interesting enough to have a book written about his life.[7] The difference between Alonso Quijano and Don Quijote is that the former could lay claim to nothing greater than

4. Although it has traditionally been claimed that the vogue of the romances of chivalry had run its course by the mid-sixteenth century, it is the opinion of the most recent critics that they remained quite popular throughout the century. See Daniel Eisenberg, "Cervantes' *Don Quijote* Once Again: An Answer to J. J. Allen," p. 109; L. P. Harvey, "Oral Composition and the Performance of Novels of Chivalry in Spain," p. 279; and Maxime Chevalier, *Lectura y lectores en la España de los siglos XVI y XVII*, p. 66.

5. Compare Marthe Robert's description of the life of Alonso Quijano in *The Old and the New: From Don Quixote to Kafka*, p. 127.

6. Juan Bautista Avalle-Arce, *Don Quijote como forma de vida*, pp. 90, 147. Avalle-Arce, a major Cervantine scholar whose work has rarely been translated into English, has developed his idea of the life of Don Quijote as a work of art in several versions in different essays. Readers who do not know Spanish should consult "Vital and Artistic Structures in the Life of Don Quixote," pp. 104–21.

7. Avalle-Arce, *Forma de vida*, p. 30.

simply being (*ser*), while the latter chose to be worth something (*valer*).[8] Surely, there can be no question that, for the reader, Alonso Quijano—comfortable, conformist, hollow—merely exists,[9] while the life of Don Quijote is of great interest and value.

Thus, Alonso Quijano, frustrated and dissatisfied, existentially aware that "cada uno es hijo de sus obras" ("everyone is the son of his works") and that his own works were insufficient to justify his continued existence, escaped into madness and fantasy. He chose to break with conventional reality to discover a different and superior one, remaking himself and his world in the image of literature. He decided, in what is described as "el más extraño pensamiento que jamás dio loco en el mundo" ("the strangest notion that ever madman in this world hit upon"), to become a knight-errant:

> le pareció convenible y necesario, así para el aumento de su honra como para el servicio de su república, hacerse caballero andante, y irse por todo el mundo con sus armas y caballo a buscar las aventuras y a ejercitarse en todo aquello que él había leído que los caballeros andantes se ejercitaban, deshaciendo todo género de agravio, y poniéndose en ocasiones y peligros donde, acabándolos, cobrase eterno nombre y fama. (I, 1, 36)

> (He fancied it was right and requisite, no less for his own greater renown than in the service of his country, that he should make a knight-errant of himself, roaming the world over in full armor and on horseback in quest of adventures. He would put into practice all that he had read of as being the usual practices of knights-errant: righting every kind of wrong, and exposing himself to peril and danger from which he would emerge to reap eternal fame and glory.) (p. 27)

---

8. Ibid., p. 34.

9. Alonso Quijano's life can properly be described as idle (p. 34): "los ratos que estaba ocioso—que eran los más del año" ("his leisure (which was mostly all year round)," p. 25). This idleness is, for Cervantes, undoubtedly a negative characteristic and must be counted against Don Quijote. See Luis Pérez, "La ociosidad-muerte en el *Quijote*," pp. 355–62; and Guillermo Díaz-Plaja, *En torno a Cervantes*, pp. 170–74. The lives of his friends, the priest and the barber, are comparably nonproductive.

And so he collected his armor, chose a significant new name—
Don Quijote de la Mancha[10]—and prepared to sally forth in
quest of adventure and fame.

This "prehistory" of Don Quijote, which consists primarily
of a few paragraphs at the beginning of the first chapter of the
book, is important as background and motivation for his chivalric career. As Don Quijote again assumes the identity of
Alonso Quijano in the final pages of the last chapter of the
novel—the life and death of Alonso Quijano thus composing
the frame for the story of Don Quijote—it will eventually be
necessary to return to the modest Manchegan *hidalgo* in order to
complete this study.

1.2 Chivalric Archaism

A knight-errant lives according to a rigidly prescribed set of
standards; innovation is not his goal. Instead, as J. Huizinga
says, "the essence of chivalry is the imitation of the ideal hero."[11]
Therefore, one of Don Quijote's primary characteristics as a
knight-errant is his insistence on the imitation of models; for
Marthe Robert, "the most radical quixotic act . . . is never the
accomplishment of some personal ambition, but on the contrary, the imitation of an ideal fixed by tradition, indeed by literary convention, and consequently stripped of all originality."[12]
Don Quijote gives the idea its fullest and most eloquent expression during his penance in the Sierra Morena:

> Quiero, Sancho, que sepas que el famoso Amadís de Gaula
> fue uno de los más perfectos caballeros andantes. No he dicho
> bien *fue uno*: fue el solo, el primero, el único, el señor de todos

10. The multiple comic aspects of this name are important but not
pertinent here; see Howard Mancing, "The Comic Function of Chivalric Names in *Don Quijote*," pp. 221–22. More important is the symbolic
significance of any change in name in the Judeo-Christian tradition, for
example, Saul of Tarsus–Saint Paul; see Avalle-Arce, *Forma de vida*, p.
34, note 18.

11. J. Huizinga, *The Waning of the Middle Ages*, p. 39.

12. Robert, *Old and New*, p. 12. See also Edward C. Riley's essential
article on the subject, "Don Quixote and the Imitation of Models," pp.
3–16.

cuantos hubo en su tiempo en el mundo. Mal año y mal mes
para don Belianís y para todos aquellos que dijeren que se le
igualó en algo, porque se engañan, juro cierto. Digo asimismo
que, cuando algún pintor quiere salir famoso en su arte, procura imitar los originales de los más únicos pintores que sabe;
y esta mesma regla corre por todos los más oficios o ejercicios
de cuenta que sirven para adorno de las repúblicas, y así lo ha
de hacer y hace el que quiere alcanzar nombre de prudente y
sufrido, imitando a Ulises, en cuya persona y trabajos nos
pinta Homero un retrato vivo de prudencia y de sufrimiento,
como también nos mostró Virgilio, en persona de Eneas, el
valor de un hijo piadoso y la sagacidad de un valiente y entendido capitán, no pintándolo ni describiéndolo como ellos fueron, sino como habían de ser, para quedar ejemplo a los veni-
deros hombres de sus virtudes. Desta mesma suerte, Amadís
fue el norte, el lucero, el sol de los valientes y enamorados
caballeros, a quien debemos de imitar todos aquellos que debajo de la bandera de amor y de la caballería militamos.
Siendo, pues, esto ansí, como lo es, hallo yo, Sancho amigo,
que el caballero andante que más le imitare estará más cerca de
alcanzar la perfección de la caballería. (I, 25, 257–58)

(I would have you know, Sancho, that the famous Amadís of
Gaul was one of the most perfect knights-errant. I am wrong
to say he was *one*. He stood alone, the first, the only one, the
lord of all that were in the world in his time. A fig for Don
Belianís and for all who say he equaled him in any respect,
for, my oath upon it, they are deceiving themselves! I say, too,
that when a painter desires to become famous in his art, he
endeavors to copy the originals of the finest painters that he
knows. The same rule holds good for all the most important
crafts and callings that serve to adorn a state. Thus must he
who would be esteemed prudent and patient imitate Ulysses,
in whose person and labors Homer presents to us a lively picture of prudence and patience. Virgil, too, shows us in the
person of Aeneas the virtue of a dutiful son and the sagacity
of a brave and skilful captain. These are not represented or
described as they were, but as they ought to be, so as to leave
the example of their virtues to posterity. In the same way
Amadís was the pole star, day star, sun of valiant and devoted
knights, whom all we who fight under the banner of love and
chivalry are bound to imitate. This, then, being so, I consider,
friend Sancho, that the knight-errant who imitates him most

closely come[s] nearest to reaching the perfection of chivalry.)
(pp. 177–78)

To be a knight-errant, Don Quijote must not only act like a
knight (by righting wrongs, rescuing damsels in distress, and so
forth), he must also talk like a knight. The most prominent stylistic feature of Don Quijote's rhetoric of chivalry is its archaism
(see the next section). In order to sound like Amadís de Gaula
and other fictional knights-errant, Don Quijote employs a mod-
erately archaic vocabulary and several phonological and morphological forms that were no longer current in the Spanish language of the seventeenth century. Don Quijote's invocation of
Dulcinea del Toboso in chapter 2, the first time he employs an
archaism, can be used to illustrate his chivalric style.[13]

> ¡Oh princesa Dulcinea, señora deste *cautivo* corazón! Mucho
> agravio me *habedes fecho* en despedirme y reprocharme con el
> riguroso *afincamiento* de mandarme no parecer ante *la vuestra*
> *fermosura*. *Plégaos*, señora, de *membraros deste vuestro* sujeto co-
> razón, que tantas cuitas por vuestro amor padece. (p. 42)

> (O Princess Dulcinea, lady of this captive heart, a grievous
> wrong hast thou done to me to drive me forth with scorn,
> and with inexorable obduracy banish me from the presence of
> thy beauty. O lady, deign to hold in remembrance this heart,
> thy vassal, that thus in anguish pines for love of thee.) (p. 30)

The authorial comment immediately following these words is
significant: "Con éstos iba ensartando otros disparates, todos al
modo de los que sus libros le habían enseñado, *imitando en cuanto*
podía su lenguaje" (p. 42; my italics) ("So he went on stringing
together these and other absurdities, all of the sort his books had
taught him, *imitating their language as well as he could*," p. 30).
    The words and phrases italicized in the invocation to Dulcinea
were clearly archaic or obsolete in the early seventeenth century
and would immediately have been recognized as such by contemporary readers of the book. This archaism, however, is not

---

13. In order to call archaic forms and vocabulary to the reader's attention, I have italicized them in this and all subsequent passages. Since
the English equivalents generally carry no archaic connotations, I have
not italicized them in the translations.

readily apparent to twentieth-century readers; in fact, Martín de Riquer considers it the aspect of the novel's style most likely to be overlooked today.[14]

Don Quijote employs three major archaisms. The presence of even one of the three is a clear, automatic, and unmistakable sign of chivalric archaism and of a conscious imitation of the romances of chivalry. These three major archaisms are

1. *f-* for *h-* (*facer, fermoso, ferida,* and so on, for *hacer, her-*

14. "En la ironía de la prosa del *Quijote*, el aspecto que más fácilmente puede escapar a un lector moderno es el del humorismo producido a base de los arcaísmos" ("In the irony found in the prose of the *Quijote*, humor based on archaisms is the aspect that can most easily escape the modern reader"); Riquer, introduction, *Don Quijote*, p. lxxvi. For years, Riquer has insisted on this aspect more frequently and more emphatically than any other critic, discussing it in "Don Quijote, caballero por escarnio," pp. 47–50; in his earlier editions of *Don Quijote* (1944 and 1962; the latter was reissued in 1975 as number 1 in the series "Hispánicos Planeta" and is the Spanish text used throughout this book); in his book *Aproximación al "Quijote"*; and in his article "Cervantes y la caballeresca," pp. 273–92, which has been translated by Joseph R. Jones as "Cervantes and the Romances of Chivalry" for the Norton edition, pp. 895–913. Although other critics rarely do more than refer to the matter in passing, some have stressed its importance: Maria Grazia Profeti, "'Afectación' e 'descuido' nella lingua del *Palmerín*," pp. 45–73; Enrique Moreno Báez, *Reflexiones sobre el "Quijote,"* pp. 109–10; John J. Allen, *Don Quixote: Hero or Fool?*, 1:56–57; Angel Rosenblat, *La lengua del "Quijote,"* pp. 26–32; Luis Rosales, "Pequeña historia de un mito," pp. 160–62; and Howard Mancing, "Cervantes and the Tradition of Chivalric Parody," pp. 177–91. G. Díaz-Plaja (*En torno*, p. 70) estimates that fully 80 percent of the comedy in the novel is derived from Don Quijote's anachronistic speech and deeds. Robert provides an example of how an otherwise excellent critic can commit a series of unfortunate blunders by not recognizing the existence and function of Don Quijote's archaic chivalric style (*Old and New*, pp. 121–22): "Because of the fixed division of epic and prosaic elements in the novel, Don Quixote is the victim of yet another kind of sorcery that compels him to betray his ideal. This ideal is, by its very nature, poetic and in principle should be expressed in the lofty language that has always been its inseparable ally. But this is not the case. Lost as he may be in his dream, rebellious and estranged, Don Quixote does not speak in verse but in prose. On this point there is no difference between him and the other characters in the novel. Aside from certain lyric digressions, precious transpositions of Homer inspired by thoughts of future literary glory ('No sooner had the rubicund Apollo . . . '), his speech

moso, *herida*, and so on). This substitution is by far the most obvious and most frequent of all archaisms used in the novel. Of Don Quijote's 172 archaisms, 81, or 48 percent, are the *f-*. The narrator and other characters who are less inventive than Don Quijote use the *f-* even more frequently: 73 (74 percent) of 99 archaisms.[15] Thus, of the 271 archaisms in *Don Quijote*, 154, or 57 percent, are the *f-*. If this study of archaism in the novel were reduced merely to an examination of this one phonological form, its essential nature would remain unchanged.

2. Second-person-plural verb forms retaining the *-d-* (*mostredes*, *hayades*, and so on, for *mostréis*, *hayáis*, and so on). Used a dozen times by Don Quijote and twice by other char-

---

is ordinarily even more prosaic than that of his companions, the amorous shepherds or cultivated gentlemen he meets on the road whose favorite pastime is to amuse each other with songs and poems. Truthfully, no one speaks in such crude language so frequently as Don Quixote does, especially in Part I where his conversations with Sancho might shock even the least fastidious readers. This is not a trivial paradox; for language is the only thing that binds Don Quixote to reality, it is his truth, the root of his faith and his last hope. He can scoff at reality until he is quite mad, but if he does not want to destroy himself completely, he must at least treat words with respect." Don Quijote does not, as Robert observes, speak in verse, but neither do his models, who are Amadís and the other heroes of the prose romances of chivalry rather than the Cid or some other hero of classical or Spanish epic poetry. Don Quijote, however, consciously uses archaism in order to achieve what he considers a lofty, even poetic, style. There is nothing "prosaic" about his chivalric style. Even at the start of the novel, his language is thoroughly divorced from reality. Only after Sancho Panza enters the work and Don Quijote finds that he cannot dismiss physical pain does he begin to retreat stylistically from his own private, poetic, archaic, chivalric world in order to accommodate reality (see section 2.1).

15. I have not included the comic archaic sonnet from Solisdán to Don Quijote that precedes part I, chapter 1. This poem has one of the highest densities of archaism and contains some of the most original archaisms in the entire book: *maguer*, *vos*, *cerbelo*, *home*, *vuesas*, *fazañas*, *joeces*, *desfaciendo*, *vegadas*, *cautivos*, *rehaces*, *la vuesa*, *desaguisado*, *vuesas*, *talante*, *vueso*, *conorte*. This sonnet, absurdly comic precisely because of the concentration of archaisms, is not a part of the novel proper but does function as the agent that introduces the technique of archaism in the book. See Pierre Ullman, "The Burlesque Poems Which Frame the *Quijote*," p. 227.

acters, the archaism of the form is immediately apparent to readers of Spanish.

3. The adjective *cautivo* in the sense of *miserable* or *desdichado*.[16] *Cautivo* is the favorite word in Don Quijote's archaic vocabulary; he uses it ten times. Other characters and the narrator use it only three times.

In addition, there are several other forms and words that reinforce (and make far more comic) passages that contain one or more of these three essential archaisms. I have counted the following as "supplementary" archaisms.

1. Several verb forms that were clearly not current or that were at least obsolescent in Cervantes's day: the split future (*levantarse han* for *se levantarán*, *prometérselo ha* for *se lo prometerá*); *hobiese* for *hubiese*; *plégaos* for *plázcaos*; *pluguiera* for *placiera*; *rescibió* for *recibió*; and *yoguieren* for *yacieren*.

2. The use of the definite article and, by extension, the demonstrative adjective with an unstressed possessive adjective (for instance, *la vuestra* for *vuestra*; *este su* for *su*).

3. Three obviously archaic morphological forms from Old Spanish: *non* for *no*; *vos* (direct or indirect object pronoun) for *os*; and *e* for *y*.

4. A modest archaic vocabulary as shown in Table 1.1.

The precise degree of obsolescence that a word or form might have had in the early seventeenth century is often extremely difficult to determine. Some of those I have included were clearly archaic (*hobiese*, *non*, *ál*, *ca*, *vegada*), while others were far less so (*levantarse han*, *la vuestra*, *catar*, *pro*, *talante*).[17] Still others that, for a lack of extensive documentation, I have not included (*acuitarse* for *afligirse*; *cuita* for *apremio*; *sandez* for *necedad*; *tuerto* for *agravio*) may have carried at least a degree of archaic, especially chivalric

16. Daniel Eisenberg cites this archaism as surviving primarily in the romances of chivalry; Diego Ortúñez de Calahorra, *Espejo de príncipes y cavalleros*, 1:168, note 1. See also *Don Quijote*, ed. Diego Clemencín, p. 1196, note 13. *Cautivo* is usually mistranslated (by nonspecialists who fail to perceive its archaic meaning in purposefully archaic passages) as "captive."

17. *Talante* was quite clearly archaic in the Renaissance, but its extensive use by Cervantes in *Don Quijote* appears to have been a major factor in restoring it to currency; see Juan Corominas, *Diccionario crítico etimológico de la lengua castellana*, 4:352.

Table 1.1.   Selection of the Archaic Vocabulary in *Don Quijote*

Archaic Form	Modern Equivalent
afincamiento	apremio (constraint)
ál	otra cosa (another thing)
asaz	bastante (enough)
atender	esperar (to await)
ca	porque (because)
catar	mirar (to look at)
desaguisado	agravio (wrong)
fenestra	ventana (window)
guisa	manera (manner)
infante	niño (young child)
lueñe	lejano (distant)
maguer	aunque (although)
membrarse	recordar (to remember)
prez	premio (reward)
pro	provecho (advantage)
tabla	mesa (table)
talante	voluntad (will)
vegada	vez (time)

archaic, connotation.[18] My list of archaisms (see Appendix A) is as complete and extensive as can be made with the consultation of a variety of sources.[19] At the expense of perhaps omitting an

18. The word *ínsula* for *isla* ("island") is more a Latinism than an archaism and therefore has not been included, even though it is virtually standard vocabulary in the romances of chivalry. Furthermore, its very special and very frequent use in the novel puts it into a category by itself.

19. These sources include Martín Alonso, *Enciclopedia del idioma*; Julio Cejador y Frauca, *La lengua de Cervantes*; Clemencín, ed., *Don Quijote*; Corominas, *Diccionario crítico etimológico*; Sebastián de Covarrubias, *Tesoro de la lengua castellana o española*; Rufino J. Cuervo, *Diccionario de construcción y régimen de la lengua castellana*; the *Diccionario de Autoridades*; William J. Entwistle, *The Spanish Language*; Samuel Gili y Gaya, *Tesoro lexicográfico (1492–1726)*; Friedrich Hanssen, *Gramática histórica de la lengua castellana*; Hayward Keniston, *The Syntax of Castilian Prose: The Sixteenth Century*; Rafael Lapesa, *Historia de la lengua española*; Ramón

occasional example (which would still leave virtually unaltered the general distribution and pattern of archaism in the novel), I have included only those archaic chivalric speeches and narrative passages that contain one of the three major archaisms (*f-*, *-d-*, *cautivo*), to which other supplementary archaisms are usually added.[20]

There are two reasons why twentieth-century readers are likely to overlook the nature and function of chivalric archaism in Cervantes's novel. First is the nature of literary parody,[21] which depends, for its maximum effect, on readers' familiarity with the work or genre parodied, in this case, the romances of chivalry. Today, not only the average readers of *Don Quijote* but also too many specialists are totally ignorant of the genre that

---

Menéndez Pidal, *Manual de gramática histórica espannola*; Real Academia Española, *Diccionario histórico de la lengua española*; Riquer, ed., *Don Quijote*; Alonso Fernández de Avellaneda, *Don Quijote*, ed. Martín de Riquer; Rosenblat, *La lengua del "Quijote"*; Robert K. Spaulding, *How Spanish Grew*; and Juan de Valdés, *Diálogo de la lengua*. Enrique Ruiz-Fornells, *Las concordancias de "El Ingenioso Hidalgo don Quijote de la Mancha,"* vol. 1, has been invaluable for checking every occurrence of words in *Don Quijote* beginning with the letter *A*. It is unfortunate that publication of subsequent volumes of this basic research tool has been delayed so long. The work of R. M. Flores, *The Compositors of the First and Second Madrid Editions of "Don Quixote," Part I,* raises the possibility that the presence or absence of archaic forms could have been determined by the book's compositors rather than by Cervantes alone. Flores himself, however, indicates that this is unlikely (p. 88).

20. An example of how the isolated use of one of these supplementary words, even though clearly an archaism, can fail to achieve the effect of an archaic chivalric speech is provided by the form *vos*. There is no question that *vos* is archaic for Cervantes, but when Don Quijote uses it without the immediate presence of one of the three major archaisms, as he does in II, 56, 1009, there is little, if any, sense of archaism. Allen, one of the critics genuinely sensitive to the function of chivalric archaism, states that Don Quijote employs no archaisms after II, 32; see *Hero or Fool*, 1:57; and in his edition of *Don Quijote*, 2:274, note 7.

21. Parody—not to be confused with burlesque—is best defined as "a humorous and aesthetically satisfying composition in prose or verse, usually written without malice, in which, by means of a rigidly controlled distortion, the most striking peculiarities of subject matter and style of a literary work, or author, or a school or a type of writing, are exaggerated in such a way as to lead to an implicit value judgement of the original"; J. G. Riewald, "Parody as Criticism," pp. 128–29.

Cervantes parodied.[22] This ignorance, by definition, makes difficult both the comprehension and the enjoyment of the aesthetic qualities of the parody.[23]

The second factor is the nature of archaism, which in order to achieve its intended effect, creates contrasts that attract the attention of the readers, referring them to a past state of the language with which they are familiar.[24] Therefore, readers who are not familiar with the sometimes subtle differences in the state of linguistic development of a given language often fail to appreciate the effect of archaism in a literary text. This is certainly true in the case of *Don Quijote*, where modern readers may fail to realize that, while *fablar* (*hablar*), *mostredes* (*mostréis*), *cautivo* (*miserable*), *otro día* (*el día siguiente*), *puesto que* (*aunque*), *tal vez* (*alguna vez*), and *valiente* (*grande*) are all archaic today, the first three were as archaic for Cervantes as they are for us, but the others were still quite current in the seventeenth century.[25]

22. "The unsuspecting modern reader unprepared by philological studies does not perceive Cervantes' irony when he makes Don Quixote say *non fuyades, fecho, la vuestra fermosura* . . . , since the writer himself pronounced them exactly as today: *no huyáis, hecho, vuestra hermosura*, etc."; Riquer, "Cervantes and the Romances," p. 910.

23. Riewald, "Parody as Criticism," p. 128.

24. Michael Riffaterre, "Criteria for Style Analysis," pp. 160–61.

25. Although this point is frequently made in passing with specific reference to Cervantes's novel, Fernando Díaz-Plaja accompanies this observation with an effective example of how such linguistic humor pales with age (*Nueva historia de la literatura española*, p. 114): "Uno de los aspectos cómicos más eficaces del *Quijote* se ha perdido con los años. Dado que todo el lenguaje del libro nos parece antiguo, no podemos calibrar el efecto que produciría en la gente de entonces quien hablara como un siglo antes ('non fuyan', por ejemplo, cuando ya se decía 'no huyan' en español). Lo más parecido nos sería que alguien se acercase a nosotros diciendo: 'Caballero, ¿podéis decirme si el petimetre es el cortejo de esa dama?'" ("One of the most effective comic aspects of the *Quijote* has been lost with the years. Given that all the language of the book seems archaic to us, we cannot estimate the effect that would be produced on the people of that time by someone who spoke like people of a century earlier ('non fuyan' [do not fly], for example, when one already was saying 'no huyan' in Spanish). The most similar situation for us would be someone coming up to us saying: 'Sir, can you tell me if the dandy is the escort of that lady?'"). The effect of Díaz-Plaja's example is, of course, lost in translation. The vocabulary and structure

The effect of parody is diminished with the passing of time. The effect of archaism also diminishes with age. Therefore, parody that makes use of archaism as its outstanding stylistic feature is doubly prone to pass into a state of nonrecognition by its later readers. The first step in approaching a literary work from a past age is to reconstruct to as great a degree as possible (a task never completely realizable) the significance that the text had for its contemporary readers. Once we realize the nature, extent, and importance of archaism in *Don Quijote*, we can study its role in the formation and development of the protagonist and the other characters in the novel.

1.3 The Romances of Chivalry

The language and style of the dozens of sixteenth-century Spanish romances of chivalry, *libros de caballerías*, vary considerably, but an outstanding feature of many of them is archaism.[26] The publishing history of *Amadís de Gaula* best explains why this is so. The earliest references to the work date from the mid-fourteenth century, proving that the book was known by that time. There are few extant fragments of a later edition, which Rafael Lapesa dates at around 1420.[27] It was most probably this latter edition that Garci Rodríguez de Montalvo used in the late fifteenth century when he prepared his four-volume version of the work, which was published posthumously in 1508. At the beginning of book I, Montalvo states with pride that he acted as editor and modernizer, updating "los antiguos originales que estauan corruptos y mal compuestos en antiguo estilo, por falta de

---

of the sentence are intended to evoke the Spanish of the neoclassic period, an epoch only slightly further removed from the mid-twentieth century as that evoked by Don Quijote with his *fabla* from the early seventeenth century.

26. The archaic literary style discussed in this section may be considered a function of the spirit of archaism that, as José Ortega y Gasset explains, informs epic literature, of which the romances of chivalry are a final manifestation; *Meditations on "Quixote,"* pp. 118–19.

27. Lapesa, "El lenguaje del *Amadís* manuscrito," p. 224. The manuscript fragments were published by Antonio Rodríguez-Moñino as "El primer manuscrito del *Amadís de Gaula*" in the same issue of the *Boletín*, pp. 199–216.

los differentes y malos escriptores. Quitando muchas palabras superfluas y poniendo otras de más polido y elegante estilo tocantes a la cauallería y actos della" ("the ancient originals which were corrupt and poorly composed in the antique style through the fault of diverse poor scribes, taking out many superfluous words and putting in others of a more polished and elegant style pertaining to chivalry and the deeds thereof").[28] But Montalvo's self-imposed modernization of the language of his text was only partially successful. His version of *Amadís,* which largely reflects the status of the Spanish language at the end of the fifteenth century, still contains many archaic forms carried over from the earlier versions. Though it may be possible to detect an increasing number of modern usages as the work progresses and Montalvo's original contributions become greater,[29] the 1508 *Amadís* maintains an archaic flavor throughout. Book V, *Las sergas de Esplandián,* largely by Montalvo (published in 1510), also maintains a consciously archaic style.

Several other romances of chivalry that were reworked from medieval originals reflect a similar style, but many chivalric romances composed in the sixteenth century, decades after Montalvo's pioneering work, continued to be written in a pseudoarchaic and increasingly mannered style often called *fabla* by modern critics.[30] Undoubtedly, the great popularity and prestige

28. Place, ed., *Amadís de Gaula,* 1:11. *Amadis of Gaul, Books I and II,* p. 21.

29. Samuel Gili y Gaya, *Amadís de Gaula,* p. 14, and Place, ed., *Amadís,* 3:927, have indicated that this is true, but neither demonstrates in detail the bases on which these affirmations are made. The most complete study of the language of *Amadís* is contained in the Ph.D. dissertation of Ruth Naomi Fjelsted, "Archaisms in *Amadís de Gaula.*" Fjelsted concludes that book II is the most archaic, followed by book III, book I, and book IV, but her criteria are quite different from those of Gili y Gaya and, presumably, of Place. The matter must be left unsettled, as none of these studies is complete enough, rigorous enough, or precise enough to be conclusive. Frank Pierce lists several reasons why linguistic studies of the romance should "proceed with caution"; *Amadís de Gaula,* p. 156.

30. Again, no study of the evolution in the style of the romances of chivalry published during the sixteenth century exists. I can only second Eisenberg's lament that these books have been so ignored by the critics. We need studies of such significant matters as style, themes,

of Montalvo's *Amadís de Gaula* were largely responsible for this trend, although another factor could have been the Renaissance fascination with medieval *romances viejos*, ballads composed in a language already a century or more old, whose popularity would have helped to make such a style more readily perceived and understood and more acceptable as a traditionally "authorized" style for the narration of ancient chivalric materials.[31] The archaic setting and tone in general, and the style in particular, of the books were almost certainly popular with the reading public, who could have readily perceived this characteristic of the prose of these works.[32]

---

characterization, and relationships to *Don Quijote*; see Daniel Eisenberg, "*Don Quijote* and the Romances of Chivalry: The Need for a Reexamination," pp. 511–23. Eisenberg's excellent edition of *Espejo* is invaluable in its treatment of many of these aspects.

31. The romances of chivalry were customarily set in a distant mythical past; *Amadís de Gaula* takes place (1:11) "no muchos años después de la passión de nuestro redemptor y saluador Jesu xpo" ("Not many years after the passion of our Redeemer and Savior, Jesus Christ," p. 21).

32. For Chevalier, the literary success of the romances of chivalry was largely due to their representation of an archaic set of manners in an archaic society; *Lectura y lectores*, p. 102. The same was almost certainly true of the archaic style, even though a dissenting opinion is offered by Eisenberg; introduction, *Espejo*, 1:xxxv, note 16. Juan de Valdés criticized the pseudoarchaic style of *Amadís de Gaula*; *Diálogo de la lengua*, p. 47. Diego de Mendoza wrote critically of the style of the romances of chivalry, stating that "usan de vocablos muy viejos" ("they use very old vocabulary"); cited by Clemencín, ed., *Don Quijote*, p. 1046, note 47. In 1580, Miguel Sánchez de Lima observed that "in most of [the romances] one does not find good speech, since it is all antiquated"; cited by Riquer, "Cervantes and the Romances," p. 911. The romances of chivalry are not the only genre in which we find examples of a conscious, mannered, archaic style. Menéndez Pidal has studied the serious and burlesque *romances en fabla* (*Romancero hispánico*, 2:156–58); Víctor F. García Díez has written a dissertation on *comedias en fabla* ("La fabla en algunas comedias históricas del siglo de oro"); I have previously attempted to place Cervantes within the multigenre tradition of parodic *fabla* ("Cervantes and the Tradition of Chivalric Parody"). Examples of *fabla* do not end with the seventeenth century; see, for example, Leandro Fernández de Moratín's poem to Godoy on the occasion of the latter's marriage in 1797, written "en lenguaje y verso antiquo" (*Obras*, BAE, no. 2 [Madrid: Rivadeneyra, 1857], pp. 583–

The famous citations from the works of Feliciano de Silva included in *Don Quijote*—"La razón de la sinrazón que a mi razón se hace, de tal manera mi razón enflaquece, que con razón me quejo de *la vuestra fermosura*" (I, 1, my italics) ("the reason of the unreason with which my reason is afflicted so weakens my reason that with reason I complain of your beauty") and "los altos cielos que de vuestra divinidad divinamente con las estrellas os fortifican, y os hacen merecedora del merecimiento que merece *la vuestra* grandeza" (my italics) ("the high heavens, that of your divinity divinely fortify you with the stars, render you deserving of the desert your greatness deserves," p. 26)[33]—seem to be attractive to Don Quijote for their clarity and "entricadas razones" ("complicated conceits"), presumably the *razón–sin-razón–razón* type of repetitions. In his own career as a knight-errant, Don Quijote never engages in such word-play, but it is worth noting that these passages also contain the archaic *la vues-tra* and *fermosura* and that these indeed are hallmarks of Don Quijote's rhetoric of chivalry. If there is any stylistic feature of the books of chivalry that has a direct effect on Don Quijote, it is archaism. Whether or not Don Quijote's *fabla* is an accurate reproduction of the style of any particular work is not important; what does matter is that his use of such language is directly inspired by his perception of the style of the books that he imitates.

Without the romances of chivalry, Don Quijote does not ex-

---

84); Luis de Eguílaz's play *Las querellas del rey sabio*, first staged in 1858 (3d ed., Madrid: Imprenta de José Rodríguez, 1867); and the conversation between the protagonist Jesús de Ceballos and the Marqués de Santillana in Ricardo León's 1908 novel *Casta de hidalgos* (Colección Austral, no. 481 [Buenos Aires: Espasa-Calpe Argentina, 1944], pp. 112–14). The most salient stylistic features of all these works remain constant: *f-*, *-d-*, and the standard archaic vocabulary. The use of an archaic style to create atmosphere is a universal technique. See, for instance, Ursula K. Le Guin's discussion of the "archaic manner, which Dunsany and other master fantasists use so effortlessly. . . . They know instinctively that what is wanted in fantasy is a *distancing from the ordinary*"; *The Language of the Night*, p. 89.

33. Apparently neither of these quotations comes exactly as cited from the works of Silva, but they are in fact accurate reflections of his style; see Clemencín, ed., *Don Quijote*, pp. 1013–14, note 9.

ist, a fact occasionally recalled by the novel's best readers but seldom expressed as forcefully and eloquently as by Avalle-Arce: "son los libros los que constituyen toda la basa y pedestal de don Quijote de la Mancha. . . . Los libros de caballerías son para la existencia de don Quijote *res sine qua non*" ("books make up the entire basis and foundation of Don Quijote de la Mancha. . . . The romances of chivalry are *res sine qua non* for the existence of Don Quijote").[34] In order to comprehend what is happening in *Don Quijote*, the protagonist's book-inspired existence must be acknowledged. Twentieth-century readers who learn to recognize Don Quijote's chivalric archaism gain more than an ability to appreciate a seemingly incidental comic level of parody. Their awareness of the archaic element in his speech allows them to appreciate the very essence of his concept of himself as a knight-errant.[35]

34. Avalle-Arce, *Forma de vida*, pp. 261, 267. Other important studies that stress this major point are those of Américo Castro, "La palabra escrita y el *Quijote*," in *Hacia Cervantes*, pp. 359–408; Mia I. Gerhardt, *Don Quijote, la vie et les livres*, especially pp. 17–18; Martín de Riquer, "El *Quijote* y los libros," pp. 5–24; and Michel Foucault, *The Order of Things: An Archaeology of the Human Sciences*, pp. 46–50. It is unfortunate that Herman Meyer had to rely on a translation of *Don Quijote* when writing his chapter on Cervantes in his important book *The Poetics of Quotation in the European Novel*, p. 55, note 1. Meyer's failure to recognize the nature and role of Don Quijote's archaism when quoting from the romances of chivalry is perhaps the most serious weakness in his otherwise excellent study.

35. This situation illustrates how readers who must rely on translations can miss crucial aspects of a work. No English translation of *Don Quijote* does more than hint at the presence or effect of the protagonist's chivalric archaisms. Even though Jones acknowledges in his translation of Riquer's article (see my note 21) the nature and importance of *fabla*, he seems not to realize its crucial role when commenting in the preface to his edition on the difficulties of translating passages in the novel inspired directly by the romances of chivalry: "Even more ticklish is the rendering of Don Quixote's version of the language found in his books of chivalry. It is not always easy to say just where Don Quixote's speech begins to be bookish and quaint and where it is merely elevated but normal. Cervantes makes good use of this ambiguity. I have eliminated the familiar address ('thou,' 'ye,' etc.) in ordinary conversation but used it as the equivalent of Don Quixote's chivalrous language when I thought it enhanced the effect" (p. xi). I believe that Arthur Efron is mistaken in his contention that no "major elements of *Don*

1.4 The Rhetoric of Chivalry

This section contains several tables and graphs that reflect my original fascination with the distribution of chivalric archaism in *Don Quijote*. By simply observing which characters speak, when they speak, and how they speak, we can begin to perceive the outline of their roles and functions in the novel.

To begin with, a simple but effective way to measure the importance of a character in a work is to count the number of times that that character speaks. As a measurement to which I refer with some frequency and as a background against which to measure Don Quijote's archaic chivalric rhetoric, Table 1.2 presents a breakdown of the frequency of speeches[36] in the ten subdivisions to which I have found it convenient to refer in part I of *Don Quijote*:

1. Chapter 1: Alonso Quijano el Bueno
2. Chapters 2–5: The first sally
3. Chapter 6: The scrutiny of Don Quijote's library
4. Chapters 7–10: The second sally
5. Chapters 11–14: A pastoral interlude
6. Chapters 15–22: Adventures

Quijote have ever been demonstrated to be untranslatable"; *Don Quixote and the Dulcineated World*, p. vi. Allen states correctly that the characteristics of the archaic style "are very imperfectly communicated in translation, and no translation reflects with any precision the distribution of their use in *Don Quixote*"; *Hero or Fool*, 1:56. See also Lowry Nelson, Jr., introduction, *Cervantes: A Collection of Critical Essays*, p. 7. Don Quijote himself best comments on this essential point (II, 62, 1064): "me parece que el traducir de una lengua en otra . . . es como quien mira los tapices flamencos por el revés, que aunque se veen las figuras, son llenas de hilos que las escurecen, y no se veen con la lisura y tez de la haz ("it seems to me that translation from one language into another . . . is like looking at Flemish tapestries on the wrong side; for though the figures are visible, they are full of threads that make them indistinct, and they do not show with the smoothness and texture of the right side," p. 776).

36. I use the term *speech* to refer to words directly quoted by the narrator. Thus Sancho's "¿Qué gigantes?" ("What giants?") is a "speech" just as Don Quijote's lecture on the Golden Age is. Similarly, when Vivaldo reads Grisóstomo's "Canción desesperada" or the priest reads from the manuscript of "El curioso impertinente," Vivaldo and the priest are both credited with "speeches."

7. Chapters 23–28: In the Sierra Morena
8. Chapters 29–31: Princess Micomicona
9. Chapters 32–46: At the inn
10. Chapters 47–52: The return home

Readily apparent are the progressive decline in the frequency of Don Quijote's speeches, the importance of Sancho Panza in the central section of the work, and the increasing prominence of other characters toward the end. We see that Don Quijote dominates the action in the early part of the novel, that Sancho's importance is greatest between chapters 15 and 31, and that other characters, led by the priest and Dorotea, control events in the last half.

Figures 1.1 and 1.2 trace as precisely as possible the distribution of Don Quijote's speeches in which he uses chivalric archaism—the essence of his rhetoric of chivalry—and the number of archaisms that he employs. Before discussing the evidence suggested by these two figures, two cautionary notes need to be stressed. First, the frequency or percentage of archaism to which I refer is only indicative (but genuinely indicative, I believe) and never absolutely significant. Speeches that are only a few words long may not contain constructions or vocabulary that would lend themselves to archaism, while a comparatively lengthy

Table 1.2.   Distribution of Speeches (Part I)

Section	Don Quijote		Sancho		Others		Total
	No.	(%)	No.	(%)	No.	(%)	
1. Chap. 1	1	(100)	—	(—)	—	(—)	1
2. Chaps. 2–5	32	(56)	—	(—)	25	(44)	57
3. Chap. 6	—	(—)	—	(—)	53	(100)	53
4. Chaps. 7–10	42	(55)	26	(34)	9	(12)	77
5. Chaps. 11–14	22	(33)	3	(4)	42	(63)	67
6. Chaps. 15–22	145	(46)	116	(37)	51	(16)	312
7. Chaps. 23–28	54	(38)	54	(38)	35	(24)	143
8. Chaps. 29–31	50	(37)	36	(27)	49	(36)	135
9. Chaps. 32–46	50	(21)	19	(8)	170	(71)	239
10. Chaps. 47–52	31	(35)	23	(26)	36	(40)	90
Total	427	(36)	277	(24)	470	(40)	1,174

Figure 1.1. Don Quijote's Archaic Speeches (Part I)

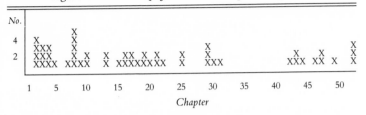

Figure 1.2. The Number of Archaisms in Don Quijote's Archaic
Speeches (Part I)

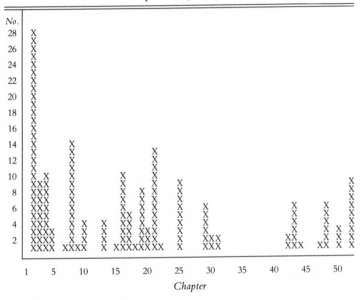

speech may contain only one or two archaisms and thus does not have the effect of a shorter speech that is full of these forms; however, even a single *fermoso*, *habedes*, or *cautivo* is a clear and unmistakable evocation of conscious *fabla*.[37] Second, Don Qui-

37. I have excluded from direct consideration archaism that is used in narration rather than in direct discourse but is still attributable to a character; for example (I, 5, 68): "y él [Don Quijote] dijo que todo era molimiento, por haber dado una gran caída con Rocinante, su caballo,

jote's chivalric archaism does not represent an infallible key to his behavior as knight-errant. Amadís de Gaula can say *fablar, fuir* one moment and *hablar, huir* the next without ceasing to act as a knight-errant, and so can Don Quijote. Don Quijote only uses this style when he is consciously acting and speaking as a knight-errant,[38] but he does not always use it when he is a knight. Archaism is a sign of Don Quijote's conscious chivalric role, but that role is not invariably signaled by archaism.[39]

With these clarifications in mind, let us observe that the frequency of Don Quijote's chivalric archaism as shown in Figures 1.1 and 1.2 indicates that Don Quijote begins his career with a very high degree of enthusiasm, but that quite early in the novel that enthusiasm begins to decline and is never again recaptured. If acting as a knight-errant is the essence of Don Quijote's existence, and if one critical aspect of this acting, his speech, is considerably modified with the progress of the story, then the character's whole being is also modified.

In order to examine more closely the pattern of archaism in Don Quijote's speech, I have provided in Table 1.3 a breakdown

combatiéndose con diez jayanes, los más desaforados y atrevidos que se pudieran *fallar* en gran parte de la tierra" ("but he [Don Quixote] said they were all bruises from having had a severe fall with his horse Rocinante when in combat with ten giants, the biggest and the boldest to be found on earth," p. 47). To have included such cases would have introduced the problem of the narrator's role in accurately reproducing the character's words. Furthermore, including such incidents of archaism would have modified the graphs only slightly without in any way altering their basic configurations.

38. That Don Quijote's chivalric archaism is employed in conscious imitation of the language used by Amadís de Gaula and other fictional knights-errant is obvious from the previously cited narrative comment following his first archaic speech (I, 2, 42), "imitando en cuanto podía su lenguage" ("imitating their language as well as he could," p. 30). Avellaneda's protagonist is equally aware of the same imitative function of his speech (I, 52): "ya que imito a los antiguos en fortaleza, . . . los quiero también imitar en las palabras" ("since I am imitating in fortitude [the] ancients . . . , I wish also to imitate them in words"; *Don Quixote de la Mancha (Part II)*, p. 22).

39. This relationship has been pointed out by Allen, *Hero or Fool*, 1:57.

of the protagonist's archaism in the ten subdivisions of the novel referred to earlier.

Anyone who has worked with statistics knows that there are a number of ways in which any given set of figures can be analyzed. In the last four columns of Table 1.3, I have provided four sets of interpretative figures in order to focus on the problem from four slightly different, but equally valid, points of view.

1. The percentage of archaism (obtained by dividing the number of speeches by the number of archaic speeches).

2. The number of archaisms per speech (obtained by dividing the number of speeches by the number of archaisms).

3. The archaic speeches per chapter (obtained by dividing the number of archaic speeches by the number of chapters in which Don Quijote speaks).

4. The archaisms per chapter (obtained by dividing the number of archaisms by the number of chapters in which Don Quijote speaks).

Table 1.3.   Analysis of Don Quijote's Archaic Speeches (Part I)

Section	Number of Chaps. in Which DQ Speaks	Number of Speeches	Number of Archaic Speeches	Number of Archaisms	Percentage of Archaic Speeches	Archaisms per Speech	Archaic Speeches per Chap.	Archaisms per Chap.
1. Chap. 1	1	1	—	—	—	—	—	—
2. Chaps. 2–5	4	32	11	50	34.4	1.6	2.8	12.5
3. Chap. 6	—	—	—	—	—	—	—	—
4. Chaps. 7–10	4	42	9	20	21.4	0.5	2.2	5.0
5. Chaps. 11–14	4	22	2	4	9.1	0.2	0.5	1.0
6. Chaps. 15–22	8	145	12	42	8.3	0.3	1.5	5.2
7. Chaps. 23–28	4	54	2	9	3.7	0.2	0.5	2.2
8. Chaps. 29–31	3	50	5	10	10.0	0.2	1.7	3.3
9. Chaps. 32–46	8	50	5	10	10.0	0.2	0.6	1.2
10. Chaps. 47–52	5	31	6	18	19.4	0.6	1.2	3.6
Total	41	427	52	173	12.2	0.4	1.3	4.2

The profiles these four measurements suggest are slightly different. The "Percentage of Archaic Speeches" column indicates the following ranking of sections from most to least archaic: 2, 4, 10, 8, 9, 5, 6, 7. The "Archaisms per Speech" column indicates the following order: 2, 10, 4, 6, 5, 7, 8, 9. The "Archaic Speeches per Chapter" column indicates: 2, 4, 8, 6, 10, 9, 5, 7. The "Archaisms per Chapter" column indicates: 2, 6, 4, 10, 8, 7, 9, 5. The consensus of these figures is that Don Quijote's language is clearly most archaic during his first sally, section 2 (chapters 2–5), and that in the early part of his second sally, section 4 (chapters 7–10), his speech is obviously still highly archaic. The third most archaic section for Don Quijote is number 10 (the final chapters, 47–52). At the opposite end of the scale, his language is least archaic during sections 5 and 7 (chapters 11–14 and 23–28), the pastoral interlude and the withdrawal to the Sierra Morena.[40] In the remainder of the novel, we see Don Quijote using chivalric archaism at a rate that is noticeably lower than that in the early chapters but that is somewhat higher than it is in these two periods of comparatively limited contact with society.

The prevailing critical consensus (see section 3.6) is that Don Quijote remains unchanged in part I of the novel, sustaining intact his fantastic and distorted vision of the world; his reconciliation with reality, it is maintained, begins to develop only in the second part. The evidence I have adduced here, suggested by the distribution of chivalric archaism, is that quite early in part I—specifically after chapter 10—Don Quijote begins to retreat from his original conception of himself. The degree to which he moves away from his chivalric fantasy ought to be directly related to the degree to which he approaches reality. Theoretically, Don Quijote could simply replace chivalry with another fantasy, but there is no evidence that he does so. Much later in the novel he briefly considers substituting pastoral for chivalric fantasy, but at this early point the alternatives seem to be either knighthood or reality.

40. Geoffery Stagg's suggestive thesis that chapters 11–14 were originally contained within the stay in the Sierra Morena might be supported by this distribution of archaism; see his "Revision in *Don Quixote*, Part I," pp. 347–66.

But it is not enough to consider archaism as the sole constituent in Don Quijote's rhetoric of chivalry. In an attempt to discover other stylistic elements related to chivalry that also characterize Don Quijote's speech, I have identified a series of clichés, formulas, and topics that can also be taken as characteristic of his chivalric discourse.

The key passage quoted in section 1.1, the "extraño pensamiento" ("strangest notion") that Alonso Quijano has when he decides to become a knight-errant, contains some of these elements. His decision is to go in quest of adventures in order to gain "honra . . . nombre y fama" ("honor . . . fame and glory") as well as to serve humanity by "deshaciendo todo género de agravio" ("righting every kind of wrong"). This he will achieve, it is added, by "el valor de su brazo" ("the might of his arm"). Figures 1.3, 1.4, and 1.5 indicate the distribution of Don Quijote's speeches in which there are references to these three elements—fame, chivalric mission, and strength—in his rhetoric of chivalry (see Appendix B for a complete list of Don Quijote's use of these motifs).

Don Quijote's references to his own fame (for example, by the use of adjectives like *famoso, nombrado,* and *alabado*) occur just often enough in his speech to appear as a recognizable motif (see Figure 1.3). Helmut A. Hatzfeld first pointed out that the most constant and salient idea in the novel is Don Quijote's consciousness of his chivalric mission: *desfacer agravios y enderezar tuertos* ("to right wrongs and correct injustices").[41] This motif is cited

Figure 1.3.   Don Quijote's References to His Own Fame (Part I)

No.										
2	X					X			X		X
	XX XX XX			X	X	X		XX		X
	1	5	10	15	20	25	30	35	40	45	50

Chapter

41. Helmut A. Hatzfeld, *El "Quijote" como obra de arte del lenguaje,* p. 8. The historical background for the chivalric mission, discussed in these precise terms, is examined by José Antonio Maravall, *Utopía y contrautopía en el "Quijote,"* pp. 123–24.

by Don Quijote in a variety of forms (see Figure 1.4): "el des-facedor de agravios y sinrazones"; "Favorecer y ayudar a todos los menesterosos y desvalidos"; "dar libertad a los encadenados, soltar los presos, acorrer a los miserables, alzar los caídos, re-mediar los menesterosos" ("undoer of wrongs"; "To help and aid needy and unprotected people"; "to free those enchained, to release prisoners, to help the unfortunate, to raise the fallen, to assist the needy"), and so forth.

If Don Quijote is to have any claim to greatness as a knight-errant, it must be through the chivalric deeds—"cada uno es hijo de sus obras" ("everyone is the son of his works")—that will be accomplished by the strength of his arm (see Figure 1.5). Don Quijote frequently refers to "el valor de mi brazo," "la bondad de mi espada," "la fuerza de mi incansable brazo" ("the might of my arm," "my good sword," "the strength of my untiring arm"), and so on, during the novel.

In order to attempt to complete the picture of the distribution of Don Quijote's chivalric rhetoric, I have chosen to chart three more elements that seem most characteristic of his speech in the early part of the novel and that are conceptually related to the practice of chivalry.

Figure 1.4.   Don Quijote's References to His Chivalric Mission (Part I)

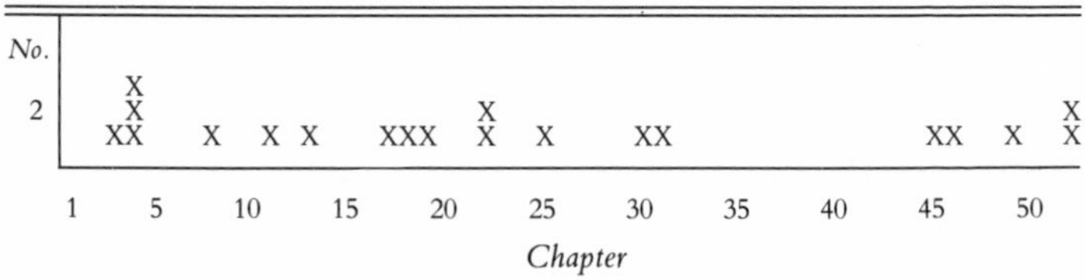

Figure 1.5.   Don Quijote's References to His Own Strength (Part I)

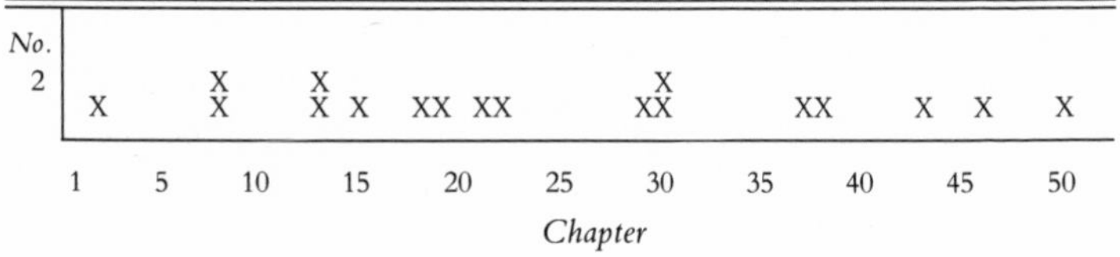

First are Don Quijote's very frequent references to the laws, rules, and customs of the order of chivalry and of knighthood in general,[42] which he cites in order to validate his actions (see Figure 1.6): "costumbre muy usada de los caballeros andantes"; "en pena de haber pasado las leyes de la caballería"; "sería contravenir a las órdenes de caballería" ("a very common custom of knights-errant"; "as a penalty for having transgressed the laws of knighthood"; "it would be to violate the rules of chivalry"). I have also included Don Quijote's custom of swearing by his oath of chivalry[43]: "yo te juro ∴ . . . a la fe de caballero andante"; "yo os prometo, por la orden de caballero que recibí"; "juro por la orden de caballería que profeso" ("I swear to you . . . on my word as a knight-errant"; "I promise to you, by the order of knighthood that I received"; "I swear by the order of chivalry that I profess").

Next are citations of the names of chivalric characters— whether from the romances of chivalry (Amadís de Gaula, Oriana, Belianís de Grecia), from popular tradition and the ballad tradition, the *Romancero* (Lanzarote, Angélica, Montesinos), or from history (Juan de Merlo, Pedro Barba, Gutierre Quijada)— who serve as Don Quijote's models and authorities in chivalric matters. The frequency with which these names, which were very familiar to seventeenth-century readers, reappear is in itself

Figure 1.6. Don Quijote's References to the Order of Chivalry (Part I)

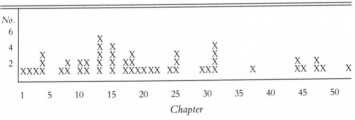

42. See Maravall, *Utopía y contrautopía*, p. 83.
43. Clemencín points out that swearing on one's order of chivalry was very common among both historical and literary knights-errant and was one of those oaths that contained the strongest commitment; *Don Quijote*, p. 1041, note 15.

a constant reminder of the presence of the chivalric world (see Figure 1.7).[44]

Finally, there is Don Quijote's frequent praise of Dulcinea del Toboso—"la sin par," "la incomparable señora mía," "aquella por quien yo vivo" ("the peerless," "my incomparable lady," "the one for whom I live")—another of the motifs originally studied by Hatzfeld (see Figure 1.8).[45]

None of these six figures (1.3–1.8) has enough evidence, given the comparatively few occurrences of each element, to be significant in itself, but the cumulative effect of all six of them does present an interesting pattern (see Figure 1.9).

It does not seem necessary to prepare a detailed analysis of this

Figure 1.7.   Don Quijote's Use of Chivalric Onomastics (Part I)

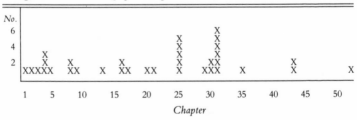

Figure 1.8.   Don Quijote's Speeches in Praise of Dulcinea (Part I)

44. See Mancing, "Chivalric Names," p. 220.
45. Hatzfeld, *El "Quijote" como obra*, pp. 13–15. I have not chosen to discuss the other two motifs that Hatzfeld associates with Don Quijote as a knight-errant—*sosiego* and *cólera* (pp. 15–17)—because calmness and anger are not inherently chivalric in nature, and, furthermore, they function more in narration than in the protagonist's speech.

Figure 1.9.   Don Quijote's Use of All Chivalric Motifs (Part I)

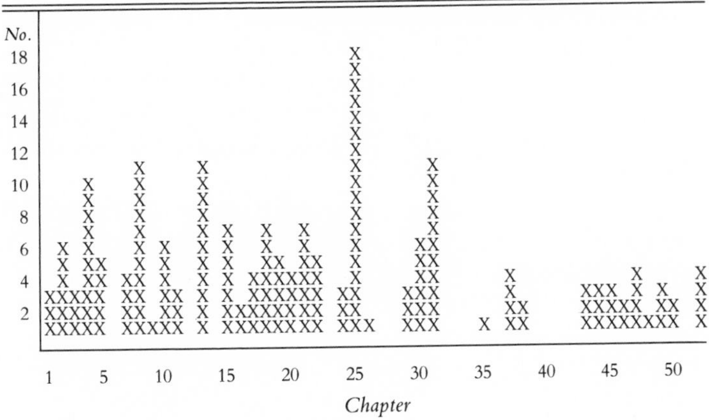

graph comparable to that in Table 1.3. It is clear that in the second half of part I there is a great decline in Don Quijote's use of these chivalric motifs. Again, the conclusion is evident: Don Quijote's entire chivalric rhetoric tends to decline as the novel progresses. If his mode of discourse changes, it would seem to follow that he himself changes.

The statistics, tables, and graphs that make up the substance of this section are important in that they point to a direction that can be followed in studying Don Quijote's conception of himself as a knight-errant; they do not, in and of themselves without further supporting evidence, form anything even resembling a definitive statement on the nature of the chivalric world of Don Quijote. Let us now examine the knight-errant's career to see if it is possible to confirm the evidence suggested by this quantitative analysis.

1.5 Chapters 2–5: The First Sally

In order to trace any evolution in the character of Don Quijote, it is essential to define exactly what he is at the beginning of his career so that what he becomes later on can be viewed in a contrastive light. Don Quijote is, or at least believes himself to be, a knight-errant; all his thoughts, words, and deeds are conditioned by this fact. In this section, we see that on his first sally he never compromises in the slightest his chivalric vision of himself and the world.

On his first outing, Don Quijote sallies forth as a living anachronism dressed in armor from the days of Ferdinand and Isabella and speaking an affected archaic language reminiscent of that period over a hundred years in the past.[46] Literally everything Don Quijote does and says in these pages of the novel is inspired directly or indirectly by the romances of chivalry.

Anxious to undertake his chivalric mission, Don Quijote thinks (I, 2, 40) of "los agravios que pensaba deshacer, tuertos que enderezar, sinrazones que emendar, y abusos que mejorar, y deudas que satisfacer" ("the wrongs that had to be righted, grievances redressed, injustices made good, abuses removed, and duties discharged," p. 29). As he recalls that he has not yet formally been dubbed a knight-errant and that, therefore (p. 41), "conforme a la ley de caballería" ("according to the law of chivalry"), he cannot enter into battle with other knights, he decides to have the first knight he encounters confer that honor upon him, "a imitación de otros muchos que así lo hicieron, según él había leído en los libros que tal le tenían" ("following the example of others in the same situation, as he had read in the books that brought him to this pass," p. 30). He has no particular destination and proceeds "sin llevar otro [camino] que aquel que su caballo quería, creyendo que en aquello consistía la fuerza de las aventuras" ("taking that [road] which his horse chose, for in this he believed lay the essence of adventures"), thus imitating another convention from the romances of chivalry.[47] Don Quijote's thoughts concern the style in which this first sally will be recorded by a future historian, for all knights-errant have their deeds immortalized by one or more enchanter-chroniclers. He

46. Martín de Riquer uses the phrase "a living relic" to describe the effect of Don Quijote's ancient armor and antiquated speech; "Cervantes and the Romances," p. 910.

47. A knight-errant who is not committed to a specific mission, knowing full well that adventures can be found anywhere, frequently loosens his reins and allows his horse to choose the path. See Eisenberg in Ortúñez de Calahorra, *Espejo*, 3:41, note 12.

then turns to his imaginary lady and addresses the famous invocation studded with archaisms cited earlier (section 1.2) ("¡Oh princesa Dulcinea . . . "), continuing in this style, "imitando en cuanto podía su lenguaje" ("imitating as far as he could their language").

As the uneventful day comes to an end, Don Quijote approaches an inn (p. 43), and "como a nuestro aventurero todo cuanto pensaba, veía o imaginaba le parecía ser hecho y pasar al modo de lo que había leído" ("as everything our adventurer thought, saw, or imagined seemed to him to be fashioned and to happen on the same lines as what he had been reading," p. 31), as soon as he sees the prosaic inn, he transforms it into a grand castle, complete even to the details of silvered towers, drawbridge, and moat, "con todos aquellos adherentes que semejantes castillos se pintan" ("and every feature usually ascribed to such castles"). A pig-herder's blast on his horn becomes a dwarf's trumpeting notes announcing the arrival of the adventure-seeking knight. A pair of prostitutes standing outside the door are perceived as ladies and addressed thus (pp. 43–44): "No *fuyan las vuestras* mercedes ni teman *desaguisado* alguno; *ca* a la orden de caballería que profeso *non* toca ni atañe *facerle* a ninguno, cuanto más a tan altas doncellas como vuestras presencias demuestran" ("Flee not, your ladyships, nor fear ye any harm, for it belongs not nor pertains to the order of knighthood which I profess to harm anyone, much less highborn maidens as your appearance proclaims you to be," p. 31). Their natural reaction—laughter—prompts Don Quijote to issue a mild rebuke (p. 44): "Bien parece la mesura en las *fermosas*, y es mucha sandez además la risa que de leve causa procede; pero *non vos* lo digo porque os *acuitedes* ni *mostrades* mal *talante*; que el mío *non* es de *ál* que de serviros" ("Modesty becomes the fair, and moreover laughter that has little cause is great folly. This, however, I say not to pain or anger you, for my desire is none other than to serve you," p. 32). Don Quijote's archaic speech and appearance evoke this narrative comment: "El lenguage, no entendido de las señoras, y el mal talle de nuestro caballero acrecentaba en ellas la risa" ("The incomprehensible language and the unpromising looks of our cavalier only increase the ladies' laughter").

The clever, picaresque innkeeper reinforces Don Quijote in his chivalric role by responding in kind to the knight's recitation of a famous chivalric *romance*. The malice in the comment he adds (p. 45)—"bien se puede apear, con seguiridad de hallar en esta choza ocasión y ocasiones para no dormir en todo un año, cuanto más en una noche" ("So you may dismount and count on enough opportunities for sleeplessness under this roof for a twelvemonth, not to say for a single night," p. 32)—is not perceived by Don Quijote. After dismounting, Don Quijote cites the figure of Lancelot, uses several more archaisms (*fasta, fazañas, fechos, pro, las vuestras*), and offers (p. 46) "el valor de mi brazo" ("the might of my arm," p. 33) in defense of the two ladies. During his dinner, he ingenuously perceives codfish as trout and filthy bread as pure *candeal*; the sound of a pig-castrator's whistle is further confirmation that he is indeed lodged within a castle.

After dinner, Don Quijote and the innkeeper act out, to an absurd extreme, the chivalric convention of asking for (*pedir*) and conceding (*otorgar*) a boon (*don*).[48] The innkeeper decides to humor his guest's desire to be dubbed a knight-errant (I, 3, 49), "por tener que reír aquella noche" ("to provide sport for the night"), adding that he too, in his youth, had practiced the same profession, "aquel honroso ejercicio" ("the same honorable calling"), which he describes in a manner that parodies Don Quijote's chivalric mission: "andando por diversas partes del mundo, buscando sus aventuras [in several well-known low-life haunts], haciendo muchos tuertos, recuestando muchas viudas, deschaciendo algunas doncellas y engañando a algunos pupilos" ("roaming in quest of adventures in various parts of the world . . . doing many wrongs, courting many widows, ruining a few maidens and swindling a few minors," p. 35). Don Quijote's failure to react to such a blatant statement of antichivalric activities can only be attributed to his willingness to give the form of the classic statement of chivalric mission greater value than its

48. In the romances of chivalry, the *don* is not always *pedido* on bended knee, and it is frequently *otorgado* at once, but occasionally the ceremony is nearly as elaborate as it is in this scene (and in the later scene between Dorotea and Don Quijote; I, 29, 318–19). See Clemencín, *Don Quijote*, p. 1293, note 27, and pp. 1294–95, note 30.

actual content.[49] Next, the innkeeper modifies the rules of chivalry in order to put Don Quijote on display during his vigil over his armor and to assure the future knight-errant that he should always be prepared with money,[50] clean shirts, and a first-aid kit. Don Quijote's two victories over the daring knights (muleteers) who disturb his armor are accompanied by a classic chivalric challenge (pp. 51–52)—"¡Oh tu, quienquiera que seas, atrevido caballero" ("O thou, whoever thou art, rash knight")—and by invocations of his lady—"Acorredme, señora mía," "¡Oh señora de la *fermosura*" ("Aid me, lady mine," "O Lady of Beauty," pp. 36–37). After the burlesque dubbing ceremony takes place (p. 54),[51] Don Quijote is prepared to sally forth "buscando las aventuras" ("in quest of adventures," p. 39), and departs at the hour of dawn.

As he passes a thicket, he hears (I, 4, 56) "unas voces delicadas, como de persona que se quejaba" ("feeble cries as of some one in distress"). Don Quijote, assuming that the cries he hears are (p. 56) "sin duda, son de algún menesteroso o menesterosa, que ha menester mi favor y ayuda" ("no doubt from some man or woman in want of help and needing my aid and protection"), immediately thanks heaven that he already has an opportunity to start fulfilling "lo que debo a mi profesión" ("the obligation I have undertaken," p. 39). He is completely convinced that all that he sees can only be explained in accordance with the ro-

49. Allen, *Hero or Fool*, 2:54.

50. Clemencín (*Don Quijote*, p. 1034, note 11) points out that Don Quijote's protestations that knights-errant never carry money are in error.

51. The ceremony by which Don Quijote is made a knight-errant is, as Riquer says (*Don Quijote*, p. 47, note), a burlesque parody of the solemn pseudoreligious act performed in many romances of chivalry. It is also technically invalid, as Riquer goes on to point out, on several grounds. But it does fulfill the two most necessary requisites; see Eisenberg in Ortúñez de Calahorra, *Espejo*, 2:22, notes 4–5: "La ceremonia de armar un caballero constaba de dos partes, primero el espaldarazo, que era lo inprescindible, y si faltaba tiempo, suficiente. El ceñir la espada era hecho por otro, generalmente una mujer" ("The ceremony of dubbing a knight consisted of two parts, first the tap on the shoulder with a sword, which was absolutely necessary, and, if time was lacking, sufficient. The buckling on of the sword was done by another person, generally a woman").

mances of chivalry.[52] He refuses to acknowledge that Juan Haldudo, though perhaps severe, has good reason to punish Andrés (the boy admits to being a thief and promises not to steal again) and insists that the oppressor swear by what is most sacred to any knight-errant (p. 58): "y con que él me lo jure por la ley de caballería que ha recebido" ("and as he has sworn to me by the order of knighthood which he has received," p. 40). The unscrupulous Haldudo is perfectly willing to swear "por todas las órdenes que de caballerías hay en el mundo" ("by all the orders of knighthood there are in the world," p. 41) in order to placate Don Quijote. The knight naively accepts his adversary's word and assumes that the adventure is successfully completed, announcing, in order to spread his fame and receive the proper credit, his identity: "sabed que yo soy el valeroso don Quijote de la Mancha, el *desfacedor* de agravios y sinrazones" ("know that I am the valorous Don Quixote of La Mancha, the undoer of wrongs and injustices"). After the knight has departed, Haldudo escalates his punishment of Andrés and mocks the simplistic and ineffective righter of wrongs by parodying his words (p. 59): "Llamad, señor Andrés, ahora . . . al *desfacedor* de agravios; veréis cómo no *desface* aquéste" ("Now, Master Andrés . . . call on the undoer of wrongs. You will find he won't undo that," p. 41). Don Quijote's postvictory invocation of Dulcinea is filled with archaisms (*e, talante, rescibió, desfecho, infante*) and pride (p. 60)—"un tan valiente y tan nombrado caballero, como lo es y será don Quijote de la Mancha" ("a knight so renowed as is and will be Don Quixote of La Mancha," p. 42).

When Don Quijote arrives at a crossroads, he briefly wonders which route a knight-errant would choose to follow, and, for the sake of imitation, again decides to leave the matter to pure chance by allowing his horse Rocinante to make the choice. An innocent group of travelers—six merchants from Toledo—immediately presents the knight with material for a new adventure, and so (p. 60) "por imitar en todo cuanto a él le parecía posible los pasos que había leído en sus libros, le pareció venir

52. For an example from *Belianís de Grecia* of a chivalric adventure that begins with voices heard by a knight as he passes a forest, see Clemencín, *Don Quijote*, p. 1040, note 6.

allí de molde uno que pensaba hacer" ("To help him imitate as far as he could those armed encounters he had read of in his books, here seemed to come one made on purpose, and he decided to act," p. 42). The knight plants himself in the path of "aquellos caballeros andantes" ("these knights-errant") and arrogantly issues the challenge that they all admit that "la emperatriz de la Mancha, la sin par Dulcinea del Toboso" ("the Empress of La Mancha, the peerless Dulcinea del Toboso") is the most beautiful maiden in the world. Such a challenge is, of course, frequent in the romances of chivalry.[53]

The encounter with the merchants is a classically symbolic confrontation between pragmatic, materialistic reality (p. 61)— "Señor caballero, nosotros no conocemos quién sea esa buena señora que decís; mostrádnosla" ("Sir knight, we do not know who this good lady is that you speak of. Show her to us")—and absolute dogmatic faith—"La importancia está en que sin verla lo habéis de creer, confesar, afirmar, jurar y defender" ("The essential point is that without seeing her ye must believe, confess, affirm, swear, and defend it," p. 42). As is often the case, the former easily wins out over the latter. Don Quijote states his position; issues a challenge, "donde no, conmigo sois en batalla" ("else ye have to do with me in battle"); insults his opponents, "gente descomunal y soberbia" ("monstrous, arrogant rabble that ye are"); and appeals to the rules of chivalry, "como pide la orden de caballería" ("as the order of chivalry requires")—all in accord with the actions of his fictional heroes. When he attacks and poor Rocinante stumbles and falls, Don Quijote maintains his chivalric arrogance (p. 62): "*Non fuyáis*, gente cobarde; gente *cautiva*, *atended*; que no por culpa mía, sino de mi caballo, estoy aquí tendido" ("Fly not, cowards and caitiffs! Stay, for not

53. Clemencín (*Don Quijote*, p. 1045, note 41) cites an episode from *Caballero de la Cruz* that is similar to this one in many details. Dámaso Alonso has suggested that the figure of Camilote (from Gil Vicente's play *Don Duardos*, which is based on the romance of chivalry *Primaleón*), an extravagant and comic figure who attempts to make others swear to the unrivaled beauty of his lady (who is hardly deserving of the title), is the direct source for this scene and, in part, for Cervantes's original conception; "El hidalgo Camilote y el hidalgo don Quijote," pp. 392–93.

by my fault, but my horse's, am I stretched here," p. 43).[54] After receiving a gratuitous beating from one of the merchants' servants, Don Quijote remains nearly ecstatic in his pain (p. 62): "Y aún se tenía por dichoso, pareciéndole que aquélla era propia desgracia de caballeros andantes, y toda la atribuía a la falta de su caballo, y no era posible levantarse, según tenía brumado todo el cuerpo" ("Yet he considered himself fortunate, as it seemed to him that this was a real knight-errant's mishap and entirely, he believed, the fault of his horse. However, battered in body as he was, to rise was beyond his power," p. 44).

As Don Quijote lies unable to move, he again resolves (I, 5, 63) to take recourse to "su ordinario remedio, que era pensar en algún paso de sus libros" ("his usual remedy, which was to think of some passages in his books," p. 44). This statement is somewhat misleading, however, as his inspiration throughout most of this chapter is not the books of chivalry but several traditional *romances* about Valdovinos and the popular short story of Abindarráez.[55] Don Quijote's near delirious raving represents a height in his chivalric madness; it is ironic that his famous (p. 66) "Yo sé quién soy" ("I know who I am," p. 46) is uttered precisely at the moment when he assumes multiple identities.

Interestingly, chivalric archaism comes into general use at the end of this section: by the niece as she recalls her uncle's madness (p. 67), "y el sudor que sudaba del cansancio decía que era sangre de las *feridas*" ("and the sweat that flowed from him when he was weary he said was the blood of the wounds," p. 46); by the charitable Pedro Alonso as he goes along with his neighbor's mad ravings (p. 68), "Abran vuestras mercedes al señor Valdovinos y al señor marqués de Mantua, que viene mal *ferido*" ("Open, your worships, to Señor Baldwin and the Marquis of

54. Even this excuse of Don Quijote's has chivalric precedents (*Amadís*, I, 326): "porque bien cuydaua [Galaor] que la culpa de su cauallo le quitaua tan tarde la vitoria" ("because he really thought that the default of his horse was taking victory from him so late in the fight," p. 385).

55. Cervantes's inspiration for most of this chapter seems to be the anonymous *Entremés de los romances*. See Ramón Menéndez Pidal, "Un aspecto en la elaboración del *Quijote*," pp. 9–60, and Juan Millé y Giménez, *Sobre la génesis del "Quijote."*

Mantua, who comes badly wounded," p. 47); by Don Quijote, "que vengo *malferido* . . . y llámese, si fuere posible, a la sabia Urganda, que cure y *cate* de mis *feridas*" ("for I am sore wounded . . . and if possible send for the wise Urganda to cure and see to my wounds"); even in narration, "Lleváronle luego a la cama, y *catándole* las *feridas*, no le hallaron ninguna" ("They carried him to bed at once. After searching for his wounds they could find none"); and again in narration, but this time reproducing the words of Don Quijote, "que se pudieran *fallar* en gran parte de la tierra" ("to be found on earth").

I have summarized and commented on the adventures of these early chapters at some length in order to illustrate that virtually everything that takes place at the beginning of Don Quijote's career is directly inspired by the romances of chivalry. Many readers of the novel fail to perceive that nearly every word, every detail, is related to the protagonist's concept of how a knight-errant should act and talk. These first chapters,[56] when Don Quijote's dedication to his chosen profession of chivalry is absolute and when form matters more to him than content, can serve as a yardstick with which to measure his later retreat from his initial self-conception.

1.6 Chapters 7–10: The Second Sally

After his first brief sally, Don Quijote spends two full weeks at home, and although he appears reconciled to reality (I, 7, 85)—"sin dar muestras de querer segundar sus primeros devaneos" ("without showing any signs of a desire to take up with his former delusions," p. 56)—he is in fact carefully preparing to set out again in quest of adventures. He recruits his neighbor Sancho Panza to act as his squire, gathers together a fair sum of money, and prepares his armor. It must be added that his friends almost seem to encourage him in his chivalric madness: the priest and the barber invent the enchanter who steals away his library; the niece and the housekeeper, in carrying out this idea,

56. Gonzalo Torrente Ballester uses the awkward but accurate term *Protoquijote* to describe chapters 1–6 of the novel; *El "Quijote" como juego*, pp. 22, 89.

stumblingly supply Don Quijote with the name Frestón when they identify the enchanter as Muñatón or Fritón.[57] Don Quijote on his own might eventually have hit upon the idea of an evil enchanter who constantly works against him, but the fact is that this device, so convenient in rationalizing his defeats (the excuse of Rocinante's weakness, used appropriately and to effect in chapter 4, could not have been called on very often) and thus of the greatest importance in sustaining his chivalric vision, is provided by others.[58]

Similarly, the priest and the barber keep engaging Don Quijote in conversations concerning matters of chivalry (p. 85): Don Quijote "pasó graciosísimos cuentos con sus dos compadres el cura y el barbero, sobre que él decía que la cosa de que más necesidad tenía el mundo era de caballeros andantes y de que en él se resucitase la caballería andantesca" ("held lively discussions with his two friends, the priest and the barber, concerning his insistence that knights-errant were what the world stood most in need of, and that through him was to be accomplished the revival of knight-errantry," p. 56). Don Quijote most probably would have returned to his chivalric quest without this encouragement. He had suffered only one serious beating—after the encounter with the merchants in chapter 4—nothing had occurred to cause his enthusiasm to wane, and the stimulus provided by his friends only intensifies this desire.

The windmill episode, the first witnessed by Sancho Panza, contains all the elements that are characteristic of the quixotic adventure (I, 8, 88–90).

1. Reality is stated in narration: "En esto, descubrieron treinta o cuarenta molinos de viento que hay en aquel campo" ("At this point they came in sight of thirty or forty windmills that are on the plain," p. 58).

57. When Don Quijote settles on Frestón as the identity of his archenemy, he commits his only—and very uncharacteristic—onomastic error in matters of chivalry. The evil enchanter from *Belianís de Grecia* is called *Fristón*; the kitchenbound housekeeper's comic Fritón (from *frito*, "fried") is as close an approximation as the name Don Quijote chooses; Mancing, "Chivalric Names," pp. 229–30.

58. Torrente Ballester considers it very possible that Don Quijote might never have invented this excuse for himself; *Como juego*, p. 149.

2. Don Quijote willfully transforms reality: "ves allí, amigo Sancho Panza, donde se descubren treinta o pocos más, desaforados gigantes" ("Look there, friend Sancho Panza, where thirty or more monstrous giants rise up").

3. Sancho Panza points out the reality of the situation: "Mire vuestra merced . . . que aquellos que allí se parecen no son gigantes, sino molinos de viento" ("Look, your worship . . . What you see there are not giants but windmills," p. 59).

4. Don Quijote rejects Sancho's interpretation: "Bien parece . . . que no estás cursado en esto de las aventuras: ellos son gigantes" ("It is easy to see . . . that you are not used to the business of adventures. Those are giants").

5. Don Quijote either invokes or commends himself to Dulcinea: "y encomendándose de todo corazón a su señora Dulcinea" ("he commended himself with all his heart to his lady Dulcinea").

6. Don Quijote undertakes the adventure: "con la lanza en el ristre, arremetió a todo el galope de Rocinante y embistió con el primero molino que estaba delante" ("With lance braced and covered by his shield, he charged at Rocinante's fullest gallop and attacked the first mill that stood in front of him").

7. During (or immediately before or after) the adventure Don Quijote uses archaism: "*Non fuyades*, cobardes y viles criaturas" ("Fly not, cowards and vile beings").

8. During (or immediately before or after) the adventure Don Quijote uses at least one of his nonarchaic chivalric motifs: name—"aquel sabio ["that same"] Frestón"; strength—"la bondad de mi espada" ("my good sword").

9. The outcome, when it is not a victory, is unfortunate for Don Quijote: "y dándole una lanzada en el aspa, la volvió el viento con tanta furia, que hizo la lanza pedazos, llevándose tras sí al caballo y al caballero, que fue rodando muy maltrecho por el campo" ("as he drove his lance-point into the sail, the wind whirled it around with such force that it shivered the lance to pieces. It swept away with it horse and rider, and they were sent rolling over the plain, in sad condition indeed").

10. Don Quijote, when not victorious, blames his defeat on enchantment: "que yo pienso, y es así verdad, que aquel sabio Frestón que me robó el aposento y los libros ha vuelto estos gigantes en molinos por quitarme la gloria de su vencimiento" ("I think, and it is the truth, that the same sage Frestón who

carried off my study and books, has turned these giants into mills in order to rob me of the glory of vanquishing them").

This adventure is commonly considered emblematic of the entire novel and does indeed capture the spirit of Don Quijote's original chivalric inspiration as well as or better than any other (see section 3.3).

The adventure with the windmills is soon followed by the encounter with the Benedictine friars in which Don Quijote transforms reality, ignores Sancho's warning, and wins a stunning victory, rescuing—so he believes—a captive princess whom he orders to report to Dulcinea in Toboso (pp. 93–94). The sword battle with the Biscayan servant of the lady in the coach should be considered a related but separate adventure. This time—after the reader finds the narration interrupted, as it often is in the romances of chivalry, at a dramatic moment[59]— Don Quijote wins outright his most obviously authentic chivalric battle so far. His inflated pride (I, 10, 106)—"¿has visto más valeroso caballero que yo en todo lo descubierto de la tierra?" ("have you ever seen a more valiant knight than I in all the world?," p. 70)—more than compensates, at least for the time being (see section 2.1), for the loss of half of his left ear.

This section of the novel closes with a long conversation in which Don Quijote attempts to explain to Sancho some of the characteristics of knight-errantry. To this point in his career, Don Quijote has allowed no compromise in his chivalric world, but that will change very shortly.

59. For examples, see Clemencín, *Don Quijote*, p. 1100, note 44.

2

Knighthood Compromised

Que la oreja me duele más de
lo que yo quisiera (I, 10, 108)

(for my ear pains me more than I could wish, p. 71)

2.1 Sancho Panza: Reality

The most important single event in Cervantes's novel, after
the original exposition, is the introduction of Sancho Panza.
Once Sancho with his nonchivalric reality rides beside Don
Quijote, the latter can never again be the same. Sancho's effect
on Don Quijote's rhetoric can be considered in three ways. First
and most important is the squire's role as "Reality Instructor."[1]
Sancho's nagging voice asking (I, 8, 88) "¿Qué gigantes?"
("What giants?") and adding more specifically, "Mire vuestra
merced . . . que aquellos que allí se parecen no son gigantes,
sino molinos de viento" ("Look, your worship . . . What we see
there are not giants but windmills"), can never be effectively
silenced by Don Quijote's mere will (pp. 88–89)—"Bien parece
. . . que no estás cursado en esto de las aventuras: ellos son gigantes" ("It's easy to see . . . that you are not used to the business of adventures. Those are giants," p. 59). The knight's chivalric fantasy must from now on attempt to withstand repeated
assaults of reality from his squire.

A second concern is one of practicality. On his first sally, Don
Quijote traveled all day until he and Rocinante were exhausted,

1. I borrow this term as being both concise and accurately descriptive
from the character of Simkin in Saul Bellow's very Cervantine novel
Herzog (New York: Viking Press, 1964), p. 30. For a discussion of Sancho's role in pointing out reality to Don Quijote, see Carlos Varo,
Génesis y evolución del "Quijote," pp. 153–56.

his only conversation being with himself as he imagined how his history would be written by a benevolent wizard and as he invoked (with appropriate chivalric archaism) the support of Dulcinea (I, 2, 41–42). In contrast, his second sally begins with a conversation with Sancho Panza that deals partly with the *ínsula* that the squire is to receive and partly with the nature of the latter's wife (I, 7, 86–87). This discussion contains no archaism. Luis Rosales has shown how beginning with this conversation an essential change in Don Quijote's character takes place. Previously he has employed a "borrowed" language, using only his chivalric style and never really communicating with anyone. Now, with the simultaneous introduction of Sancho Panza and practical social dialogue, Don Quijote becomes more humanized.[2] One of the main reasons why Don Quijote's frequency of archaic speech declines is that it is simply not practical to sustain such an artificial style in his conversations with Sancho.

Third, Sancho Panza introduces into the novel an element of humor that even Don Quijote cannot ignore. In the early chapters, there is not recorded a single instance of laughter by Don Quijote: madmen do not sustain their visions of fantasy through humor. But when the knight-errant explains (I, 8, 90) to his squire "si no me quejo del dolor es porque no es dado a los caballeros andantes quejarse de herida alguna, aunque se le salgan las tripas por ella" ("if I make no complaint of the pain it is because knights-errant are not permitted to complain of any wound, even though their bowels be coming out through it"), Sancho responds, "De mí sé decir que me he de quejar del más pequeño dolor que tenga, si ya no se entiende también con los escuderos de los caballeros andantes eso del no quejarse" ("For

2. Luis Rosales, "Pequeña historia de un mito," pp. 155–56. Alfred Schutz makes the same point from a psychological and philosophical point of view, citing William James's essay on the relative reality of different individuals' "sub-universes" and concluding that Don Quijote "has to establish a 'sub-universe of discourse' with the fellow-men with whom he shares a face-to-face relationship within the world of common sense. This refers first of all to Sancho Panza, his squire"; "Don Quixote and the Problem of Reality," p. 142. See also Hans Jörg Neuschäfer, "Don Quijote como ser social. Nuevo aspecto de la dialéctica cervantina," 2:406–7.

my part, I confess I must complain however small the ache may be, unless this rule about not complaining applies to the squires of knights-errant also"), and the narration adds: "No se dejó de reír don Quijote de la simplicidad de su escudero" ("Don Quixote could not help laughing at his squire's simplicity," p. 60).[3]

Throughout the novel, Sancho will point out reality, will engage Don Quijote in nonchivalric conversation, and will make his master laugh. The cumulative effect of Sancho's influence will be the gradual undermining of Don Quijote's chivalric fantasy. Ironically, Sancho Panza himself will become increasingly caught up in that fantasy world and will at times seem as quixotic as his master, but his effect on Don Quijote will consistently be contrary to the sustaining of a chivalric role.

Reality is not, however, first introduced into Don Quijote's chivalric world by Sancho Panza; it is present from the very first chapter when, after destroying the week's work that went into the making of a helmet, he prudently decides not to test the strength of his second effort (I, 1, 37): "él quedó satisfecho de su fortaleza, y sin querer hacer nueva experiencia della, la diputó y tuvo por celada finísima de encaje" ("he was satisfied with its strength. Then, not caring to try any more experiments with it, he accepted and commissioned it as a helmet of the most perfect construction," p. 28).[4] It is also possible that the surreptitiousness of his departure on both his first and second sallies (I, 2, 40)—"Y así, sin dar parte a persona alguna de su intención, y sin que nadie le viese, una mañana, antes del día, . . . por la puerta falsa de un corral salió al campo" ("So, without informing anyone of his intentions, and without anybody seeing him, one morning before dawn . . . by the back door of the yard sallied forth upon the plain," p. 29)—and (I, 7, 86)—"sin despedirse Panza de sus hijos y mujer, ni don Quijote de su ama y sobrina, una noche se salieron del lugar sin que persona los viese" ("without taking leave, Sancho Panza of his wife and children, or Don Quixote of his housekeeper and niece, they sallied

3. See Varo, *Génesis y evolución*, p. 170.

4. Salvador de Madariaga, *Don Quixote: An Introductory Essay in Psychology*, p. 110.

forth, unseen by anybody, from the village one night," p. 57)—
belies a tacit recognition that his chivalric intention is inappropriate.[5]

The first major incursion of reality that directly contradicts
Don Quijote's chivalric vision is the loss of half of his ear in the
battle with the Biscayan. Previously, physical pain had been
readily accepted by Don Quijote as part of the rigors of knight-
errantry. His first serious, painful beating occurs at the time of
the adventure of the Toledan merchants. Don Quijote is left
lying on the ground unable to rise, but with his chivalric spirit
intact (I, 4, 62): "Y aún se tenía por dichoso, pareciéndole que
aquélla era propia desgracia de caballeros andantes, y toda la
atribuía a la falta de su caballo, y no era posible levantarse, según
tenía brumado todo el cuerpo" ("Yet he considered himself fortunate, as it seemed to him that this was a real knight-errant's
mishap and entirely, he believed, the fault of his horse. However, battered in body as he was, to rise was beyond his power,"
p. 44). His next adventure is that of the windmills, and though
he receives a hard and painful fall, he announces to Sancho, in
the words previously cited, that knights-errant were not permitted to complain when they were wounded.

Cervantes describes the wound inflicted by the Biscayan with
brilliant comic understatement.

> mas la buena suerte, que para mayores cosas le tenía guardado,
> torció la espada de su contrario, de modo que, aunque le
> acertó en el hombro izquierdo, no le hizo otro daño que de-
> sarmarle todo aquel lado, llevándole, de camino, gran parte
> de la celada, con la mitad de la oreja; que todo ello con espan-
> tosa ruina vino al suelo, dejándole muy maltrecho. (I, 9, 103)

> (But that good fortune which reserved him for greater things
> turned aside the sword of his adversary so that, though it
> smote him upon the left shoulder, it did him no more harm
> than to strip all that side of its armor, carrying away a great
> part of his helmet with half of his ear. It all fell to the ground
> with a fearful din, leaving him in sorry plight.) (p. 68)

5. I say that this is possible because a secret departure is a characteristic of the knights-errant whom Don Quijote imitates. See Daniel Eisenberg, "*Don Quijote* and the Romances of Chivalry: The Need for a
Reexamination," pp. 520–21.

Don Quijote completes the adventure, an authentic chivalric victory, as previously observed, and goes on his way, inflated with pride, without mentioning his wound. It is, appropriately, his Reality Instructor, Sancho, who advises his master (I, 10, 107) to take steps to cure himself, "que le va mucha sangre de esa oreja" ("because a great deal of blood is flowing from that ear," p. 70). Don Quijote ecstatically raves about the magic universal healing balm of Fierabrás but is forced to admit (p. 108) that "la oreja me duele más de lo que yo quisiera" ("my ear pains me more than I would like," p. 71). An authentic fictional knight-errant from the romances of chivalry does not complain about his wounds, but Don Quijote—who is thus implicitly inauthentic according to his own norms—does, and does again (p. 109)—"porque yo te voto a Dios que me va doliendo mucho la oreja" ("for I swear to God, this ear is giving me great pain," p. 72)—and again (I, 11, 118)—"sería bien, Sancho, que me vuelvas a curar esta oreja, que me va doliendo más de lo que es menester" ("it would be well if you would dress this ear of mine again, for it is giving me more pain than it should," p. 78).[6]

The reality is that the ear hurts. Sancho's first-aid kit is insufficient and Don Quijote does not have any magic balm of Fierabrás. Finally the ear is cured not by chivalric ideals or chivalric magic but by simple, rustic, practical knowledge. One of the goatherds, on seeing his guest's wound, offers a cure by applying a mixture of a few rosemary leaves, saliva, and salt to the ear and covering it with a bandage. This treatment, he assures, will be sufficient (I, 11, 118): "y así fue la verdad" ("and so it

---

6. Varo (*Génesis y evolución*, p. 177) notes that Don Quijote's ability to feel pain further humanizes his character. Both Marthe Robert and Arthur Efron must ignore these passages in order to make a similar erroneous point. Robert states that Don Quijote "refuses to believe in the reality of his wounds . . . It is impossible to make any contact with him, even by the radical means of cruelty and violence"; *The Old and the New: From Don Quixote to Kafka*, pp. 135–36. Efron discusses the issue at some length before concluding that "like the ideals of the Knight, his pain and his sorrow exist only so that they may be perpetuated further. They become goals in themselves, stock roles blithely masquerading as the height of life's possibilities. The possible emergence of real value from the experience of pain . . . is thus truncated"; *Don Quixote and the Dulcineated World*, p. 47.

proved," p. 78); Don Quijote never again complains of the pain of his ear. Later, when he is again bleeding and in pain (I, 17, 166)—"porque se me va mucha sangre de la herida que esta fantasma me ha dado" ("I am losing much blood from the wound that the phantom gave me")—Don Quijote, in a tacit admission of the efficacy of this remedy, recalls the identical ingredients when he prepares to manufacture the balm of Fierabrás: "procura que se me dé un poco de aceite, vino, *sal* y *romero* para hacer el salutífero bálsamo" ("have him give me a little oil, wine, *salt*, and *rosemary* to make the salutary balm," p. 113; my italics). The reality of physical pain cannot be dismissed by Don Quijote; his many stonings, beatings, falls, and various battle wounds, like the presence of Sancho Panza, have a cumulative destructive effect on his chivalric career.

2.2 Chapters 11–14: A Pastoral Interlude

Chapters 11–14 represent a deliberate and effective change in the pace of narration and a disaster for Don Quijote's career. Knight and squire arrive at the camp of some goatherds and are invited to join them for a simple, rustic dinner. In a long, uninvited postdinner speech (I, 11, 113–14), Don Quijote contrasts the "Dichosa edad y siglos dichosos" ("Happy the age, happy the time," p. 74) of a mythical Golden Age with "estos nuestros detestables siglos" ("this hateful age of ours," p. 75) in order to justify, with considerable rhetorical skill and eloquence, the establishment of knight-errantry—"Para cuya seguridad . . . se instituyó la orden de los caballeros andantes" ("In defense of these . . . the order of knights-errant was instituted")—and his own adherence to this order—"Desta orden soy yo" (p. 115). Unfortunately, this standard set-piece is wasted on the unlettered goatherds (but not on Sancho Panza; see section 2.5), who maintain a respectful, probably slightly embarrassed, silence.

With the arrival of Antonio and his song to Olalla, chivalric matters are thrust into the background. The subsequent news that the feigned shepherd (I, 12, 119), "aquel famoso pastor estudiante" ("the famed student-shepherd"), Grisóstomo, has died of love for the pseudoshepherdess Marcela—"aquella que se anda en hábito de pastora por esos andurriales" ("the girl who wanders about in these lonely places in the dress of a shepherdess," p. 79)—introduces a brilliant series of ironic contrasts, especially literature versus life (the literary pastoral of Grisóstomo and Marcela in contrast with the genuine pastoral of the goatherds) and literature versus literature (the literary pastoral of Grisóstomo as opposed to the literary chivalric of Don Quijote). Grisóstomo has played his role to the ultimate extreme, dying of love—or committing suicide—for the disdainful Marcela. Don Quijote, meanwhile, has found it increasingly difficult to suffer even the loss of part of an ear for the nonexistent Dulcinea.

The next day's journey to the site of Grisóstomo's burial is enlivened by the presence of the cultured and slightly malicious Vivaldo, who is described (I, 13, 128) as a "persona muy discreta y de alegre condición" ("person of great shrewdness and with a merry disposition," p. 85) and is implicitly—and unfavorably—contrasted with the reserved and respectful goatherds. Vivaldo is the first cultured person Don Quijote meets who is very familiar with the romances of chivalry[7] and who amuses himself at Don Quijote's expense, drawing him out in matters of chivalry, concentrating on the vulnerable point of the knight's near sacrilegious devotion to his lady. Don Quijote has obviously met his match in Vivaldo and is forced into an overstatement (p. 130)—"digo que no puede ser que haya caballero andante sin dama . . . y a buen seguro que no se haya visto historia donde se halle caballero andante sin amores" ("I say it is impossible there could be a knight-errant without a lady . . . Quite assuredly no history has ever been written concerning a knight-errant without a lady," p. 86)—which is exposed by Vivaldo who cites Amadís de Gaula's brother, Don Galaor, who never devoted himself to a single lady.[8] Don Quijote, trapped, reacts

7. Obviously, Vivaldo anticipates the type of character that Don Quijote will encounter more frequently later in the novel: Dorotea, the duke and duchess, Don Antonio Moreno, and so on.

8. In effect, as Galaor has no need to remain faithful to any particular lady, he is able to sleep with several whom he rescues during the four volumes of *Amadís de Gaula*. Place calls Galaor (*Amadís*, III (1962), 934)

in a manner that anticipates the classic Sancho Panza, by citing a proverb (p. 131)—"Señor, una golondrina sola no hace verano" ("Sir, one solitary swallow does not make a summer")—and then by contradicting himself with an outright lie: "Cuanto más, que yo sé que de secreto estaba ese caballero muy bien enamorado . . . ; averiguado está muy bien que él tenía una sola a quien él había hecho señora de su voluntad, a la cual se enco-mendaba muy a menudo y muy secretamente" ("Moreover, that knight, as I am aware was in secret very deeply in love. . . . it is well established that he had one alone whom he made mistress of his will. To her he commended himself very frequently and secretly," p. 87). Vivaldo continues to press on this matter and on the identity of Dulcinea, and Don Quijote is saved only by their arrival at the funeral. Don Quijote's lie is important. Since later in the novel he will state (I, 25, 263) that "las órdenes de caballería . . . nos mandan que no digamos mentira alguna" ("the ordinances of chivalry . . . forbid us to tell any lie," p. 182), the statement about Galaor is a clear sign that Don Qui-jote has failed to maintain his own chivalric standards during the conversation with Vivaldo.

Don Quijote is again thrust into the background during the funeral but is able to assert himself dramatically and, perhaps, effectively in his defense of Marcela at the very end of chapter 14. Clearly, Don Quijote finds his chivalric role more difficult to sustain in the face of nonchivalric pastoral reality and well-executed pastoral-inspired literature. Overall, Don Quijote comes off quite badly in these chapters. In the company of the simple but generous and attractive goatherds, he looks foolish in forcing Sancho to sit beside him in order to illustrate the uni-versality of chivalry, absurdly and uselessly rhetorical in his Golden Age speech, and unnecessarily pedantic in his frequent corrections of Pedro's speech. He is on the defensive throughout the conversation with Vivaldo and clearly loses their debate. He is superfluous at the funeral of Grisóstomo, whose ultimate lit-erature-inspired act makes those of Don Quijote pale in con-

---

"un alegre seductor, realmente más donjuanesco que don Juan" ("a merry seducer, really more Don Juan–like than Don Juan"). See also Clemencín, *Don Quijote*, p. 1134, note 38.

trast. Even his defense of Marcela may have been ineffective (I, 14, 144): "O ya que fuese por las amenazas de don Quijote, o porque Ambrosio les dijo que concluyesen con lo que a su buen amigo debían, ninguno de los pastores se movió ni apartó de allí" ("Whether it was because of the threats of Don Quixote, or because Ambrosio told them to fulfil their duty to their good friend, none of the shepherds moved or stirred from the spot," p. 96).

2.3 Rocinante

After attending the burial of Grisóstomo and searching in vain for Marcela, Don Quijote and Sancho pause to rest (I, 15, 146) in "un prado lleno de fresca yerba, junto del cual corría un arroyo apacible y fresco" ("a meadow covered with tender grass. Alongside ran a pleasant cool stream," p. 99). In this lush meadow, typical of the setting for Neoplatonic love laments in the pastoral romances, Sancho unbridles his *rucio* and Don Quijote's Rocinante to graze, confidently assuming that the latter is (p. 147) "tan manso y tan poco rijoso, que todas las yeguas de la dehesa de Córdoba no le hicieran tomar mal siniestro" ("of [such a] staid, continent temperament, that all the mares in the Córdoba pastures would not lead him into error," p. 99). However, Sancho misjudges Rocinante's tastes, for it turns out that the horse's sexual interests are indeed aroused by some nearby mares. Their rejections of his overtures and the beating that ensues for the knight, squire, and erotically inclined horse provide the framework for a highly comic situation.

In this scene, there is another level of comedy involving linguistic subtleties that deserves analysis and comment. The first mention of the mares is in a reference to "una manada de hacas galicianas" ("a drove of Galician ponies"). What is important here is the use of *hacas* rather than the alternate form *jacas*. While it is possible that Cervantes's orthography could be the result of mere coincidence, or even of a deliberate intent to create alliteration in the phrase "una manada de *hac*as *gal*icianas de unos arrieros *gal*legos," an even more plausible explanation of his preference for the *h-* spelling is his desire to set up a phonetic contrast with the comic archaic *f-* in the beginning of the following paragraph (p. 147): "Sucedió, pues, que a Rocinante le vino en deseo de refocilarse con las señoras *facas*" ("It was at this moment that Rocinante took a fancy to disport himself with the ladies," p. 99). Although the comic personification and irony implicit in the phrase "las *señoras* hacas," especially in the light of what follows, might have been sufficient to achieve a considerable comic effect, the substitution of *facas* for *hacas* cannot help but remind the reader of Don Quijote's frequent use of the archaic *f-*. Reinforcing the assumption of a deliberate choice of the *h- < f-* archaism is the subsequent presence of the equally archaic *ál*: "Mas ellas, que . . . debían de tener más gana de pacer que de *ál*" (p. 147) ("They, however, seemed to prefer their pasture to him").[9] It is almost as though Rocinante takes on human and even, like his master, chivalric characteristics (see note 15); the horse seems to be "thinking" in *fabla* about his erotic chivalric adventure.[10]

The significance of this scene, which casts an ironic light on the preceding episode of pure and idealized love in the case of Marcela,[11] is augmented by what occurs in the following chapter in the inn of Juan Palomeque el Zurdo where Don Quijote and Sancho take refuge.[12] The Manchegan knight, unable to sleep,

9. The use of *ál* here recalls the well-known line of Celestina to Pármeno: "Este es el deleyte; que lo al, mejor lo fazen los asnos en el prado" ("That's the real pleasure. As for the other thing, the donkeys in the field can do it better than we can"); Francisco de Rojas, *La Celestina*, 1:108 (*The Spanish Bawd*, trans. J. M. Cohen, p. 51). In fact, it is quite likely that Cervantes had this specific passage (largely responsible, perhaps, for making *ál* less than acceptable in polite language) in mind when writing this scene.

10. This aspect of the personification of Rocinante, together with any consideration of archaism in the passage, is absent in the stylistic analysis and subsequent discussion of this paragraph by Charles W. Steele in his article "Functions of the Grisóstomo–Marcela Episode in *Don Quijote*: Symbolism, Drama, Parody," pp. 14–15.

11. Helena Percas de Ponseti, *Cervantes y su concepto del arte*, 1:132. See also Steele, "Grisóstomo–Marcela Episode," pp. 15–16.

12. Joaquín Casalduero, noting the setting of Rocinante's misadventure, sees it as a burlesque exaggeration of pastoral elements that sets up a parody of chivalric love in the Don Quijote–Maritornes scene in the next chapter; *Sentido y forma del "Quijote,"* p. 91. There is a fusion of pastoral and chivalric elements here, but the literary *parody*—which

imagines that the daughter of the lord of the castle in which he is lodged is smitten with love for him—in accord with what takes place in many romances of chivalry—and intends to visit him in his bedchamber. In fact, the innkeeper's daughter is sound asleep; up and about, however, is the servant girl Maritornes, who intends to keep an appointment with a mule driver whose bed is located near that of Don Quijote (I, 16, 157): "Había el arriero concertado con ella que aquella noche se refocilarían juntos" ("The mule driver had made an arrangement with her for recreation that night," pp. 106–7). Noteworthy is the use of the same verb, *refocilarse*, that was associated with Rocinante's misadventure (which also involved *arrieros*) in the previous chapter. This word appears only one other time in the novel (II, 22, 742), and then with no sexual connotation.

Don Quijote used some archaic words on his arrival at the inn (p. 157): *fermosa* (twice), *este vuestro*, *habedes fecho*, and *pluguiera*. Now in bed (pp. 159–60), lying "mal *ferido*" ("sorely wounded"), he imagines that the approaching maiden has come looking for him "a *furto* de sus padres" ("without the knowledge of her parents"), and as she passes, he reaches out his arms "para recebir a su *fermosa* doncella" ("to receive his beauteous damsel," p. 108). These archaisms occur in narration, perhaps reflecting Don Quijote's thoughts, as was the case in the scene dramatizing Rocinante's amorous disaster in the previous chapter. Thus, holding the girl tightly, he says (p. 160): "Quisiera hallarme en términos, *fermosa* y alta señora, de poder pagar tamaña merced como la que con la vista de vuestra gran *fermosura* me *habedes fecho*" ("Would that I found myself, lovely and exalted lady, in a position to repay the favor that thou, by the sight of thy great beauty, hast granted me," p. 108). While stating his intention to defend his chastity and remain faithful to Dulcinea, Don Quijote's actions strongly suggest an inclination to do just the opposite.[13] The scene, of course, ends in chaos.

---

must involve a distortion of "the most striking peculiarities of subject matter *and style*" (my italics) of a work—is specifically chivalric. See the definition of parody cited in Chapter 1, note 20.

13. The contrast between Don Quijote's words and his deeds is also pointed out and commented on by Efron, *Don Quixote and the Dulcineated World*, p. 53.

Rocinante's aborted sexual adventure takes place in a perfect setting for an idealized human love scene, but that of Don Quijote takes place in a garret that (p. 155) "daba manifiestos indicios que había servido de pajar muchos años" ("showed signs of having formerly served for many years as a hayloft," p. 105), in fact, a stable, "aquel estrellado [star-lit] establo." [14] The presence of the muleteer, with his bed made of (p. 158) "las enjalmas y . . . todo el adorno de los dos mejores mulos que traía" ("the packsaddles and all the trappings of the two best mules he had," p. 107), contributes to the animal imagery that informs the scene. If Celestina's proverbial statement is that donkeys do it better in the field (see note 9), the implicit corollary is that people do it worse in the hayloft. [15]

14. Henry Mendeloff describes it as "more fit for animals than humans," but his subsequent analysis of the farcical aspects of the scene in the inn contains no reference to the related events in the previous chapter; "The Maritornes Episode (*DQ*: I, 16): A Cervantine Bedroom Farce," pp. 753–59.

15. The humanization of Rocinante and the *rucio* is a process that goes on throughout the novel. The friendship between the two animals is described at some length and a comparison is made with classical heroes (II, 12, 662–63). After Rocinante's unfortunate erotic episode, Sancho refers to him (I, 15, 150) as a "persona casta y tan pacífica como yo" ("a virtuous person and as quiet as myself," p. 102) and (p. 152) as a "caballero andante" ("knight-errant," p. 103). On his first sally, Don Quijote refers to Rocinante (I, 2, 42) as "compañero eterno mío" ("constant companion," p. 30); the tearful Sancho who leaves his governorship calls the *rucio* (II, 53, 987) "compañero mío y amigo mío" ("comrade and friend and partner," p. 720), and when he falls into the pit (II, 55, 1000), he observes that "nunca Sancho Panza se apartó de su asno, ni su asno de Sancho Panza" ("Sancho Panza is never separated from his donkey, nor his donkey from Sancho Panza," p. 729) and again calls his ass "compañero y amigo mío." In general, the relationships between tall, thin Don Quijote and long, lanky Rocinante and between short, fat Sancho Panza and his well-fed *rucio* tend to blur the distinctions between man and beast. Completing the process of animal–human reversal are statements by Sancho (II, 11, 653)—"Señor, las tristezas no se hicieron para las bestias, sino para los hombres; pero si los hombres las sienten demasiado, se vuelven bestias" ("Sadness, señor, was made not for beasts but for men, but if men give in to it they turn beasts," p. 478)—Don Quijote (II, 28, 799)—"Asno eres, y asno has de ser, y en asno has de parar cuando se te acabe el curso de la vida; que para mí tengo que antes llegará ella a su último término que tú caigas y des en

   There is an interesting recollection of this scene later in the
novel when Don Quijote, at the same inn, goes outside to guard
the "castle." In order to play a trick on him, Maritornes and the
innkeeper's daughter, the two "semidoncellas" ("demi-damsels"),
have him reach his hand up to (I, 43, 478) "un agujero de un
pajar" ("a hole in the wall of a straw-loft," p. 349)—probably
the same one where the previous action took place—where they
tie his wrist and then leave him to spend the night, arm uplifted,
standing on Rocinante's back. In the morning, some travelers
arrive at the inn. One of their mounts sniffs at Rocinante who
after all, being made of flesh and bone (p. 483), "aunque parecía
de leño" ("though he looked as if he were made of wood"),
cannot resist responding to "quien le llegaba a hacer caricias"
("the one who had come to offer him attentions," p. 348).
Whereupon, he moves and leaves his master dangling by his tied
wrist. Don Quijote's pride and belief that the daughter of the
lord of the castle is in love with him get him into difficulties; his
horse's erotic interests compound his misfortune.

   The attempts of both Rocinante and Don Quijote at erotic
adventures end in frustration and disaster. In both cases, chivalric archaism, especially the *f-*, provides a key to interpretation.
Rocinante, with his own version of his master's style of speech
and sexual desires, anticipates and parodies Don Quijote in the
Maritornes adventure. Again, as always in the novel, there are
multiple images and structural and thematic relationships that
make a simple, comic scene much richer and more significant

---

la cuenta de que eres bestia" ("Ass you are, ass you will be, and ass you
will end when the course of your life is run; for I know it will come to
its close before you perceive or discern that you are a beast," p. 585)—
and Cide Hamete Benengeli (II, 29, 807)—"Volvieron a sus bestias, y
a ser bestias, don Quijote y Sancho" ("Don Quixote and Sancho returned to their animals—and to their beastly life," p. 590). In the inn,
Sancho is tossed in a blanket like a dog (I, 17, 170–71) and later Don
Quijote is incited like a dog (*azuzado*) by the people watching him fight
with the goatherd (I, 52, 551; see section 3.4). Maese Pedro owns an
ape who can talk to him (II, 25); men bray like donkeys (II, 25, 27, 55);
enchanters turn human beings into grotesque statues of animals (II, 39,
876); Dulcinea is compared (quite suggestively) with a rabbit (II, 73,
1127); and so on. The novel's rich underlying animal–human imagery,
especially in part II, is a topic worthy of further study.

than it seems at first glance. If there is a single cardinal principle to be observed when dealing with *Don Quijote*, it is that nothing is as simple and obvious as it first appears.

2.4 Chapters 15–22: Chivalric Adventures

Chapters 15–22 form what may be artistically the best section of *Don Quijote*. In a series of brilliant—and brilliantly narrated—scenes, knight and squire come alive as have no other characters before them, and few after them, in the history of literature. The comic genius of these pages, properly called "la cumbre del humor" ("the pinnacle of humor") by Carlos Varo,[16] has seldom been rivaled. In this part of the novel, the figure of Sancho Panza receives its fullest development (see the following section) and that of Don Quijote simultaneously declines in knightly perfection and grows in human stature.

After the frustration and humiliation that Don Quijote experiences during the Grisóstomo episode, the knight wisely turns down the offer of Vivaldo and his friends to accompany them to Seville (I, 14, 145), "por ser lugar tan acomodado a hallar aventuras, que en cada calle y tras cada esquina se ofrecen más que en otro alguno" ("this being a convenient place for finding adventures, which rose up in every street and around every corner oftener than anywhere else," p. 96).[17] Don Quijote conceivably realizes that he would continue to be an object of ridicule and mockery among these people, for his reason for turning them down is an outright lie. He says that "por entonces no quería ni debía ir a Sevilla, hasta que hubiese despojado todas

16. Varo, *Génesis y evolución*, p. 187.

17. Clemencín (*Don Quijote*, p. 1143, note 37) notes that Seville would be the worst possible place for chivalric adventures. He is obviously correct: when Don Quijote visits a comparable big city, Barcelona, in part II, he acts more like a tourist than a knight-errant (see section 4.5). When Sansón Carrasco, whose fun-loving personality is anticipated here by Vivaldo, plays the role of the Caballero de los Espejos, he tells Don Quijote that he has defeated the famous Sevillan giantess Giralda (II, 14, 674), which could be a hint of the type of adventure that Vivaldo and his friends might have prepared for Don Quijote had he accepted their offer.

aquellas sierras de ladrones malandrines, de quien era fama que todas estaben llenas" ("he could not go to Seville until he had cleared all those mountains of the highwaymen and robbers who were said to infest them"), but in fact he has made up his mind to "ir a buscar a la pastora Marcela y ofrecerle todo lo que él podía en su servicio" ("go in quest of the shepherdess Marcela and offer her all the services he could render," p. 97).

In the episode of Rocinante's unfortunate attempt to satisfy his sexual desires, Don Quijote does not transform reality at all. He realizes from the start that he is dealing with (I, 15, 147) "gente soez y de baja ralea" ("base people of low birth," p. 100). Sancho's realistic observation that they are outnumbered by more than ten to one piques Don Quijote's pride and evokes his famous response (p. 148), "Yo valgo por ciento" ("I count for a hundred," p. 100). After their drubbing, when Sancho calls his master in a voice described as "enferma y lastimada" ("weak and doleful"), Don Quijote—in anger, humiliation, frustration, and pain—answers "con el mesmo tono afeminado y doliente" ("in the same feeble, suffering tone"). Don Quijote is able to rationalize this defeat, blaming himself for having exceeded the laws of chivalry by raising his sword against men who were not knights-errant. He is still able to boast (p. 149) of "el valor de este mi fuerte brazo" ("the might of my strong arm"), which leads the narrator to comment that "tal quedó de arrogante el pobre señor con el vencimiento del valiente vizcaíno" ("Such was the poor gentleman's arrogance, because of his victory over the stout Biscayan," p. 101). Later, he attempts to console his squire by delivering a lecture (p. 151) on how "la vida de los caballeros andantes está sujeta a mil peligros y desventuras" ("the life of knights-errant is subject to a thousand dangers and reverses," p. 102), and by citing examples of how famous knights-errant, Amadís de Gaula and the Caballero del Febo, were able to overcome adversity. Unfortunately, his statement about the lashing given to Amadís by his archrival Arcaláus is either a lie or the result of a confused memory.[18]

The famous night of Maritornes described in the last section

18. See Clemencín, *Don Quijote*, p. 1149, note 28.

comes about (I, 16, 158–59) because "los pensamientos que
siempre nuestro caballero traía de los sucesos que a cada paso se
cuentan en los libros autores de su desgracia, le trujo a la imaginación una de las estrañas locuras que buenamente imaginarse
pueden" ("the thoughts, ever present to our knight's mind, of
the incidents described at every turn in the books that were the
cause of his misfortune, delivered up his imagination to the most
extraordinary delusion that one could possibly conceive," p.
108). In the aftermath of the beating he receives, Don Quijote
resorts to his classic excuse (I, 17, 163–64): "sin duda . . . o yo
sé poco, o este castillo es encantado" ("Assuredly . . . for either
I know little about it, or this castle is enchanted," p. 111). This
ought to obviate any possible intrusion of reality, but there is a
subtle, tacit acknowledgment of reality in Don Quijote's request
for ingredients (suspiciously reminiscent of those used by the
goatherd who cured the knight's ear) for the balm of Fierabrás.
There is, shortly after, when Sancho has been incapacitated by
the magic healing potion, an even more startling implicit admission of nonchivalric reality on Don Quijote's part. According to
the narration, Don Quijote (p. 168), "aliviado y sano" ("relieved
and well"), is anxious to depart in order to go "buscar aventuras,
pareciéndole que todo el tiempo que allí se tardaba era quitársele
al mundo y a los en él menesterosos de su favor y amparo, y
más, con la seguridad y confianza que llevaba en su bálsamo"
("in quest of adventures. It seemed to him that all the time he
lingered was a deprivation for the world and those in it who
stood in need of his help and protection, and all the more since
he had the security and confidence his balm afforded him"), and
so, "forzado deste deseo, él mismo ensilló a Rocinante y enal-
bardó al jumento de su escudero, a quien también ayudó a vestir
y a subir en el asno" ("urged by this impulse, he saddled Rocinante himself and put the packsaddle on his squire's beast. He
also helped Sancho to dress and to mount the ass," p. 114). It
would be, to say the least, an extraordinary breach of propriety
for an authentic knight-errant to saddle not only his own horse
but also his squire's and then, even worse, to help his servant to
get dressed and mounted. It is proper and even common for
someone who has just inadvertently caused a close friend to suf-

fer innocently to do such things, but these acts are thoroughly out of keeping with the practices of the order of chivalry.

Finally, when Sancho Panza is tossed in a blanket (p. 170) by some "gente alegre, bien intencionada, maleante y juguetona" ("lively fellows all, well-disposed, fond of a joke and playful," p. 116), Don Quijote is unable to come to his assistance (p. 171): "Probó a subir desde el caballo a las bardas; pero estaba tan molido y quebrantado, que aun apearse no pudo" ("He tried to climb from his horse on to the top of the wall, but he was so bruised and battered that he could not even dismount," p. 116). The narration here directly contradicts its own words of just three pages before when it stated that Don Quijote felt "aliviado y sano" and was so anxious to continue his quest that he acted as servant to his squire. "Molido y quebrantado" ("bruised and battered")—and, one might add, humiliated and repentant for the harm he has caused Sancho—rings more true here than the alternative. Furthermore, the blanketing, which Sancho Panza will never forget nor let his master forget, proves a constant source of embarrassment for the ineffective Don Quijote, who will repeatedly change his lies to his squire in no fewer than four attempts to find one that might be acceptable:

1. "no me fue posible subir por ellas, ni menos pude apearme de Rocinante, porque me debían de tener encantado" (I, 18, 173) ("it was beyond my power to climb it [the wall] nor could I even dismount from Rocinante, because they no doubt had me enchanted," p. 117).

2. "Fue porque no pude yo saltar las paredes del corral" (I, 19, 186) ("it was because I was unable to leap the walls of the yard," p. 126).

3. "Que, bien apurada la cosa, burla fue y pasatiempo; que, a no entenderlo yo ansí, ya yo hubiera vuelto allá, y hubiera hecho en tu venganza más daño que el que hicieron los griegos por la robada Elena" (I, 21, 211) ("For jest and sport it was, properly regarded, and had I not seen it in that light I would have returned and done more mischief in revenging you than the Greeks did for the kidnap of Helen," p. 144).

4. "que si así fuera, yo te vengara entonces, y aun agora; pero ni entonces ni agora, pude ni vi en quién tomar venganza de tu agravio" (I, 46, 506) ("for had it been so, I would have

avenged you that instant, or even now. But neither then nor now could I do so, not having seen anyone I could punish for it," p. 365).[19]

It is immediately after his humiliating tossing in the blanket that Sancho Panza introduces his return-home motif (I, 18, 174)—"sería mejor . . . el volvernos a nuestro lugar" ("The best and wisest thing . . . would be for us to return home," p. 118). For a knight-errant to be abandoned by his squire would be an embarrassing experience; for a squire to talk a knight-errant into giving up the quest and returning home would be utterly unacceptable. From now on, Don Quijote will periodically have to face the pressure of coming up with inducements to keep his squire at his side. On this first occasion, he creates one of his greatest spectacles, that of the warring armies of sheep. The narration states that Don Quijote "tenía a todas horas y momentos llena la fantasía de aquellas batallas, encantamentos, sucesos, desatinos, amores, desafíos, que en los libros de caballerías se cuentan, *y todo cuanto hablaba, pensaba o hacía* era encaminado a cosas semejantes" (p. 175; my italics) ("At all times and seasons his fancy was full of the battles, enchantments, adventures, reckless feats, loves, and challenges that are recorded in the books of chivalry, *and everything he said, thought, or did* had reference to such things," p. 119; my italics), but, as we have already seen, this statement has less validity than it would have had earlier in the novel. Still, Don Quijote's fantastic description of the knights-errant who compose the two armies is a chivalric masterpiece. Sancho believes his master for a while but finally sees the reality of the situation. Don Quijote enters the fray convinced that he can, like so many of his fictional heroes, decide the question (p. 179): "que solo basto a dar la victoria a la parte a quien yo diere mi ayuda" ("for alone I suffice to bring victory to the side I choose to aid," p. 122).[20] Defeated and wounded

19. See also Don Quijote's comment that he (spiritually) shared fully in Sancho's (physical) pain (II, 2, 593).

20. See Clemencín, *Don Quijote*, pp. 1439–40, note 37. Daniel Eisenberg also discusses such an adventure but perhaps goes too far in rationalizing the relative verisimilitude of his hero's feat; Ortúñez de Calahorra, *Espejo de príncipes y cavalleros*, 4:98–99, note for lines 21ff.

again, Don Quijote once more resorts to the excuse of enchantment but is unwilling to have Sancho put the matter to a test:

> porque te desengañes y veas ser verdad lo que te digo: sube en tu asno y síguelos bonitamente, y verás cómo, en alejándose de aquí algún poco, se vuelven en su ser primero, y, dejando de ser carneros, son hombres hechos y derechos, como yo te los pinté primero . . . Pero no vayas agora, que he menester tu favor y ayuda. (p. 181)

> ("to undeceive yourself, and grasp that what I say is true. Mount your ass and follow them quietly, and you will see that when they have gone some little distance they will return to their original shape. Ceasing to be sheep, they will become men exactly as I described them to you. But do not go just yet, for I want your help and assistance.") (p. 123)

In order to placate his obviously dejected squire (p. 182), Don Quijote modifies his "sube en tu jumento. Sancho el bueno, y vente tras mí" ("Sancho the Good, mount your beast and come along with us," p. 124) to (pp. 183–84) "y guiá tú por donde quisieres; que esta vez quiero dejar a tu elección el alojarnos. . . . Sube, amigo, y guía, que yo te seguiré al paso que quisieres" ("and lead on where you will, for this time I leave our lodging to your choice. . . . Mount, friend, and lead the way, and I will follow you at whatever pace you wish," pp. 124–25).

The nocturnal encounter with the funeral procession gives Don Quijote a chance to recover some chivalric stature in a classic adventure.[21] Don Quijote's challenge is appropriately archaic.

> Deteneos, caballeros, o quienquiera que seáis, y dadme cuenta de quién sois, de dónde venís, adónde vais, qué es lo que en aquellas andas lleváis; que, según las muestras, o vosotros habéis *fecho*, o *vos* han *fecho*, algún *desaguisado*, y conviene y es menester que yo lo sepa, o bien para castigaros del mal que *fecistes*, o bien para vengaros del tuerto que *vos ficieron*. (I, 19, 187)

21. Riquer points out that, while the modern reader might well find this adventure absurd, Cervantes's contemporaries readily perceived it as a conscious parody of a particular episode from *Palmerín de Inglaterra*; *Don Quijote*, p. 184, note. See also Clemencín, *Don Quijote*, p. 1178, note 11.

("Halt, knights, or whoever ye may be, and render me account of who ye are, whence ye come, where ye go, and what
it is ye carry upon that bier. To judge by appearances, either
ye have done some wrong or some wrong has been done you,
and it is fitting and necessary that I should know, either that I
may chastise you for the evil ye have done, or that I may
avenge you for the injury inflicted upon you.") (p. 127)

The challenge, "Deteneos" ("Halt"), is repeated (p. 188) with
the traditional "si no, conmigo sois todos en batalla" ("Otherwise ye must all do battle with me," p. 127). Don Quijote is able
to rout his adversaries and evoke the admiration of his doubting
squire: "Sin duda este mi amo es tan valiente y esforzado como
él dice" ("Clearly, this master of mine is no less bold and valiant
than he says he is," p. 128). After learning that the man has died
a natural death and that the knight's opportunity for vengeance
is thus obviated, Don Quijote goes on to announce his identity
(p. 189): "Y quiero que sepa vuestra reverencia que yo soy un
caballero de la Mancha, llamado don Quijote, y es mi oficio y
ejercicio andar por el mundo enderezando tuertos y *desfaciendo*
agravios" ("I would have your reverence know that I am a
knight of La Mancha, Don Quixote by name, and it is my business and calling to roam the world straightening out wrongs and
redressing injuries," p. 129). Incongrously, broken leg and Don
Quijote's potential wrath notwithstanding, Alonso López mocks
Don Quijote's chivalric mission through a series of puns: "No
sé cómo pueda ser eso de enderezar tuertos . . . , pues a mí de
derecho me habéis vuelto tuerto . . . ; y el agravio que en mí
habéis deshecho ha sido dejarme agraviado . . . ; y harta desven-
tura ha sido topar con vos, que vais buscando aventuras" ("I do
not understand the part about straightening out wrongs . . . for
from straight you have made me crooked. . . . The injury you
have redressed in my case has left me so injured. . . . It was the
height of misadventure for me to fall in with you, on your
search for adventures"). Don Quijote's response is the inane
"No todas las cosas . . . suceden de un mismo modo" ("Things
do not always happen in the same way"). The knight is brought
to nonchivalric laughter by Sancho's explanation of the new chivalric name he gives his master—El Caballero de la Triste Figura

(The Knight of the Mournful Countenance)—and his comments about Don Quijote's appearance.

The adventure of the fulling mills will be analyzed in the next section as one of Sancho Panza's finest moments. Don Quijote's pompous self-inflation (I, 20, 194)—"Sancho amigo, has de saber que yo nací, por querer del cielo, en esta nuestra edad de hierro, para resucitar en ella la de oro, o la dorada, como suele llamarse. Yo soy aquel para quien están guardados los peligros, las grandes hazañas, los valerosos hechos" ("Friend Sancho, know that I by Heaven's will have been born in this iron age to revive in it the age of gold, or the golden as it is called. I am he for whom perils, mighty achievements, and valiant deeds are reserved," p. 132)—is neutralized by Sancho's *industria* in "enchanting" Rocinante. The comedy of the next morning's anticlimactic reality is perceived by both knight and squire, who break into rollicking laughter. Sancho, however, goes too far and parodies his master's words, impertinently exaggerating the rhetoric and escalating the chivalric archaism (p. 204): "'Has de saber, ¡oh Sancho amigo!, que yo nací, por querer del cielo, en *esta nuestra* edad de hierro, para resucitar en ella la dorada, o de oro. Yo soy aquel para quien están guardados los peligros, las hazañas grandes, los valerosos *fechos*'" ("Friend Sancho, know that I by Heaven's will have been born in this our iron age to revive in it the age of gold, or the golden as it is called. I am he for whom perils, mighty achievements, and valiant deeds are reserved," p. 140).[22] In spite of his ire, Don Quijote admits (p. 205) that the episode is "cosa digna de risa" ("worth laughing at") but goes on to affirm that "no es digna de contarse; que no son todas las personas tan discretas que sepan poner en su punto las cosas" ("it is not worth making a story about, for not everyone is shrewd enough to put things in the right place," p. 140). What he really means, of course, is that he recognizes that what has happened is incompatible with the maintenance of his chivalric vision—another tacit recognition of reality—and must therefore be suppressed.

In a very revealing speech, Don Quijote attempts to establish

22. See John J. Allen, *Don Quixote: Hero or Fool?*, 1:57; see also 1:37.

a new relationship with Sancho. He begins with praise for his squire (p. 206)—"eres discreto y sabes que los primeros movimientos no son en mano del hombre" ("you are shrewd enough to know that our first impulses are beyond our control")—and then imposes the condition that Sancho talk less and with greater respect, for, he adds—correctly—"en cuantos libros de caballerías he leído, que son infinitos, jamás he hallado que ningún escudero hablase tanto con su señor como tú con el tuyo" ("In all the books of chivalry I have read, and they are innumerable, I never met with a squire who talked so much to his lord as you do to yours," pp. 140–41). As stated in section 2.1, the mere fact that Sancho talks and forces Don Quijote to talk about nonchivalric matters in a nonchivalric style compromises Don Quijote's chivalric world. Don Quijote takes advantage of Sancho's ignorance of the romances of chivalry in order to describe the comportment of Amadís de Gaula's squire Gandalín (if Amadís is his own model, he reasons, Gandalín should logically be Sancho's): "se lee dél que siempre hablaba a su señor con la gorra en la mano, inclinada la cabez y doblado el cuerpo, *more turquesco*" ("We read of him that he always addressed his lord with his cap in his hand, his head bowed down, and his body bent double, *more turquesco* [in Turkish fashion]"). This is, purely and simply, another lie, unethical, unscrupulous, and very unbecoming of one who claims to adhere to the rules of chivalry.[23]

The winning of Mambrino's helmet allows Don Quijote to transform reality (gray ass to dappled gray steed, barber to knight-errant, basin to helmet) (I, 21, 209): "que todas las cosas que veía con mucha facilidad las acomodaba a sus desvariadas caballerías y malandantes pensamientos" ("For he made everything he saw fall in with his crazy chivalry and aberrant notions"); issue a mildly archaic challenge, "¡Defiéndete, *cautiva criatura*, o . . . !" ("Defend thyself, miserable being, or . . . "); and win another outright victory. Don Quijote seems to waver only on the matter of the nature of the animal ridden by the

23. Clemencín (*Don Quijote*, p. 1193, note 64) notes that Don Quijote does not tell the truth here but rationalizes that the knight should be excused on account of his madness. In the following note, Clemencín observes that Don Quijote's statement that the squires of knights-errant were typically silent is in error.

barber (p. 212): "Así que, Sancho, deja ese caballo, o asno, o lo que tú quisieres que sea" ("Therefore, Sancho, leave this horse, or ass, or whatever you will have it to be," p. 145).

Don Quijote's summary for the benefit of his squire of the life cycle of a typical knight-errant, another carefully structured and modulated piece of oratory that has the desired effect—Sancho listens attentively and exclaims (p. 216), "Eso pido, y barras derechas . . . : a eso me atengo" ("That's what I want, plain and simple! . . . That's what I'm waiting for," p. 148)—is the longest speech in the novel in which Don Quijote employs archaism (*fenestras, fermosos, fablar, furto, Levantarse han, tablas, fermosas, pro, talante, fablado, prométerselo ha*), though their effect is diminished by their comparative infrequence in such a long speech.

The encounter with the galley slaves enables Don Quijote to exercise his chivalric mission (I, 22, 221)—"aquí encaja la ejecución de mi oficio: *desfacer* fuerzas y socorrer y acudir a los miserables" ("here is a case for the exercise of my office, to put down force and to succor and help the wretched," p. 151)—although he fulfills the letter rather than the spirit of that calling. Don Quijote does not transform reality; rather he interprets reality according to his own, very strictly literal preference. The stoning he receives (p. 231) leaves the knight "mohinísimo de verse tan malparado por los mismos a quien tanto bien había hecho" ("[fuming] at finding himself treated thus by the very persons for whom he had done so much," p. 159).

Overall, Don Quijote seems to vacillate during the events of this series of chapters. He is still capable of willfully transforming reality to conform to his chivalric vision, of speaking in archaism and using all the formulaic clichés of his chivalric rhetoric, of gloating with pride over his victories and rationalizing his nonencounters or defeats. In short, during this period Don Quijote still maintains a reasonable degree of faithfulness to his chivalric vision. But at the same time, it is undeniable that Don Quijote is unable to sustain his chivalric role with the same degree of fidelity as in the earlier chapters. In virtually every adventure, Don Quijote makes minor but very important concessions to physical and psychological reality, and the degree to which he does this is directly proportional to the degree to which he invalidates his original concept of himself and his chivalric world. The most important single cause of these concessions to reality is Sancho Panza.

2.5 Sancho Panza: Chivalry

Sancho Panza enters the novel, for better or worse, in order to play a major role in Don Quijote's chivalric world. The manner in which he undermines that world from within has been discussed earlier. But Sancho is more than just another element in a consideration of Don Quijote's progression from chivalry to reality. Sancho's own development is a major aspect of Cervantes's novel, and this development too can be more fully understood when considered in terms of the rhetoric of chivalry.

In section 1.4, in a brief comment following Table 1.2, I observed that the distribution of Sancho's speech reflects his comparatively minor role at the beginning and at the end of part I of *Don Quijote*. More specifically, it is between chapters 15 and 31 that Sancho's role is most prominent. To look at Sancho's figures in a different way, 206 of his 277 speeches, that is, 74 percent, fall within the section between chapters 15 and 31, which include the adventures discussed in the last section and the events that take place in the Sierra Morena.

It is significant that the pattern of Sancho Panza's archaic speech also centers on the same part of the novel. Sancho uses no archaism before chapter 15 nor any after chapter 31, as seen in Figure 2.1. This figure indicates a gradual adaptation to Don Quijote's rhetoric of chivalry, as well as a growing linguistic self-confidence on Sancho's part. The squire's first archaism comes after the beating by the Yanguesans when he asks his master (I, 15, 148) for "dos tragos de aquella bebida del feo Blas"

Figure 2.1.   Sancho Panza's Archaic Speeches (Part I)

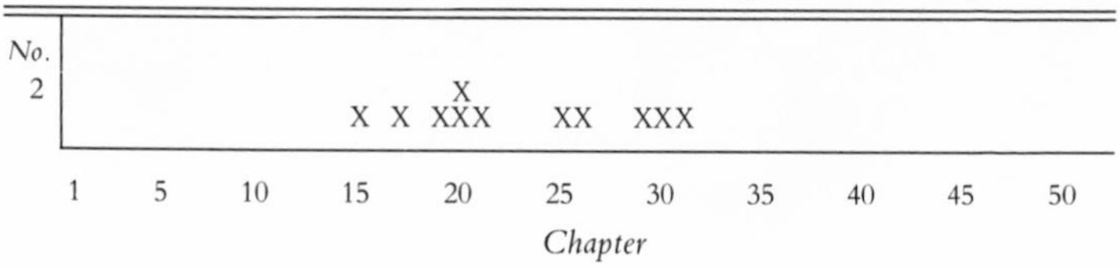

No. 2										
				X						
			X X XXX		XX	XXX				
1	5	10	15	20	25	30	35	40	45	50

Chapter

("a couple of sips of that potion of Fear-o'-brass," p. 100), reasoning that it might "de provecho para los quebrantamientos de huesos como lo es para las *feridas*" ("serve for broken bones as well as for wounds"). This is typical of Sancho's use of archaism, which usually consists of a single *f-*, the most frequent and most easily perceived archaic form used by his master (see Appendix B). There is one occasion, however, when Sancho Panza employs a string of archaisms: when he delivers his most sophisticated and rhetorical speech in part I.

In chapter 20 (p. 193), Don Quijote and Sancho hear the sound of "unos golpes a compás, con un cierto crujir de hierros y cadenas, . . . acompañados del furioso estruendo del agua" ("strokes that fell with a measured beat, and a certain rattling of iron and chains. Together with the furious din of the water," pp. 131–32). The mysterious nature of this unknown noise is heightened by the absolute blackness of the night. Sancho is at least as frightened, if not more so, as he was by the spectral lights in the night not so long before. Don Quijote proposes separating from his squire in order to go and discover the source of the noise. Sancho, terrified by the prospect of being left alone in such circumstances (p. 195), begins to "llorar con la mayor ternura del mundo" ("weep in the most pathetic way," p. 132). In this context, motivated by fear, in the midst of tears and trembling, Sancho delivers the following extraordinary speech.

> Señor, yo no sé por qué quiere vuestra merced acometer esta tan temerosa aventura; ahora es de noche, aquí no nos vee nadie, bien podemos torcer el camino y desviarnos del peligro, aunque no bebamos en tres días; y pues no hay quien nos vea, menos habrá quien nos note de cobardes; cuanto más que yo he oído predicar al cura de nuestro lugar, que vuestra merced bien conoce, que quien busca el peligro perece en él; así, que no es bien tentar a Dios acometiendo tan desaforado hecho, donde no se puede escapar sino por milagro, y basta los que ha hecho el cielo con vuestra merced en librarle de ser manteado, como yo lo fui, y en sacarle vencedor, libre y salvo de entre tantos enemigos como acompañaban al difunto. Y cuando todo esto no mueva ni ablande ese duro corazón, muévale el pensar y creer que apenas se habrá vuestra merced

apartado de aquí cuando yo, de miedo, dé mi ánima a quien quisiere llevarla. Yo salí de mi tierra y dejé hijos y mujer por venir a servir a vuestra merced, creyendo valer más y no menos; pero como la cudicia rompe el saco, a mí me ha rasgado mis esperanzas, pues cuando más vivas las tenía de alcanzar aquella negra y malhadada ínsula que tantas veces vuestra merced me ha prometido, veo que, en pago y trueco della, me quiere ahora dejar en un lugar tan apartado del trato humano. Por un solo Dios, señor mío, que *non* se me *faga* tal *desaguisado*; y ya que del todo no quiera vuestra merced desistir de acometer este *fecho*, dilátelo, a lo menos, hasta la mañana; que, a lo que a mí me muestra la ciencia que aprendí cuando era pastor, no debe de haber desde aquí al alba tres horas, porque la boca de la bocina está encima de la cabeza, y hace la media noche en la línea del brazo izquierdo. (pp. 195–96)

(Señor, I do not know why your worship wants to attempt this dreadful adventure. It is night now, no one sees us here, we can easily turn around and take ourselves out of danger, even if we don't drink for three days to come. As there is no one to see us, all the less will there be anyone to call us cowards. Besides, I have heard the priest of our village, whom your worship knows well, preach that "he who seeks danger perishes in it." So it is not right to tempt God by trying so tremendous a feat from which there can be no escape except by a miracle, and Heaven has performed enough of them for your worship in delivering you from being blanketed as I was, and bringing you out victorious and safe and sound from among all those enemies that were with the dead man. If all this does not move or soften that hard heart, let it be moved by this thought and reflection, that you will have hardly left this spot when from pure fear I shall give my soul up to anyone that will take it. I left home and wife and children to come and serve your worship, trusting to do better and not worse. But as "greed bursts the bag" it has torn my hopes open, for just as I had them highest about getting that wretched, unlucky island your worship has so often promised me, I see that instead and in exchange for it you mean to desert me now in a place so far from human contact. For God's sake, master, let not so great an injustice be done to me. And if your worship will not entirely give up attempting this feat, at least put it off till morning. According to what I learned when I was a shepherd, dawn cannot be more than three hours off, because the Little Dipper is overhead and its handle shows that it's midnight.) (pp. 132–33)

The first thing that strikes the reader is the length of the speech, which is over 50 percent longer than anything Sancho has said previously.[24] But more than the length, the careful, logical construction; the rhetorical embellishment; and the shifts in style make it truly remarkable. Sancho begins with a brief introductory statement, or *exordium*, in which he succinctly states his purpose: to dissuade Don Quijote from undertaking the adventure. He launches immediately into his *narratio*, describing the facts—"es de noche, . . . no nos vee nadie" ("it is night . . . no one sees us")—and the logical consequence of these facts—"pues no hay quien nos vea, menos habrá quien nos note de cobardes" ("As there is no one to see us, all the less will there be anyone to call us cowards"). Next he appeals to recognized authority (as he has often heard Don Quijote appeal to the authority of the romances of chivalry)—in this case, the local priest—citing the truism, both popular and Christian, that "quien busca el peligro perece en él" ("he who seeks danger perishes in it"), and the logical corollary that "no es bien tentar a Dios" ("it is not right to tempt God"), and offering the opinion that God, who intervened to spare Don Quijote in earlier adventures, might exhaust his patience. After the first sentence,[25] which ends with the word

24. The speech occupies thirty-one lines in the Riquer edition. Sancho's longest speech prior to this, when he described his blanketing and suggested returning home, was nineteen lines (I, 18, 173–74). The only time that Sancho speaks at greater length (about thirty-eight lines) is when he learns that Dulcinea del Toboso is really Aldonza Lorenzo (I, 25, 265–66). The longest of his other speeches are: twenty-nine lines, when he narrates the story of Torralba (I, 20, 199–200); twenty-five lines, when he reproaches the priest for "enchanting" Don Quijote (I, 47, 515–16); twenty lines, when he discusses chivalric procedures with his master (I, 21, 213); and twenty lines, when he learns that a princess in distress is searching for Don Quijote (I, 29, 316–17).

25. This sentence is one of the longest and most sophisticated ever uttered by Sancho. However, simply measuring the length of Sancho's sentences is less revealing than might be hoped because of the sometimes arbitrary punctuation in the Spanish passage, as seen in these examples: "tres días; y pues" and "al difunto. Y cuando."

difunto, we can assume that there is a pause, during which Don
Quijote's silence is observed.

With the failure of his logical petition, the *logos* of classical
rhetoric, Sancho modifies his technique, employing the other
two standard means of rhetorical persuasion, *pathos* and *ethos*;
that is, if he cannot evince a response from Don Quijote with an
intellectual appeal, he will speak to him in emotional terms and
will even allude to his own moral character. The eloquent squire
announces this change, saying, "Y cuando todo esto no mueva
. . . , muévele el pensar y creer que" ("If all this does not move
. . . , let it be moved by this thought and reflection"). He speaks
now of his personal sacrifice—"Yo salí . . . y dejé . . . creyendo
valer más" ("I left . . . and I abandoned . . . trusting to do better")—which has never been rewarded properly—"mis esperanzas . . . aquella . . . ínsula que tantas veces vuestra merced me
ha prometido" ("my hopes . . . that . . . island that your worship has so often promised me")—but which has terminated in
rejection—"me quiere ahora dejar" ("you mean to desert me").

This progression from fact and universal (that is, theological)
truth to personal appeal, the progression from *logos* to *pathos* and
ethos, is accompanied by a variety of stylistic devices, the *elocutio*
of classical rhetoric:

1. Preplaced adjectives: "tan temerosa aventura," "tan desaforado hecho," "ese duro corazón," "aquella negra y malhadada ínsula."

2. Exaggeration with *tan* and *tanto*: "tan temerosa," "tan desaforado," "tantos enemigos," "tantas veces," "tan apartado."

3. Parallel constructions: "ahora es . . . aquí no nos vee,"
"torcer el camino y desviarnos del peligro," "pues no hay
quién nos vea, menos habrá quien nos note," "quien busca
. . . perece," "en librarle . . . y en sacarle," "cuando . . . no
mueva . . . muévale," "apenas se habrá vuestra merced apartado . . . cuando yo . . . dé mi ánima," "Yo salí . . . y dejé."

4. Sententious statements: "quien busca el peligro perece en
él," "la cudicia rompe el saco."

5. Near synonymous pairs of adjectives, verbs, and nouns:
"libre y salvo," "no mueva ni ablande," "pensar y creer," "negra y malhadada," "pago y trueco."

6. Hyperbolic paraphrase: "tan desaforado hecho" ("so tremendous a feat") for "esta aventura" ("this adventure"), "ese

duro corazón" ("that hard heart") for "vuestra merced" ("your worship"), "dé mi ánima a quien quisiere llevarla" ("I shall give my soul to anyone that will take it") for "meura" ("I will die"), "un lugar tan apartado del trato humano" ("a place so far from human contact") for "aquí" ("here").

We can suppose another pause after *trato humano* during which Sancho sees that his rhetoric has not, in fact, moved Don Quijote's "duro corazón." Abruptly changing tactics, Sancho replaces rhetorical logic with the heaviest concentration of chivalric archaism that he ever employs—"que *non* se me *faga* tal *desaguisado . . .* este *fecho*" ("let not so great an injustice be done to me . . . this feat")—and then switches again, this time to a stylistically more appropriate account of a shepherd's popular astronomy. While the astronomical calculations briefly engage Don Quijote's curiosity—"¿Cómo puedes tú . . . ver donde hace esa línea?" ("How can you see . . . where the handle is?")—the knight remains determined to continue "hacer lo que debía a estilo de caballero" ("fulfilling knightly usage") and "acometer ahora esta tan no vista y tan temerosa aventura" ("to undertake now this so unexampled and terrible adventure"). The result is that Sancho must resort to the device he knows best: "Viendo, pues, Sancho la última resolución de su amo, y cuán poco valían con él sus lágrimas, consejos y ruegos, determinó de aprovecharse de su industria, y hacerle esperar hasta al día, si pudiese" ("When Sancho realized that this was his master's final resolve, and saw how little his tears, counsels, and entreaties prevailed, he decided to employ his own ingenuity and compel him, if he could, to wait till daylight"). Sancho ties Rocinante's feet and suggests that it is divine intervention (or perhaps, by implication, an "enchantment") that keeps the knight from leaving his squire.

It is ironic that Sancho's eloquent speech, combined with an appeal in his master's own chivalric archaism, has no effect on Don Quijote. But its ineffectiveness in no way diminishes the fact that this is a remarkable speech to have been articulated by Sancho Panza. It is equally remarkable that, as far as I know, no critic of the novel has ever commented on this extraordinary passage. Perhaps this inattention is due in part to the fact that other, more obviously comic scenes in the same chapter have attracted greater attention: Sancho's amusing folkloric tale; the scatological scene (p. 201) in which the squire must do "lo que otro no pudiera hacer por él" ("what no one could do for him," p. 137); and the absurd discovery of the fulling mills. Another factor in the lack of recognition accorded this passage is its incongruity: how could Sancho have ever learned such a mode of discourse? I suggest that, although he has had no formal training in oratory, Sancho has a good ear for style and a natural ability to mimic speech patterns. For years, he has heard mass and sermons at church—recall his statement that he has "oído predicar al cura de nuestro lugar" ("heard our priest preach")—and is therefore familiar with the rhetoric of the pulpit. Then, of course, he has recently been in the company of a truly outstanding orator, Don Quijote. More specifically, within the last few days, Sancho has witnessed and has undoubtedly heard with admiration Don Quijote's celebrated rhetorical discourse on the Golden Age and Marcela's equally rhetorical harangue at the burial of Grisóstomo.[26] With such recent impressive examples of classical rhetoric still fresh in his mind, it is less difficult than one would have expected to accept the squire's eloquence in this scene.

Furthermore, this speech is not a sudden and incongruous event; rather, it is possible to see it as a logical culmination of an increasing sophistication on the part of the squire. Sancho Panza is introduced (I, 7, 85) as an "hombre de bien . . . pero de muy poca sal en la mollera" ("a good man . . . but with very little grey matter in his skull," p. 57), and it is generally assumed that Don Quijote recruits him as his squire simply by appealing to his material interests by promising him an *ínsula* to govern and exploit.[27] The scene of this recruitment is merely summarized by the narrator, but there is a suggestion that the appeal is to more than mere greed: "En resolución, *tanto* le dijo, *tanto* le per-

26. See the excellent analyses of the speeches by Don Quijote and Marcela by Mary Mackey, "Rhetoric and Characterization in *Don Quijote*," pp. 51–66; and Thomas R. Hart and Steven Rendall, "Rhetoric and Characterization in Marcela's Address to the Shepherds," pp. 287–98.

27. See, for example, Franklin O. Brantley, "Sancho's Ascent to the Spheres," pp. 37–38.

suadió y prometió . . . Decíale, *entre otras cosas*, . . . Con estas promesas y *otras tales*" (p. 85; my italics) ("Finally, Don Quixote convinced him with *such* persuasions and promises . . . *among other things*, told him . . . On these and *the like* promises," p. 57; my italics). We can never know all that Don Quijote said to Sancho Panza, but it is at least possible that some of the knight's appeal was to Sancho's higher instincts.

From the beginning, Sancho fails to impress as genuinely stupid ("de muy poca sal en la mollera")[28] but is at first comparatively timid and submissive, believing naively that his master's victory over the Biscayan can bring him his governorship (I, 10, 105). He demonstrates an ability to make subtle distinctions when he corrects Don Quijote's oath of vengeance against the Biscayan (p. 108). Sancho stays in the background and merely observes the events leading up to and during the burial of Grisóstomo, but immediately thereafter, following Rocinante's amorous misadventure, he begins to use the chivalric archaisms that he has heard so often in his master's speech.

When they arrive at the inn, Sancho lies for the first time in the novel, saying (I, 16, 154) that Don Quijote "había dado una caída de una peña abajo" ("had fallen down from a cliff," p. 104). The innkeeper's wife almost catches him up by suggesting that "también debistes vos de caer" ("then you must have fallen also"), forcing Sancho to lie again (pp. 155–56): "No caí . . . ; sino que del sobresalto que tomé de ver caer a mi amo, de tal manera me duele a mí el cuerpo, que me parece que me han dado mil palos" ("I did not fall, but from the shock I got at seeing my master fall, my body aches so that I feel as if I had had a thousand whacks," p. 105). The innkeeper's daughter rescues Sancho from her mother's suspicions by supporting this last absurdity. Thus reinforced, Sancho proceeds very condescendingly to explain (p. 156) to Maritornes what a "caballero aventurero" ("knight-adventurer") is: "¿Tan nueva sois en el mundo que no

28. Gonzalo Torrente Ballester makes the same observation; *El "Quijote" como juego*, p. 91. Unfortunately, Sancho's natural stupidity is assumed by the great majority of the novel's readers, including, for example, one of his best biographers, Hipólito R. Romero Flores, who calls Sancho "un porro" ("a dolt"); *Biografía de Sancho Panza, filósofo de la sensatez*, p. 107.

lo sabéis vos?" ("Are you so new in the world that you don't know?," p. 106). During all of this, Don Quijote has been silent; Sancho has had to maintain on his own for the first time the chivalric world of his master, and he has responded well to the pressure, finding out in the process how advantageous lying can be.

Fear seems to bring out both the best and the worst in Sancho, for it is after Don Quijote's nocturnal victory over the white-shirted mourners that the enthusiastic squire, without any prompting, invents for his master the genuinely chivalric name of El Caballero de la Triste Figura (I, 19, 190). After this adventure, Sancho, both euphoric and anxious to get Don Quijote to a safe refuge, combines a bit of rhetoric and his first proverb (I, 19, 192): "El jumento está como conviene, la montaña cerca, la hambre carga, no hay que hacer sino retirarnos con gentil compás de pies, y, como dicen, váyase el muerto a la sepultura y el vivo a la hogaza" ("This ass is properly loaded; the mountains are near at hand; we are hungry. All we have to do is retreat at a reasonable walk and, as the saying is, 'Let the dead man sleep; a live one has to eat,'" p. 131). Then he continues to assert himself over an uncharacteristically silent and submissive Don Quijote: "Y antecogiendo su asno, rogó a su señor que le siguiese; el cual, pareciéndole que Sancho tenía razón, sin volverle a replicar le siguió" ("And leading his ass, he begged his master to follow. Feeling that Sancho was right, Don Quixote did so without saying a word in reply"). A short while later, it is again Sancho who suggests that the abundant grass they see speaks for the presence of a nearby fountain or brook and that they should proceed to find it; the comment is added (p. 193) that "Parecióle bien el consejo a don Quijote" ("The advice seemed good to Don Quixote," p. 131).

Thus, with accelerating frequency, there have been numerous indications of Sancho Panza's growing self-confidence as he settles comfortably into his assigned role. His oratorical master-piece is then a height in his psychological ascent. Don Quijote's attempt, discussed in the last section, to force Sancho into a more subservient role is a recognition that the squire's stature has increased and rivals his own.

Don Quijote will not be able to reduce the prominence of Sancho, whom he will follow into the Sierra Morena (I, 23, 233), whose explanation he will accept in place of his own theory concerning the dead mule (p. 236), and who will bravely rush to the defense of his master in the fight with Cardenio (I, 24, 252). But if Sancho steadily gains in self-confidence and self-assertion while largely alone with Don Quijote in chapters 15–25, his chance meeting with the priest and the barber reduces him to performing a stereotyped, comic routine for their benefit as he tries to recite the letter to Dulcinea (I, 26, 278). Sancho recovers somewhat during the excitement of the Princess Micomicona adventure, chapters 29–31, but goes into a sharp decline when he is relegated to a very minor role during the long stay in the inn. As we shall see later (in section 3.4), he recovers in certain strategic ways on the return to the village.

Sancho Panza, like his master, is commonly supposed to remain a static character in the first part of the novel, but all evidence indicates that this is by no means true. It is no rustic, myopically realistic, comic farmer "de muy poca sal en la mollera" who delivers the rhetorical speech in chapter 20, but rather an extraordinarily intelligent, perceptive, and self-confident man who has already acquired from his equally extraordinary companion a new vision of life and the levels of style with which to express a variety of sophisticated thoughts.

2.6 Chapters 23–28: In the Sierra Morena

After Don Quijote frees the galley slaves, Sancho, fearing the rural police, advises flight, prudently cautioning (I, 23, 232) that "con la Santa Hermandad no hay usar de caballerías" ("chivalry is of no account with the Holy Brotherhood," p. 160). Don Quijote agrees condescendingly but insists that he does so only for Sancho's benefit and that it should never be so much as hinted that it is done out of fear. It appears that Don Quijote protests too much, and he covers his concession to reality with yet another lie.

As in chapters 11–14, Don Quijote and Sancho meet a goatherd as a prelude to the introduction of an important secondary

character, this time Cardenio, whose furious penance has the
obvious literary parallels of Amadís de Gaula and Orlando Furioso. After the fight with Cardenio and the goatherd (I, 24,
252–53), Sancho proposes returning home. In order to placate
his squire, Don Quijote lifts the ban on speaking (which had not
been effective at any rate, since in the four chapters between its
imposition and its suspension there is no noticeable change in
Sancho's frequency or style of speech) and then announces (I,
25, 256–57) that since "todo cuanto yo he hecho, hago e hiciere,
va muy puesto en razón y muy conforme a las reglas de caballería" ("everything I have done, am doing, or shall do, is well
founded on reason and in conformity with the rules of chivalry"), he intends now to perform "una hazaña, con que he de
ganar perpetuo nombre y fama en todo lo descubierto de la
tierra; y será tal, que he de echar con ella el sello a todo aquello
que puede hacer perfecto y famoso a un andante caballero"
("something that will win me eternal name and fame throughout the known world. It shall be such that thereby I shall set the
seal on all that can make a knight-errant perfect and famous," p.
177). Next Don Quijote delivers his lecture on imitation cited in
section 1.2 and reveals that he now intends to imitate Amadís,
who responded to Oriana's anger by retiring to the Peña Pobre
and calling himself Beltenebros, while simultaneously imitating
Orlando in his fury after learning of Angelica's infidelity. The
logical Sancho points out (p. 259) that "los caballeros que lo tal
ficieron fueron provocados" ("the knights who behaved in this
way had provocation"), while there is no evidence that Dulcinea
"ha hecho alguna niñería con moro o cristiano" ("has been trifling with Moor or Christian," p. 179). That is precisely the
point Don Quijote wants to make: "si en seco hago esto ¿qué
hiciera en mojado?" ("if I do this without an excuse, what I
would do if I had one?").

Don Quijote commits a tactical error[29] in revealing to Sancho
the reality behind the myth of Dulcinea and then compounds his
mistake by implying a base carnal motivation for his interest in

29. Jorge E. Sorensen calls this confession "inexplicable"; "The Importance of Sierra Morena as a Point of Transition in *Don Quijote*," p.
48.

her (pp. 265–67),[30] thus opening a little further the cracks made by reality in his chivalric construct. Don Quijote's letter to Dulcinea is a carefully executed masterpiece of chivalric rhetoric, imitating perfectly the epistolary practices of the fictional knights-errant. But any guise of nobility that the penitential act might have had is eliminated by the bare-bottomed acrobatics (p. 272) designed to illustrate his madness for his lady that he performs before Sancho goes off to deliver the message.

The very gratuity of Don Quijote's penance, which makes it a pinnacle in the knight's efforts to live according to artistic norms,[31] paradoxically reduces in great measure the authenticity of the art-inspired existence that is the hallmark of Don Quijote's chivalric world. The fictional knights-errant who withdrew from the world always believed that they had good reason to do so.[32] Amadís or Orlando would appear silly—as silly as Don Quijote—if they went sulking off to be alone with no cause. Don Quijote's early adventures always had, at least in his own eyes, some degree of substance as well as form: he really did stand vigil over his armor and really was dubbed a knight; Juan Haldudo really was beating poor Andrés; he really did defeat the Biscayan in a sword battle. Now Don Quijote is merely

30. Don Quijote cites the folkloric anecdote of the cultured widow who defends her love for a stupid *mozo motilón* ("young lay-brother") by saying (p. 267) "para lo que yo le quiero, tanta filosofía sabe, y más, que Aristóteles" ("Because for all I want with him, he knows as much and more philosophy than Aristotle," p. 184), and then he adds "por lo que yo quiero a Dulcinea del Toboso, tanto vale como la más alta princesa de la tierra" ("for all I want with Dulcinea del Toboso, she is just as good as the most exalted princess on earth"). The switch from *para*, indicating the use to which the man is to be put, to *por*, suggesting the motivation for Don Quijote's love for Dulcinea, is significant (and, sadly, lost in translation), but the fact that such an analogy should even occur to Don Quijote can only put Dulcinea in an unfavorable light. See Mac E. Barrick, "The Form and Function of Folktales in *Don Quijote*," pp. 127–28.

31. The essential critical study on this important subject is Juan Bautista Avalle-Arce's essay on "La vida como obra de arte," included in revised form as chapter 5 of *Don Quijote como forma de vida*, pp. 144–72. See also "Vital and Artistic Structures in the Life of Don Quixote," p. 104–21.

32. See Edward C. Riley, *Cervantes' Theory of the Novel*, p. 67.

playacting out of frustration with the harsh encounters he has had with reality; he has ceased to be a knight-errant and has become a jester.

Although Don Quijote's stated models for his penance are Amadís and Orlando, his real models are Cardenio, who told the goatherds (I, 23, 241–42) that he had come to these mountains and was acting as he did "porque así le convenía para cumplir cierta penitencia que por sus muchos pecados le había sido impuesta" ("since he was obliged to do so in order to work out a penance which for his many sins had been imposed upon him," p. 166), and Grisóstomo.[33] One reason (besides the fact that it is easier) why Don Quijote finally decides to imitate Amadís rather than Orlando is that Cardenio has already preempted that role in his raving madness that has so disturbed the goatherds. Just as the genuine death of Grisóstomo put Don Quijote in an unfavorable light earlier, Cardenio's authentic penance in the Sierra Morena makes the feigned one of Don Quijote all the more hollow.

During most of chapter 26, all of 27 and 28, and the beginning of 29, Don Quijote is ignored in his solitude as the narrative interest shifts to Cardenio and Dorotea and the decisive reentry of the priest and the barber into the story. Whenever the reader's attention is drawn away from Don Quijote, his chivalric world becomes more remote.

---

33. Luis Rosales has commented on the many details of Cardenio's penance that are copied by Don Quijote; *Cervantes y la libertad*, 2:305–7. For Grisóstomo as a model for Don Quijote, see Harold G. Jones, "Grisóstomo and Don Quixote: Death and Imitation," p. 88.

3

Knighthood Defeated

Será una gran prudencia dejar pasar el mal influjo
de las estrellas que agora corre (I, 52, 555)

(It will be wise to let the malign influence of
the stars which now prevails pass off, p. 400)

3.1 Chapters 29–31: Princess Micomicona

The setting for chapters 29–31 remains the Sierra Morena, but
as these three chapters introduce an important innovation in the
plot, they deserve to be considered as the beginning of the final
part of the novel of 1605. Here for the first time, an authentic
chivalric adventure, complete to the smallest detail, presents itself to Don Quijote. The knight does not have to transform or
invent anything when dealing with Dorotea in the guise of the
Princess Micomicona. Furthermore, it is not just an ordinary
adventure "de encrucijadas" ("crossroad encounter," p. 69), as
Don Quijote calls them (I, 10, 105), but the type of adventure
that is essential in almost every romance of chivalry and that he
has most dreamed of, longed for, and talked about: the princess
in distress, the heiress to a fabulous throne who will marry her
benefactor (who can then grant a prosperous *ínsula* to his loyal
squire). All these hopes were implicit in Don Quijote's words as
early as his recruitment of Sancho (I, 2), in the enamored princess (Maritornes) episode (I, 16), perhaps in the adventure of the
sheep armies where he hoped to save a Christian princess from
falling into pagan hands (I, 18), and they formed the high point
in his summary of the life of a typical knight-errant (I, 21). Specifically, after this summary (p. 217), Don Quijote worried that
if he could not be found to be of royal blood "no me querrá el

85

rey dar a su hija por mujer" ("the king will not be willing to
give me his daughter in marriage," p. 149).

The princess arrives unexpectedly before Don Quijote, properly attired, riding her *palafrén* ("palfrey")[1] and, kneeling before
the knight, "le *fabló* en esta guisa" ("addressed him while still
kneeling").

> De aquí no me levantaré, ¡oh valeroso y esforzado caballero!,
> *fasta* que *la vuestra* bondad y cortesía me otorgue un don, el
> cual redundará en honra y prez de vuestra persona y en *pro* de
> la más desconsolada y agraviada doncella que el sol ha visto.
> Y si es que el valor de vuestro fuerte brazo corrsponde a la
> voz de vuestra inmortal fama, obligado estáis a favorecer a la
> sin ventura que de tan *leuñes* tierras viene, al olor de vuestro
> famoso nombre, buscándoos para remedio de sus desdichas.
> (I, 29, 318)

> (From this spot I will not rise, O valiant and courageous
> knight, until your goodness and courtesy grant me a boon
> which will redound to the honor and renown of your person
> and render a service to the most disconsolate and afflicted
> damsel the sun has ever seen. If the might of your strong arm
> corresponds to the repute of your immortal fame, ye are
> bound to aid the helpless being who, let by the fragrance of
> your renowned name, has come from far distant lands to seek
> your aid in her misfortunes.) (p. 224)

Not only the archaism but also the appeal to knightly valor; the
repeated references to fame, honor, and reputation; and the
stress on her own misfortune contribute to the authenticity of
Dorotea's appeal. Don Quijote answers with appropriate archa-
ism (*fermosa*, *facienda*, *fasta*, *vos*, *la vuestra*, *fermosura*), courtesy,[2]
and generosity, although he must promise no less than three
times to grant her request (pp. 318–19).

Events suddenly turn sour for Don Quijote when (p. 324), in

---

1. Dorotea is riding the barber's mule; in narration, it is ironically
called a *palafrén*, the common mount for maidens in the books of chivalry (see Clemencín, *Don Quijote*, pp. 1292–93, note 24). Whether or
not Don Quijote perceives it as a *palafrén* is problematical.

2. His repeated insistence on her rising before he will *otorgar* the *don*
is, of course, highly comic and recalls the scene with the first innkeeper
in I, 3.

order both to test—"por ver lo que hacía o decía" ("to see what would be said or done by Don Quixote," p. 228)—and to embarrass the knight, the priest lies and says that a group of condemned criminals stole some money from him after they had been freed by a madman. Sancho immediately reveals the fact (which everyone already knew) that his master was the author of the deed (I, 30, 325). Don Quijote's reaction is to insult his squire, calling him a "majadero" ("blockhead"), and to defend his tenuous position that a knight-errant need only heed form and not substance in any given matter. Dorotea steps in to calm his knightly wrath by finishing her story, which is complete down to the details of her wizard father Tinacrio el Sabidor, a character who appears in several romances of chivalry, and the evil giant Pandafilando de la Fosca Vista, an invented name thoroughly in keeping with typical chivalric onomastics (p. 327).[3]

When the princess finishes her tale with a vow to marry her liberator, Don Quijote can hardly contain his excitement and gloats (p. 329): "¿Qué te parece, Sancho amigo? . . . ¿No oyes lo que pasa? ¿No te lo dije yo? Mira si tenemos ya reino que mandar y reina con quien casar" ("What do you think now, friend Sancho? . . . Do you hear that? Did I not tell you so? See how we have already got a kingdom to govern and a queen to marry," p. 232). Sancho's enthusiasm could not be greater; he exclaims, "¡Eso juro yo . . . para el puto que no se casare en abriendo el gaznatico al señor Pandahilado! Pues ¡monta que es mala la reina! ¡Así se me vuelvan las pulgas de la cama!" ("I'll swear to that! And to hell with the bastard who won't marry after slitting Señor Pandahilado's windpipe! The queen's not bad either! I wish the fleas in my bed were like that"), and gives "dos zapatetas en el aire, con muestras de grandísimo contento" ("a couple of capers in the air with every sign of extreme satisfaction"). Shortly thereafter, however, Don Quijote realizes the conflict that confronts him, as he remembers his avowed dedication to Dulcinea (pp. 330–31): "no es posible que yo arrostre, ni por pienso, el casarme, aunque fuese con el ave fénix" ("it is impossible for me for a moment to contemplate marriage, even

3. See Howard Mancing, "The Comic Function of Chivalric Names in *Don Quijote*," p. 226.

with Phoenix," p. 233). Sancho, angry, shouts back at his master:

> Voto a mí, y juro a mí, que no tiene vuestra merced, señor don Quijote, cabal juicio. . . . Cásese, cásese luego, encomiéndole yo a Satanás, y tome ese reino que se le viene a las manos de vobis vobis, y en siendo rey, hágame marqués o adelantado, y luego, siquiera se lo lleve el diablo todo. (p. 331)

> (By my oath, Señor Don Quixote, you are not in your right senses. . . . In the devil's name marry, marry, take this kingdom that has been dropped in your lap, and when you are king, make me a marquis or governor of a province, and take the rest.) (p. 233)

Don Quijote responds by striking his squire and calling him several insulting names.

Dorotea manages to pacify knight and squire, who then go off together in order to discuss Sancho's recent interview with Dulcinea. The ensuing conversation between Don Quijote and Sancho occupies a singularly ambiguous position in Cervantes's novel. Given his master's most recent exhibition of temper, Sancho is brazenly flirting with danger as he describes his imaginary interview with the nonexistent lady. Sancho has no need to base his version of the meeting that never took place on the sort of reality that might have surrounded it had it in fact occurred; there is absolutely no reason why he could not—and, indeed, given his need to remain in Don Quijote's good graces, should not—have provided a more readily appreciated version of the event. There is no doubt that the clever Sancho could have followed the outline his master was willing to provide so that Don Quijote would have virtually described the event himself, while Sancho merely confirmed the details. For his part, Don Quijote is surprisingly indulgent with his squire's apparently gratuitous proliferation of grossly unchivalric detail and seems almost gleeful as he transforms each item into its chivalric counterpart. Don Quijote's tolerance of the story that Sancho tells him could be his way of apologizing to his squire for his recent excessive anger, or it could imply that Don Quijote, as well as Sancho Panza, is prepared to discuss the matter in terms of a real Aldonza Lorenzo rather than of an imaginary Dulcinea del Toboso. In any case, the predominant tone is one of lightheartedness; it is almost as though both Don Quijote and Sancho are playing a private game in which both are aware of the rules, and neither needs to fear the noncooperation of the other.[4] In what must be considered a clear acknowledgment of their solidarity, Don Quijote concludes by saying (p. 341), "Y avísote que no digas nada a nadie, ni a los que con nosotros vienen, de lo que aquí hemos departido y tratado" ("But I counsel you not to say anything to anyone, or to those who are with us, about what we have considered and discussed," p. 241).

Dulcinea is Don Quijote's most vulnerable weakness as a knight-errant as well as his greatest strength. In his adventures, especially the earliest ones, her image infused him with both spiritual and physical strength. But Vivaldo used Dulcinea to expose Don Quijote's foolishness and to put him in a bad light (see section 2.2). In his gratuitous penance for her in the Sierra Morena, Don Quijote was shown to exist as a knight only in form and not at all in fact. Furthermore, by revealing the reality of Aldonza Lorenzo to Sancho, he lost a final veil of the mystery of genuine knighthood in the eyes of his squire and allowed the incongruous conversation just discussed to take place. Perhaps without Dulcinea, Don Quijote would not be a semifamous knight-errant sought by his friends and by a supposed princess in distress. But without Dulcinea, the lady he arbitrarily invented for himself, Don Quijote would face no conflict of interests when a truly beautiful woman approached him with an attractive marriage proposition.[5]

One further event takes place before the traveling party leaves

4. This scene is particularly important to those who see Don Quijote as being constantly at play: Arturo Serrano-Plaja, *"Magic" Realism in Cervantes: "Don Quixote" as Seen through "Tom Sawyer" and "The Idiot,"* pp. 191–93; and Gonzalo Torrente Ballester, *El "Quijote" como juego,* pp. 128–31. Richard L. Predmore suggests that Sancho purposefully paints Dulcinea in such repulsive terms in order to make his master accept the Princess Micomicona as his wife and thus bring wealth to the squire; *The World of Don Quixote,* p. 47. This explanation might suffice for Sancho, but it does not explain Don Quijote's participation in this scene.

5. The problems created by Dulcinea del Toboso in part II are, as we shall see, even greater.

the mountains: the chance encounter with Andrés. Don Quijote readily seizes on this opportunity to impress his companions
with his importance, as though a real knight-errant would have
had any reason to prove the validity of his chivalric values to a
princess and her squire or to a friend, the priest, who greets him
(I, 29, 321) as "el espejo de la caballerí, . . . la quinta esencia de
los caballeros andantes" ("the mirror of chivalry . . . the quintessence of knight-errant," p. 226): "cuán de importancia es haber caballeros andantes en el mundo, que *desfagan* los tuertos y
agravios que en él se hacen" ("how important it is to have
knights-errant to redress the wrongs and injuries done . . . in
this world"). But when the reality of his ineffectiveness is exposed and when his commitment to the Princess Micomicona
restrains him from taking any further action in the case, Don
Quijote is absolutely humiliated and is described (p. 345) as
"corridísimo" ("crestfallen," p. 244).

3.2 The Priest, the Barber, and Dorotea

I observed in section 1.4 that the frequency with which a character speaks can serve as a measurement of his importance in a
work. The relative frequency of the speech of Don Quijote,
Sancho Panza, and other characters in general proved to be an
accurate indication of their relative significance in a given section
of *Don Quijote*. In the same way, the number of times that secondary characters speak can signal the importance of their roles.
The most prominent of the more than fifty-four characters who
speak in part I are ranked in Table 3.1.[6] The priest, Pero Pérez,
and the barber, Maese Nicolás, are Don Quijote's closest friends.
The importance of their reentry into the chivalric world of Don
Quijote in I, 26, is second only to the knight's acquisition of
Sancho Panza as his squire. Because of the priest and the barber,
the final half of part I is radically different from the first half.
Their role, along with that of their accomplice, Dorotea, is thus

6. A precise total of the number of individuals who speak cannot be
determined, as an unspecified number of goatherds speak in chapters
11–14, and probably more than one of Don Luis's servants speak during
chapters 43–45. This list does not include characters from interpolated
stories (such as Anselmo and Lotario from "The Story of Ill-Advised
Curiosity") as they are not actually characters in *Don Quijote*.

Table 3.1. Frequency of Speech among Secondary Characters (Part I)

Character	Number of Speeches
The priest Pero Pérez	91
Dorotea	41
The barber Maese Nicolás	34
Cardenio	25
The innkeeper Juan Palomeque	21
The captive Ruy Pérez de Viedma	20
The canon of Toledo	14
Andrés	12
Ginés de Pasamonte	12
Fernando	10

of major importance in the story. But before examining this role more closely, it is necessary to look briefly at certain other characters.

Comparative characterization is a term I have used elsewhere[7] to describe how the reader's evaluation of the ethical status of a given character, usually the protagonist of a work, is partially determined by the impression that that character makes in comparison with other, usually secondary, characters. For example, in the first *tratado* of *Lazarillo de Tormes*, the protagonist lies, cheats, and steals during his apprenticeship with the blind beggar, but since his master is an even greater liar, cheat, thief, and hypocrite, Lazarillo is comparatively sympathetic to the reader. Don Quijote is essentially a comic character at the beginning of part I and as such the reader's natural reaction is to laugh at him. Let us examine briefly how the words and deeds of some of the characters who make brief appearances in Don Quijote's world of chivalry contribute to our reaction to him.

The first innkeeper, described (I, 2, 45) as "no menos ladrón que Caco, ni menos maleante que estudiantado paje" ("as crafty a thief as Cacus and as full of tricks as a student or a page," p. 32) and (I, 3, 49) "un poco socarrón" ("something of a wag," p. 34), whose life is a parody of the chivalric mission, puts Don

7. Howard Mancing, "The Deceptiveness of *Lazarillo de Tormes*," p. 426.

Quijote on public display for laughs and makes a farce of the dubbing ceremony, but is essentially good-natured and not unsympathetic, especially as he humors Don Quijote by counseling him always to carry money, clean shirts, and a first-aid kit. The rich Juan Haldudo is too frightened by Don Quijote to ridicule him to his face, but after the latter's departure sarcastically refers to him (I, 4, 59) as a "*desfacedor* de agravios" ("undoer of wrongs," p. 41) as he makes the youth Andrés pay doubly for his own humiliation. The Toledan merchant described (I, 4, 61) as "un poco burlón y muy mucho discreto" ("fond of a joke and very sharp-witted," p. 42) is cruel in his sarcasm about Dulcinea. The Biscayan, in his clumsy Spanish, also ridicules Don Quijote's profession when he plays on the words *caballero andante* (I, 8, 95): "Anda, caballero que mal andas" ("Go away; good riddance, gentleman," p. 63). Neither the actions nor the parodic words of these characters from the early chapters has any major effect on the reader's perception of Don Quijote, whose consistently proud self-inflation and constant stream of ridiculous chivalric rhetoric ensure that the reader will continue to perceive him as comic. The generosity and kindness of Pedro Alonso in chapter 5 contrast sharply with the knight's mad ravings. The simplicity and authenticity of the goatherds in chapters 11–14 also appear attractive when compared to Don Quijote's pomposity and erudite pettiness (as observed in section 2.2).

By implicit comparison, Grisóstomo and Cardenio most reduce the status of Don Quijote. The real death of the former and the real penance of the latter expose Don Quijote's *pro forma* suffering and gratuitous penance for Dulcinea del Toboso for the hollow gestures that they are (see sections 2.2 and 2.6). The other character who brings out the worst in Don Quijote is Vivaldo (I, 13, 128), "que era persona muy discreta y de alegre condición" ("a person of great shrewdness and with a merry disposition," p. 85). Familiar with the books of chivalry, of a social station equal or superior to that of Don Quijote—as Gristóstomo and Cardenio were, and as all those previously mentioned were not—Vivaldo directly confronts Don Quijote on the matter of Dulcinea, resulting in a major intellectual humiliation for the supposed knight-errant (see section 2.2).

In the early chapters, Don Quijote's status—both comic and

chivalric—is maintained intact. In his two periods of comparative inaction (chapters 11–14 and 23–28), however, he is definitely eclipsed by others. What happens in the series of adventures in chapters 15–22 is quite different. The Yanguesans, Maritornes and the muleteer, the shepherds of supposed armies at war, and the barber with the basin do not speak (chapters 15–18 and 21). No one is present during the night and morning of the fulling mills except knight and squire (chapter 20). The only character from this section whose words deflate Don Quijote's chivalric mission is Alonso López, the waggish but wounded *bachiller* (see section 2.4). The relative unimportance of these secondary characters is compensated for by the increasing prominence of Sancho Panza, whose major role in undermining Don Quijote's chivalric world has already been discussed (see especially sections 2.1 and 2.5).

The priest and barber encourage their friend by talking with him about chivalric matters and are thus accomplices both in Don Quijote's original decision to become a knight-errant and in his decision to leave on a second sally. Both of them, especially the priest, are presented in an essentially favorable light at the beginning of the novel. The reader naturally perceives them positively, as intelligent and discreet, helpful to the members of the Quijano household, and concerned about their friend's madness. During the inquisition of the books in I, 6, Pero Pérez clearly takes the leading role and further establishes himself as a respectable authority figure, representing Cervantes's own literary judgments.[8] But at the same time, there is a certain capriciousness in some of his statements[9] that anticipates his presentation later on in the novel.

One can imagine the two friends talking at length about the madness of Don Quijote and deciding that it was up to them to "rescue" him. So they set out, theoretically motivated by an altruistic desire to aid a comrade who has lost touch with reality. But they no sooner come across Sancho Panza than we begin to observe another aspect of their quest. After determining a few

8. John J. Allen, *Don Quixote: Hero or Fool?*, 2:58.
9. Daniel Eisenberg, "Pero Pérez the Priest and His Comment on *Tirant lo Blanch*," pp. 324–26.

facts about Don Quijote's whereabouts and what has happened to the knight and the squire since leaving home, they have no small bit of fun at Sancho's expense, having him repeat no fewer than three times what he remembers of the letter his master wrote to Dulcinea (I, 26, 278). Rather than take a truthful, logical, and direct approach to their problem by using their superior intelligence, culture, and social status to convince Sancho of the validity of their undertaking and perhaps thus directly enlist his aid, they decide to humor him (p. 279): "No quisieron cansarse en sacarle del error en que estaba, pareciéndoles que, pues no le dañaba nada la conciencia, mejor era dejarle en él, y a ellos les sería de más gusto oír sus necedades" ("They did not care to waste their effort trying to disabuse him of his error, as they considered that since it did not in any way hurt his conscience, it would be better to leave him in it, and they would have all the more amusement in listening to his foolishness," p. 193). Their aim is clearly to enjoy their task as much as possible rather than to dispatch their chore with maximum efficiency. As we shall see, having a good time and a few laughs at their friends' expense is at least as important as getting Don Quijote and Sancho to return to the village.

Apparently, the priest and the barber set out with no specific plan in mind, because it is only after they are at the inn and have already begun to take an indirect approach with Sancho that the priest conceives (p. 280) "un pensamiento muy acomodado al gusto de don Quijote, y para lo que ellos querían" ("an idea very well adapted to humor Don Quixote and effect their purpose," p. 194). The idea is to prepare a mock chivalric adventure in which the priest will dress as a *doncella andante* ("maiden-errant") in distress and will *pedir un don* ("ask for a boon") that Don Quijote cannot fail to *otorgar* ("to grant") and will thus promise to "*desfacelle* un agravio que un mal caballero le tenía *fecho*" ("redress a wrong which a wicked knight had done her," p. 194). The narration here shows that the priest simultaneously reveals his plan and rehearses his lines.

The carefully prepared script, the disguises, and the switch in the roles that the priest and barber are to play are all obviated by Dorotea's offer to play the role of the *doncella menesterosa* ("maiden in distress"), which sets up a series of ironic contrasts:

Dorotea is not a *doncella* ("maiden" or "damsel"; specifically, a virgin) but a *dueña* (used here not to mean "chaperone" or "matron" but rather a woman who is no longer a virgin), a distinction she carefully makes (I, 28, 308)—"y con volverse a salir del aposento mi doncella, yo dejé de serlo" ("so I was left by my maid, and I ceased to be one," p. 216)—and which tends to be rigorously insisted on in the romances of chivalry,[10] but she is very much in distress (*menesterosa*), so we have a *dueña menesterosa* playing the role of a *doncella menesterosa* who will appear before a mad *hidalgo* playing the role of a mad *caballero andante*; furthermore, Dorotea comes to rescue Don Quijote on the pretext that she is in need of rescue.[11] She insists that she has both the costume to play the role and the ability to do it well because (I, 29, 315) "ella había leído muchos libros de caballerías y sabía bien el estilo que tenían las doncellas cuitadas cuando pedían sus dones a los andantes caballeros" ("She had read a great many books of chivalry and knew exactly the style in which afflicted damsels begged boons of knights-errant," p. 222). We saw in the last section how well she played her part.

A good time is had by all at the expense of Don Quijote and Sancho Panza. Both the priest, accurately described (I, 27, 285) as an "hombre bien hablado" ("well-spoken man," p. 198) and (I, 29, 320) a "gran tracista" ("very clever," p. 225), and Dorotea (I, 30, 325), "que era discreta y de gran donaire" ("who was shrewd and witty," p. 227), add occasional gratuitous comic ele-

10. Just as Dorotea euphemistically describes losing her virginity as a change of status from *doncella* to *dueña* (I, 28, 308), the narrators of the romances of chivalry very frequently employ the same terminology: Amadís and Oriana (*Amadís*, I, 285): "fue hecha dueña la más hermosa donzella del mundo" ("was the most beautiful maiden in the world made a matron [i.e., *dueña*]," p. 339); Palmerín de Olivia and Polinarda, together with Tolomé and Brionela (*Palmerín de Olivia*, pp. 169–70): "E ansí aquellas dos donzellas, que de tan alta guisa eran, fueron tornadas dueñas aquella noche" ("Thus the two maidens, who were of such high rank, became *dueñas* that night"); the Caballero del Febo and Claridiana (*Espejo*, 6:245): "la real princesa Claridiana fue vencida y hecha dueña" ("the royal princess Claridiana was conquered and made a *dueña*").

11. On the last point, see Margaret Church, *Don Quixote: The Knight of La Mancha*, p. 42.

ments to their treatment of Don Quijote. The barber can barely conceal his laughter when he observes the meeting between Dorotea and Don Quijote (p. 329), and when Sancho gloats over his forthcoming *ínsula* (I, 30, 330), it "renovó la risa en todos" ("set them all laughing again," p. 232).

The world's apparent acceptance of Don Quijote's chivalric vision is a mixed blessing for the Manchegan knight. It simultaneously confirms and, because it is a sham, undermines his chivalric existence. The real enchanters in the novel are the priest, the barber, and Dorotea because they are the ones who do most to incapacitate Don Quijote.[12] Very little of what occurs in the remainder of part I is decided or controlled by Don Quijote. Rather than the inventor, the manipulator, who, as in the earliest chapters, forces others to accept his vision, he becomes little more than a pawn in the hands of the others who usurp his rhetoric and his powers and who drain his vitality.

Miguel de Unamuno's reaction to the novel in I, 29, is—in spite of its rhetorical exaggeration—essentially sound and can serve as a summary statement.

Now begins, I say, the sad part of the quixotic career. His most beautiful and spontaneous adventures lay behind him now. From now on, the majority of them will be plotted and rigged by malicious men. Until this point, the world was unaware of the hero, while he, in his turn, tried to make it over in his image. Now the world knows and accepts him, but only in order to make mock of him, and going along with his humor, makes him over into its image. Now, my poor Don Quixote, you have become forever the butt and laughingstock of barbers, curates, graduates, dukes, and idlers of every

12. See Ricardo López Landeira, "Los encantadores de Don Quijote y su crítica literaria," p. 116. López Landeira does not include Dorotea in his list of "enchanters." See also Jorge E. Sorensen, "The Importance of Sierra Morena as a Point of Transition in *Don Quijote*" (especially pp. 49–51), for a discussion of the negative influence of Dorotea, the priest, and others in Don Quijote's world of chivalry. L. A. Murillo has observed that when the priest, the barber, and Dorotea enter the novel "the elements of *burla* and *artificio*, complete with a mock plot, costumes and masks, have come to substitute for the hero's will and incentive for action"; "*Don Quixote* as Renaissance Epic," p. 63.

breed. Your Passion has begun, and the bitterest type of passion at that: passion by mockery.[13]

3.3 Chapters 32–46: At the Inn

On his return to the inn of Juan Palomeque el Zurdo, Don Quijote exchanges a few words with the innkeeper's wife about accommodations—nothing is recorded as having been said about the structure's being a castle—and then immediately goes to bed (I, 32, 346), "porque venía muy quebrantado y falto de juicio" ("since he was badly in need of rest and good sense," p. 244). Don Quijote's lack of physical strength might seem a little strange, as (since losing some teeth after attacking the herds of sheep in chapter 18) his only recent sufferings have been from the stoning by the galley slaves and from the rock thrown by Cardenio. He has just rested a few days during his period of penance, and during the short trip with Princess Micomicona and company has demonstrated no particular tiredness or weakness. Perhaps, however, there has been a cumulative effect produced by his several physical misfortunes, and perhaps his spiritual and intellectual humiliations and sufferings have also taken their toll. At any rate, to go to bed and sleep while others remain up and active is hardly the hallmark of a knight-errant. The reality of pain and exhaustion makes the fantasy of chivalry increasingly difficult to maintain.

The stay at the inn is the lowest point in Don Quijote's knightly career. He sleeps through the literary discussion and the priest's reading of the manuscript of "The Story of Ill-Advised Curiosity," interrupting the story only briefly with his ridiculous dream-adventure of the wineskin giants. Although he seems to believe that he has just completed his ideal adventure victoriously, Don Quijote returns immediately to bed—amid the laughter of almost all his companions—and goes to sleep (I, 35, 394) "con muestras de grandísimo cansancio" ("with every appearance of excessive weariness," p. 289).

After sleeping through the denouement of the Dorotea–Fer-

13. Miguel de Unamuno, *Our Lord Don Quixote: The Life of Don Quixote and Sancho with Related Essays*, p. 122.

nando–Cardenio–Luscinda episode, Don Quijote is awake for
the arrival of the captive and Zoraida. Don Quijote delivers his
arms-and-letters dinner speech, during which he again attempts
to justify his chivalric profession, to a much more appreciative
audience than the one that listened to his lecture on the Golden
Age. But immediately after Don Quijote talks theoretically
about the superiority of arms over letters, Ruy Pérez de Viedma,
the escaped captive, tells the story of his life, which graphically
illustrates the validity of his genuinely heroic exploits. Don
Quijote remains silent (or is he absent?) throughout.

Don Quijote makes an effort to reassert chivalric values when
he greets the magistrate's company at the castle with another
reference to arms and letters and with a pair of archaisms (*fermosura, fermosa*; I, 42, 467). The knight is briefly marveled at
(pp. 467–68)—"no menos le admiraba su talle que sus palabras;
. . . el talle, visaje y la apostura de don Quijote le desatinaba"
("being no less astonished by his appearance than by his talk
. . . but with the figure, countenance, and bearing of Don Quixote he was at wit's end," p. 336)—and then shunted aside during the reunion of the Pérez de Viedma brothers. After Don
Quijote offers to guard the castle (p. 472), the magistrate is in-
formed about the knight-errant's "humor estraño" ("extraordinary disposition"), from which he derives "no poco gusto"
("not a little pleasure," p. 340).

Taking a cue from the way that all the respectable guests in
the inn seem to enjoy Don Quijote's extravagance, Maritornes
and young Miss Palomeque have their own bit of fun at his expense (I, 43, 478): "determinaron las dos de hacelle alguna burla,
o, a lo menos, de pasar un poco el tiempo oyéndole sus disparates" ("The pair of them resolved to play some trick upon him,
or at any rate to amuse themselves for a while by listening to his
nonsense," p. 344). Don Quijote is all the more comic (pp. 478–
80) in his invocation of Dulcinea ("¡Oh mi señora . . . "), archaism (*fará, la tu* merced, *cautivo, este mi* cuitado corazón, *fermosa,
hayades*), transformation of reality—"agujero que a él le pareció
ventana, y aun con rejas dordas" ("the hole in the wall. To him
it seemed to be a window, and what is more, with a gilt grating,"
p. 345)—and pride—"esa mano, o, por mejor decir, ese verdugo
de los malhechores del mundo; . . . la fuerza del brazo que tal

mano tiene" ("this hand, or rather this scourge of the evil-doers of the earth. . . . the strength of the arm that has such a hand," p. 346). This is, however, another pseudoevent, conceived and staged by others, in the same class as, but on a lesser scale than, the Princess Micomicona adventure. The very painful results and the evocations of the Rocinante and Don Quijote episodes of chapters 15–16 have already been discussed in section 2.3.

The next morning, the sore and embarrassed knight-errant issues a challenge to some new arrivals that he will fight anyone who does not believe that he was enchanted, but the innkeeper informs the newcomers that they ought pay him no heed ("que no había de hacer caso dél") and they comply, at which Don Quijote (I, 44, 484–85) "moría y rabiaba de despecho y saña" ("was furious and ready to die with indignation and wrath," p. 349). Needless to say, a genuine knight-errant would never have been so ignored, or, if he had been, would not have rationalized as Don Quijote does that he is already under contract to the princess and can therefore do nothing but accept the humiliation.

When Juan Palomeque is assaulted by two guests who try to sneak out without paying their bill, Don Quijote is appealed to for assistance simply because he is the only one who has nothing to do. His phlegmatic response and his search for an excuse not to help are quite unchivalrous and are referred to (p. 489) as "cobardía" ("pusillanimity," p. 352). But while the reader's attention is waggishly turned by the narrator to the events concerning Don Luis, Don Quijote intervenes (p. 490) and persuades—"por persuasión y buenas razones de don Quijote, más que por amenazas" ("by persuasion and Don Quixote's fair words more than by threats," p. 353)—the guests to pay what they owe. It is no surprise that Don Quijote, whom we have seen speak so eloquently on previous occasions, is capable of such mediation. But at his most chivalric moments earlier in the novel (for example, with Juan Haldudo or the Biscayan), it was simply a matter of asserting the right and defending it with force. Perhaps, in spite of what Don Quijote had stated in his speech the day before, there are times when letters are superior to arms in establishing peace. Later, the great fight over the *baciyelmo* ("basin-helmet") is terminated not by Don Quijote's strong right arm but rather by his verbal persuasion (I, 45, 499). The events at the inn are brought to a conclusion with the "enchantment" of Don Quijote by his friends. After two days and nights of being ignored, laughed at, humiliated, and incapacitated as a knight-errant, this enchantment comes almost as a welcome relief.

If the fortunes of Don Quijote ebb during the stay in the inn, those of Sancho Panza virtually evaporate. In ten of the fifteen chapters, Sancho remains completely silent; his role is minor at best in every event that takes place. He listens to part of the discussion about the romances of chivalry and learns that knights-errant no longer exist and that the books written about them, so important to his master, are (I, 32, 351) "necedades y mentiras" ("foolishness and lies," p. 248), which causes him to consider again the possibility of leaving Don Quijote's service. Sancho is laughed at along with his master when he believes that Don Quijote has actually beheaded the enemy giant and must be consoled by Dorotea, taking solace in the long history of enchantments in matters that occur in the inn.

Sancho is present for the reuniting of Dorotea and Fernando and sees (I, 37, 411) "la reina convertida en una dama particular" ("the queen turned into a private lady," p. 294). Thoroughly dejected and disillusioned, his spirits as low as possible, he complains bitterly and accusingly to Don Quijote (p. 410): "Bien puede vuestra merced, señor Triste Figura, dormir todo lo que quisiere, sin cuidado de matar a ningún gigante, ni de volver a la princesa su reino; que ya todo está hecho y concluido" ("Sir Mournful Countenance, your worship may as well sleep on as much as you like, without troubling yourself about killing any giant or restoring her kingdom to the princess. For that is all over and settled now," p. 293). The clever Dorotea is able to assure knight and squire that nothing has changed (p. 413)—"la misma que ayer fui me soy hoy" ("I am the same as I was yesterday," p. 295)—and promises that she still expects to complete the adventure. Sancho asserts himself only during the dispute over the barber's basin and the ass's trappings when he literally has to fight in order to retain what small material advantage has come his way as a squire. Later, Sancho again accuses the supposed princess of petting shamelessly with another man (Fernando) and jeopardizing his promised *ínsula*, which brings forth Don Quijote's angriest outburst yet (I, 46, 504–5). Once more, Dorotea is able to reconcile the two, this time by suggesting enchantment.

Outnumbered and outclassed, the Sancho Panza who previously gained so much self-confidence and self-assurance is reduced to a peripheral figure during these chapters. His hopes of immediate material reward disappear before his eyes. When his friend the priest and the others tie and encage Don Quijote, pretending to enchant him, Sancho maintains a wary silence, hoping against hope that all is not lost (p. 508).

If Don Quijote and Sancho suffer while at the inn, other characters, led by the priest, reach unprecedented heights.[14] Pero Pérez leads the book discussion while Don Quijote is asleep. His curiosity is responsible for his reading the manuscript of a story about curiosity to the assembled guests. After helping to get Don Quijote back to bed following the interruption of the wineskins, he completes the story and offers his criticism of the author. The priest takes the lead in arranging the reunion between the captive and his brother. He assists Maese Nicolás and Fernando in determining that the barber's basin is in fact a helmet.[15] He convinces the *cuadrilleros* (rural police officers) not to arrest and incarcerate Don Quijote, but rather to leave it to him to keep this dangerous madman from doing more damage. Finally, it is the priest who conceives and directs the enchantment of Don Quijote.

The small-town priest does well for himself indeed in the midst of well-to-do and educated people like Fernando and the magistrate. He thoroughly enjoys the opportunity to occupy center stage both in Don Quijote's world of chivalry and in the

14. The priest's preeminence is readily seen in the fact that he speaks thirty-one times during these seventeen chapters, far more than any other character except Don Quijote.

15. A remark he makes when the barber's goods are being transformed illustrates as well as any his playful spirit. One of Don Luis's servants who is not a party to the fun that can be had by humoring Don Quijote refuses to believe that "ésta no sea bacía de barbero y ésta albarda de asno" ("this is not a barber's basin and that's a jackass's packsaddle"). The priest observes (I, 45, 496), "Bien podría ser de borrica" ("It might easily be a she-ass's," p. 357).

real world of love and intrigue, rubbing elbows with society's elite, directing the actions of others, and sharing with his newly acquired friends the good fun provided by Don Quijote. This has been, perhaps, the finest moment in his life.

Maese Nicolás is rather like the priest's Sancho Panza. He is never as eloquent or assertive as his more learned companion. During events in Sierra Morena and in the inn, he is usually content to go along with and assist the priest. But he does take the initiative when the other barber arrives and the argument over the basin and trappings begins. Having seen the success of the priest's efforts to get laughs at Don Quijote's expense, the barber decides (I, 45, 493) to "esforzar su desatino y llevar adelante la burla para que todos riesen" ("back him in his delusion and stretch out the joke for the amusement of all," p. 355) and affirms along with Don Quijote that the object in question is a helmet. With the help of Cardenio and Fernando, they all have a good laugh and a general free-for-all. The barber later is assigned the role of the enchanter who delivers the prophesy to Don Quijote and shows that he too has mastered the chivalric style (I, 46, 508), using archaism—*afincamieto, yoguieren, faga, vegadas, fecho*; metaphor—"el furibundo león manchado . . . la blanca paloma tobosina" ("the raging Manchegan lion . . . the white Tobosan dove"); chivalric clichés—"la flor de la caballería andante" ("the flower of knight-errantry," p. 366); and so on.

Dorotea, who is probably second in importance to the priest during this section, also operates effectively in both the chivalric and the real worlds. She repeatedly uses feminine charm and chivalric authority to pacify Don Quijote and Sancho and to maintain their illusions and hopes. At the same time, she is most directly responsible, in her moving, tearful plea (I, 36, 404–5), for convincing Fernando to surrender Luscinda to Cardenio and to be content with his de facto wife, Dorotea. Later, she involves herself in the Clara–Luis intrigue.

The implicit comparison between the authentic deeds of arms of the ex-captive captain and the mere rhetoric of Don Quijote has already been observed. The story of Anselmo also provides an implicit multilayered warning for Don Quijote (who, significantly, is asleep): he who becomes obsessed with a single extravagant idea may eventually pay dearly for his impertinence;

he who invites others into his private construct may find that they play their roles only too well.

3.4 Chapters 47–52: The Return Home

The final chapters of a novel, like the last act of a play or the last tercet of a sonnet, often present events and/or statements of theme that enable the reader to make ultimate and definitive judgment on the work as a whole. The end of part I of *Don Quijote* allows the reader to pause and make a tentative estimation of all that has taken place up to that point. What occurs in the final six chapters of the first part is of major importance to all the characters involved: Don Quijote, Sancho Panza, the priest, and the barber.

Chapter 47 begins with Don Quijote "confused" because of the gross and utterly nonchivalric nature of his enchantment— he is caged on an ox cart. Sancho's attempt to convey his suspicions about the "enchanters" to his master are rejected by Don Quijote. The women of the inn feign tears as they take leave of the enchanted knight, but Don Quijote maintains (p. 512) that "todas estas desdichas son anexas a los que profesan lo que yo profeso" ("All these mishaps are the lot of those who follow the profession I profess," p. 369). Although these words recall those previously cited of I, 4, 62—"Y aún se tenía por dichoso, pareciéndole que aquélla era propia desgracia de caballeros andantes" ("Yet he considered himself fortunate, as it seemed to him that this was a real knight-errant's mishap," p. 44)—the context in which they are delivered is quite different. This time, Don Quijote is not lying on the ground, badly beaten and unable to rise, railing arrogantly at his enemies, but sitting calmly in a cage after others have told him that he has been enchanted. He attributes his misfortune to envy, begs pardon for his errors—"Perdonadme, *fermosas* damas, si algún *desaguisado*, por descuido mío, os he *fecho*" ("Forgive me, fair ladies, if through inadvertence I have in aught offended you")—and states his appreciation for all that has been done on his behalf. This reposed and melancholy Don Quijote is far less comic and far more sympathetic than the figure of the early chapters.

The arrival of the canon of Toledo presents Don Quijote with the necessity to defend once again his book-inspired chivalric life and gives the priest a highly respected colleague to impress with the comedy of his caged friend, as well as an opportunity to engage in another of the literary discussions that he so enjoys, this time with a very knowledgeable and sympathetic fellow critic. But before the literary discussions take place, Sancho Panza makes the most daring move of his career, confronting not Don Quijote but the priest and his friends with an uncomfortable reality.

Sancho Panza, an Old Christian and a respectful believer in authority (especially that of the church), fully realizes that criticizing the priest—and in the presence of an important ecclesiastical figure from Toledo—is a bold and impertinent proposition. His first words (p. 515)—"Ahora, señores, quiéranme bien o quiéranme mal por lo que dijere" ("Well, sirs, you may like or dislike what I am going to say," p. 371)—reveal that he is aware of the possible consequences of his brazenness. If the priest has just stated to the canon that Don Quijote "va encantado" ("is enchanted"), Sancho corrects him—pointedly and rather crudely—by saying that "el caso de ello es que así va encantado mi señor don Quijote como mi madre" ("the fact of the matter is, my master, Don Quixote, is about as much enchanted as my mother") since none of his physical processes are suspended as is supposed to be the case with an enchantment. Then, looking accusingly at the priest, Sancho adds:

> ¡Ah señor cura, señor cura! ¿Pensaba vuestra merced que no le conozco, y pensará que yo no calo y adivino adónde se encaminan estos nuevos encantamentos? Pues sepa que le conozco, por más que se encubra el rostro, y sepa que le entiendo, por más que disimule sus embustes. En fin, donde reina la envidia no puede vivir la virtud, ni adonde hay escaseza la liberalidad. (pp. 515–16)

> (Ah, señor priest! Do you think I don't know you? Do you think I don't guess and see the drift of these new enchantments? Well, I can tell you I know you, even though your face is covered, and I can tell you I am on to you, however you hide your tricks. After all, where envy reigns virtue cannot live, and where there is miserliness there can be no generosity.) (p. 372)

First, let us note the rhetorical unity of this brief passage. After a dramatic opening, in which Sancho employs the octosyllabic reiteration ("señor cura, señor cura") that is the most distinctive stylistic characteristic of the popular *Romancero*,[16] there is a brilliant extended parallel construction:

¿Pensaba . . .	que	no le conozco,	
y pensará	que...	no lo calo y advino . . . ?	
Pues sepa	que	le conozco	por más que se encubra el rostro,
y sepa	que	le entiendo	por más que disimule sus embustes.
Do you think	[that]	I don't know you?	
Do you think	[that]	I don't guess and see the drift . . . ?	
Well, I can tell you	[that]	I know you,	even though your face is covered,
and I can tell you	[that]	I am on to you,	however you hide your tricks.

Both Don Quijote and the priest have stated that the spell was cast by an enchanter envious of Don Quijote's fame and glory. Sancho now gives an ironic literal meaning to their words by ascribing the same motive—envy—directly to the priest.[17] Rationalizing and role playing have given way to reality. Sancho's role as Reality Instructor becomes more profound than ever before, as this speech is no mere pointing out of physical reality, but an accusation of betrayal. Is it not possible that in fact the priest did become jealous and envious of his friend's notoriety? Could this not explain the priest's enjoyment of his own successful chivalric role playing, as well as his eagerness to laugh and have others laugh at Don Quijote? I suggest that Sancho's accusation is well grounded in psychological reality and that it is of major importance in encouraging the reader to shift his or her evaluation of the priest from positive to negative. Pero Pérez's stated idealistic goal of helping a friend in distress, which has already been undercut by his own cavalier attitude, is exposed as a fraud by Sancho Panza. One more scene in the final chapter, as we shall see, completes the unmasking of the priest's

16. See Ramón Menéndez Pidal, *Romancero hispánico*, 1:78.
17. See López Landeira, "Encantadores de Don Quijote," p. 122.

pettiness and meanness. Let us not underestimate the magnitude of Sancho Panza's quixotic defense of Don Quijote's chivalric world. Sancho attacks an enemy stronger than any directly confronted by his master: the ubiquitous enemy of public opinion, society's norm, in the person of a representative of society's strongest institution, the church.

Sancho then goes on to lament his lost *ínsula* (p. 516) and "todos aquellos socorros y bienes que mi señor don Quijote deja de hacer en este tiempo que está preso" ("the good deeds and acts of mercy that my lord Don Quixote leaves undone while he is a prisoner," p. 372). This debilitates his criticism of the priest, who remains silent (in anger?, in shame?) while the barber engages Sancho in a discussion of these secondary matters. Sancho loses the offensive and perhaps his nerve and ends weakly, saying: "Dios sabe la verdad; y quédese aquí, porque es peor meneallo" ("God knows the truth. Leave it as it is: it only makes it worse to stir it"). The narration continues thus:

> No quiso responder el barbero a Sancho, porque no descubriese con sus simplicidades lo que él y el cura tanto procuraban encubrir; y por este mesmo temor había el cura dicho al canónigo que caminasen un poco delante: que él le diría el misterio del enjaulado, con otras cosas que le diesen gusto. (p. 517)

> (The barber did not wish to answer Sancho lest by his plain speaking he should disclose what the priest and he himself were trying so hard to conceal. The priest, sharing his apprehension, had asked the canon to ride on a little in advance so that he might tell him the mystery of this man in the cage and other things that would amuse him.) (p. 373)

These "enchanters" realize only too well that Sancho could reveal the truth about their actions and their motives to Don Quijote and the canon of Toledo (as well as to the reader). The priest takes the canon aside in order to explain things from his own point of view and to enlist another ally in the campaign to derive *gusto* from Don Quijote's madness. The canon, it turns out, is very much a kindred spirit to the priest (I, 48, 526), "de quien ya iba aficionado" ("to whom he had begun to take a fancy," p. 379). We shall pass over the literary discussion between the two churchmen and between the canon and Don Quijote, except to observe that the latter, who "lost" to Vivaldo earlier, seems to emerge victorious in this debate (I, 49, 537), reducing his opponent to an equivocal "Todo puede ser" ("All that may be," p. 386).[18]

Sancho, frustrated in his attempt to confront the priest with the truth, turns to his only alternative, Don Quijote. After the latter rejects as absolutely unthinkable the suggestion that their friends the priest and the barber have enchanted him, Sancho appeals to his master's sense of authenticity in chivalric matters, citing the popular and literary belief, to which he had alluded earlier, that a person under a spell has no urge to satisfy his ordinary physical needs. As Don Quijote has stated that he does indeed feel compelled by such necessities, this proves, as far as the astute Sancho is concerned, that he cannot be enchanted. After his dream-encounter with enchantment in the cave of Montesinos, Don Quijote will confirm what Sancho says, stating (II, 23, 757) that enchanted people "no comen . . . ni tienen excrementos mayores" ("neither eat, nor are they subject to the greater excretions," p. 555), but now he offers the opinion that, since in these days enchantments are themselves of an unusual sort (that is, they involve an ox cart), perhaps the rules governing enchanted knights-errant are also modified. Don Quijote is desperately clinging to enchantment in order to maintain a guise of chivalry, for to admit the obvious truth of his companion's assertions would be to admit his own inauthenticity (I, 49, 529): "Yo sé y tengo para mí que voy encantado, y esto me basta para la seguridad de mi conciencia; que la formaría muy grande si yo pensase que no estaba encantado y me dejase estar en esta jaula perezoso y cobarde" ("I know and feel that I am enchanted, and that is enough to ease my conscience, for it would weigh heavily on it if I thought I was not enchanted and that in a faint-hearted and cowardly way I allowed myself to lie in this cage," pp. 381–82). In an anticipation of the deathbed scene at the very end of

18. For a brilliant, detailed discussion of this debate, see Alban K. Forcione, *Cervantes, Aristotle, and the "Persiles,"* pp. 91–130.

the novel, Sancho Panza, Reality Instructor par excellence, attempts to rekindle his master's lost chivalric enthusiasm by exhorting him to return to the quest (p. 530): "probásemos otra vez la suerte de buscar más aventuras" ("we might try our chance in looking for adventures again," p. 382). Don Quijote laconically responds that he will try what Sancho suggests, but he actually holds out no hope: "pero tú, Sancho, verás como te engañas en el conocimiento de mi desgracia" ("But you will see, Sancho, how wrongly you interpret my misfortune").

Poor Sancho finds that the truth can be difficult to defend in the face of fanaticism, madness, the need to save face, the desire to impress others, and the enjoyment of a friend's misfortune. As the other barber learned at the inn, both the norms of fantasy and society's standards are often better served by lies and deceits than by the simple truth. One sustains the emperor by applauding his new clothes, not by pointing out that he is naked.

The final chapter of part I merits close scrutiny for its three major scenes: the fight with the goatherd, the adventure of the penitents, and the arrival at the village. Don Quijote cannot accept the crude insults of the goatherd and, although the man is obviously not a knight-errant and therefore not a proper opponent, bloodies his nose—very unchivalrously—by hurling part of a loaf of bread at him. Eugenio responds violently (p. 551): "saltó sobre don Quijote, y asiéndole del cuello con entrambas manos, no dudara de ahogalle, si Sancho Panza no llegara en aquel punto" ("he sprang on Don Quixote, seizing him by the throat with both hands. He would no doubt have throttled him, had not Sancho Panza that instant come to his rescue," p. 397). Notice that it is Sancho and not any of the others who comes to Don Quijote's aid and prevents him from being strangled (literally to death?). As Eugenio is outnumbered two to one, he becomes more desperate: "andaba buscando a gatas algún cuchillo de la mesa para hacer alguna sanguinolenta venganza" ("he was on all fours feeling about for one of the table knives to take a bloody revenge with"). But this time, the priest and the canon intervene to prevent bloodshed (perhaps the messiness of a knifing is more offensive than mere strangulation). Meanwhile, Maese Nicolás also steps in: "mas el barbero hizo de suerte que el cabrero cogió debajo de sí a don Quijote" ("but the barber so contrived it that he got Don Quixote under the goatherd"). In a more advantageous position, and with Sancho being restrained by one of the canon's servants, the choleric goatherd is able to bloody his opponent's face as badly as his own.

What is the attitude of the illustrious company watching this scene? "Reventaban de risa el canónigo y el cura, saltaban los cuadrilleros de gozo, zuzaban los unos y los otros, como hacen a los perros cuando en pendencia están trabados; sólo Sancho Panza se desesperaba" ("The canon and the priest were bursting with laughter, the officers were capering with delight, and both the one and the other egged them on as they do dogs in a fight. Sancho alone was frantic"). Surely this scene must dissipate any sympathy the reader might still have for the priest and the others. There can no longer be any pretext of their acting in Don Quijote's behalf. One of the reasons why Sancho's blanketing was so great a humiliation for him was because it was so dehumanizing. Dogs, traditionally mistreated by Spaniards, were tossed in blankets during carnival diversions. This dehumanization of Don Quijote, the equivalent to Sancho's blanketing, is the most humiliating event in his chivalric career. If nothing that has occurred previously has awakened in the reader any sympathy for Don Quijote, surely this scene does. Perhaps no event in the novel better illustrates the concept of comparative characterization.[19]

19. This vitally important scene has received far too little critical attention, perhaps precisely because it casts such an unfavorable light on the priest and barber (together with the canon of Toledo) whose altruistic motives have rarely been doubted. Occasionally, nonspecialist, impressionistic readers have reacted negatively to these and other comparable characters in the novel (an example is John Cowper Powys, who calls them "capricious and brutal magnates"; *Enjoyment of Literature*, p. 189), but such isolated and insubstantial opinions have carried little weight. Among Hispanists, it has been rare to find little more than some misgivings: Bruce Wardropper, for example, asks, "Should we sympathize with a village priest whose good intentions, love of his friend and desire for his cure are negated by his fondness for play-acting?"; "*Don Quixote*: Story or History?," p. 11. Allen feels in I, 52, a "slight note of ambivalence" toward these characters who "have been presented very sympathetically throughout"; *Hero or Fool*, 1:40. This is essentially the same reaction that Clemencín had over a century ago; *Don Quijote*, p. 1495, note 13. Carlos Varo (*Génesis y evolución del "Qui-*

The adventure of the penitents represents an almost frantic attempt by Don Quijote to recover some of his chivalric stature. Although he stated immediately prior to his fight with Eugenio that his enchantment prevented his undertaking any adventure, he now feels the need to show his companions (p. 552) "cuánto importa que haya en el mundo caballeros que profesan la orden de la andante caballería" ("how important it is that there should be knights in the world professing the order of knight-errantry," p. 398). The action that follows has a structure reminiscent of a classic quixotic adventure: reality, established in narration, is transformed by Don Quijote, who ignores Sancho's warning; Don Quijote issues a challenge, uses archaism, and states his chivalric mission (pp. 552–53). The main difference is that Don Quijote offers no excuse after his defeat. He could have fallen back on enchantment, cited his error in undertaking an adventure when technically indisposed because of his own enchanted state, or he could even have rationalized that his opponents were not knights-errant. Instead, he merely admits the reality of de-

---

jote," p. 288) says that the "grotescas carcajadas" ("grotesque guffaws") of those watching the fight between Don Quijote and Eugenio are repugnant, which indicates for him that the scene is badly written ("poco acertada"). The opinion of Enrique Moreno Báez (*Reflexiones sobre el "Quijote*," p. 33) is simply that such laughter on the part of respectable people merely points out that our modern concept of humor is quite different from that of Cervantes's day. Until very recently, the only major Cervantine critic who has challenged the standard opinion that the priest, barber, canon of Toledo, and the like, represent the novel's positive social norm (see the discussion of the article by Oscar Mandel in section 3.6) has been the iconoclastic Arthur Efron, who is not a traditional Hispanist; *Don Quixote and the Dulcineated World*, p. 98. More recently, in a paper read at the Fordham Cervantes conference, New York City, 8 December 1977, entitled "Critics Attend Human Dogfight and Miss the Action—Headline 1977," Efron issued a challenge to Cervantine scholars, stating his belief that one cannot honestly read the crucial fight scene in I, 52, and deny the importance of violence and the negative values represented by these characters. Then, at the I Congreso Internacional sobre Cervantes, Madrid, 3–9 July 1978, no fewer than three papers were presented in which the priest and others were criticized to varying degrees: Peter N. Dunn, "Una ironía estructural en el *Quijote*"; Howard Mancing, "Alonso Quijano y sus amigos"; and Manuel Ferrer Chivite, "El cura y el barbero o Historia de dos resentidos."

feat and pain (p. 555): "Ayúdame, Sancho amigo, . . . porque tengo todo este hombro hecho pedazos" ("Aid me, friend Sancho . . . as this shoulder is all knocked to pieces," p. 400). To Sancho's suggesion that they return home Don Quijote responds submissively: "Bien dices, Sancho, . . . y será gran prudencia dejar pasar el mal influjo de las estrellas que agora corre" ("You are right, Sancho. It will be wise to let the malign influence of the stars which now prevails pass off"). Thoroughly broken in body and spirit, Don Quijote makes no attempt to maintain his chivalric vision. The uneventful six-day journey back to the village must be particularly anguishing for the defeated knight.

At the end of the first sally (I, 5, 66), Pedro Alonso took Don Quijote home and, arriving at dusk, waited "a que fuese algo más noche, porque no viesen al molido hidalgo tan mal caballero" ("until it was a little later, so that the battered gentleman might not be seen riding in such a shameful way," p. 46), a thoughtful act by a mere acquaintance who wants to spare Don Quijote some embarrassment. In contrast, the return from the second sally takes place at midday on a Sunday, when everyone is in the town square through which Don Quijote's cart passes. It would never occur to the priest and the barber to take any precautions to avoid ridicule for Don Quijote. With friends like these, Don Quijote has no need of enemy enchanters.

The niece and housekeeper receive Don Quijote and put him immediately to bed. This scene is dismissed with a few lines; no conversation involving Don Quijote is recorded. His last quoted words in part I were, significantly, those to Sancho cited earlier, "Bien dices . . ." In these final pages, Don Quijote is no longer a participant; rather, he is a mere object, evoking laughter, pity, or anger.

The homecoming scene that is recorded is the triumphal one of Sancho Panza. Even though his once high hopes for fabulous wealth have vanished, and even though his master has been ridiculed, exposed, and degraded in spite of his own heroic intellectual and physical efforts, Sancho has been so affected by his experience that he is already anxious to return to the chivalric life (p. 556): "siendo Dios servido de que otra vez salgamos en viaje a buscar aventuras" ("if it please God that we should again go on our travels in search of adventures," p. 401). All his complaints to Don Quijote are forgotten as he espouses quixotism, assuring his wife that

> no hay cosa más gustosa en el mundo que ser un hombre hon-rado escudero de un caballero andante buscador de aventuras. . . . es linda cosa esperar los sucesos atravesando montes, es-cudriñando selvas, pisando peñas, visitando castillos, alojando en ventas a toda discreción, sin pagar ofrecido sea al diablo el maravedí. (p. 557)

> (there is nothing in the world more delightful than to be a person of consideration, squire to a knight-errant, and a seeker of adventures. . . . it is a fine thing to be on the look-out for what may happen, crossing mountains, searching woods, climbing rocks, visiting castles, putting up at inns, all free, and devil take the *maravedí* to pay.) (pp. 401–2)

In contrast to Don Quijote's defeat and dejection, Sancho Panza's spiritual exaltation ends part I on a positive note.

3.5 The Pattern of Adventure

The phrase *pattern of adventure* is used with two distinct mean-ings in this section. First, it refers to a certain sequence of ele-ments, or a pattern, that characterizes Don Quijote's adventures. Second, it refers to the general pattern into which these adven-tures fall. The structure of the latter recalls Figures 1.1 to 1.9 and represents a visual description of Don Quijote's career as a knight-errant.

When discussing Don Quijote's battle with the windmills (section 1.6), I suggested that there were ten elements that could be considered typical of a quixotic adventure. In Table 3.2, these ten criteria are applied to each of the sixteen adventures that Don Quijote has in the first part of the novel.[20] First, I review the ten

20. My list of chivalric adventures is based essentially on Predmore's; *World of Don Quixote*, pp. 17–22. Predmore's definition ("All of them involve battle or the probable risk of battle," p. 17) is quite acceptable. Allen discusses this list and suggests a few modifications; *Hero or Fool*, 1:41–42, note 6. Oscar Mandel has a "table of 'foes'" that is of interest; "The Function of the Norm in *Don Quixote*," p. 161. Edmund de Chasca has made a useful list of adventures for the first half of part I; "Algunos aspectos del ritmo y del movimiento narrativo del *Quijote*,"

categories, indicating what must be present in order to comply completely with the criteria and thus to put an x in that category for an adventure or to comply partially or incompletely and thus put an *(x)* in the category.

1. Reality is stated in narration, before Don Quijote undertakes the adventure. If the reality is revealed during the course of events, as in the cases of Andrés, the herds of sheep, the dead body, or the wineskins, the condition is only partially fulfilled.[21]

2. Don Quijote willfully transforms reality. On two occasions—the episodes involving Andrés and the galley slaves—Don Quijote does not actually transform physical reality but rather alters the significance of the events that he sees. During the wineskins adventure, Don Quijote is asleep, and therefore his transformation of reality can hardly be considered willful.

3. Sancho Panza points out the reality of the situation. Occasionally another participant in the adventure, such as Juan Haldudo or Alonso López, or another person who observes what has happened, Juan Palomeque in the case of the wineskins, acts as Reality Instructor. Twice when Don Quijote does not actually transform physical reality—the adventures of the Yanguesans and the galley slaves—Sancho points out the probable result of their intervention.

4. Don Quijote rejects Sancho's interpretation. Again in the cases of the Yanguesans and the galley slaves, Don Quijote rejects Sancho's advice not to undertake the adventure, rather than his interpretation of physical reality.

---

pp. 297–98. See also the list of Luis Morales Oliver, *Sinópsis de "Don Quijote,"* p. 21. Most recently, Colbert I. Nepaulsingh has provided a list of fourteen adventures, "acts that pertain to arms," that is more complete than any of those previously mentioned; "Cervantes, *Don Quijote*: The Unity of the Action," p. 241. My own list is somewhat more inclusive than any of these but does not include Don Quijote's nonchivalric brawls with Cardenio (I, 24) and Eugenio (I, 52) or the gratuitous blow on the head that he receives from the *cuadrillero* (I, 17), all cited by Allen or de Chasca, or the free-for-all at the inn (I, 45). My division of these engagements into "victories" and "defeats" is also occasionally at variance with the opinions of these critics.

21. Juan Bautista Avalle-Arce and Edward C. Riley suggest a progression—with several significant exceptions—in which reality is fully revealed from the start in chapters 1–17 and then presented more from Don Quijote's perspective in chapters 18–52; "*Don Quijote,*" pp. 65–67.

5. Don Quijote either invokes or commends himself to Dulcinea. In the case of Andrés, the invocation follows the actual adventure, while in those of the merchants, Maritornes, the fulling mills, and the Princess Micomicona, Dulcinea is not invoked but is discussed by Don Quijote and other participants.

6. Don Quijote undertakes the adventure. Don Quijote is prepared (and actually begins) to undertake the adventure of the fulling mills and only sets out to undertake the Princess Micomicona adventure, which is never completed.

7. During (or immediately before or after) the adventure, Don Quijote uses archaism.

8. During (or immediately before or after) the adventure, Don Quijote uses at least one of his nonarchaic chivalric motifs.

9. The outcome, when it is not a victory (shown as V in Table 3.2), is unfortunate for Don Quijote. In the adventure of the fulling mills, Don Quijote is not harmed physically, but he is thoroughly humiliated. In the case of the galley slaves, Don Quijote wins a clear victory over the guards; the unfortunate outcome—the stoning he receives—technically occurs after the adventure.

10. Don Quijote, when not victorious, blames his defeat on enchantment. At times, he uses a different excuse, as in the adventures of the merchants, the Yanguesans, and the galley slaves. In the adventure of the wineskins, the excuse of enchantment is suggested by Dorotea and accepted later by Don Quijote, who at first believes that he has won a victory.

Don Quijote has surprisingly few actual adventures. Many of the most memorable moments in the novel fall far short of this status: the arrival at the inn, the penance in Sierra Morena, the dispute over the basin-helmet, and so on. In the first ten chapters, Don Quijote has six adventures, four of which are victories. In the brilliant section of the novel that consists of chapters 15–22, there are seven more adventures, of which only three are concluded victoriously by Don Quijote. In the final thirty chapters, there are only three more episodes that can be considered as adventures. In this section, Don Quijote scores no victories (the apparent victory in the wineskins adventure turns into another case of enchantment), and there is one adventure, that of

Table 3.2.   The Pattern of Adventure⋆

Chapter	Adventure	Reality Stated	DQ Transforms Reality	SP Points out Reality	DQ Rejects SP	DQ Invokes Dulcinea	DQ Undertakes Adventure	Archaism	Chivalric Motif	Unfortunate Results	DQ Blames Enchanters
3	Muleteers	x	x		x	x	x	x	x		V
4	Andrés	(x)	(x)	(x)	(x)	(x)	x	x	x		(V)
4	Merchants	x	x			(x)	x	x	x	x	(x)
8	Windmills	x	x	x	x	x	x	x	x	x	x
8	Friars	x	x	x	x		x	x	x		V
8–9	Biscayan	x	x			x	x	x	x		V
15	Yanguesans	x		(x)	(x)		x		x	x	(x)
16	Maritornes	x	x			(x)	x	x	x	x	x
18	Sheep	(x)	x	x	x		x	x	x	x	x
19	Dead body	(x)	x	(x)			x	x	x		V
20	Fulling mills				(x)	(x)	x	x	(x)		
21	Basin	x	x	x	x		x	x	x		V
22	Galley slaves	x	(x)	(x)	(x)		x	(x)	x	(x)	V
29–31	Micomicona	x				(x)	(x)	x	x		
35	Wineskins	(x)	(x)	(x)			x		x		(x)
52	Penitents	x	x	x	x		x	x	x	x	

⋆Legend: x—conforms to criterion; (x)—partially conforms to criterion; V—victory for Don Quijote; (V)—partial victory for Don Quijote.

the Princess Micomicona, that is staged by others and is drawn out over several chapters and never really concluded.

The pattern suggested by these adventures corresponds to the cumulative evidence of Figures 1.1–1.9 and to the discussion of Don Quijote's chivalric career in preceding chapters. Once again, the inevitable conclusion is that there is a noticeable evolution away from the original concept of chivalry as the novel progresses. At the end of the final adventure, when Don Quijote is defeated and, for the first and only time, offers no excuse, his chivalric career is terminated.

Referring again to Table 3.2, we can see that the adventure of the windmills is the only one that meets all ten of the criteria. In its own way, it thus represents the quintessence of quixotism, but it is not an accurate reflection of Don Quijote throughout part I and even less of Don Quijote throughout the two parts of the novel as a whole. Yet this episode has come to symbolize Cervantes's novel, even in the eyes of those who have never read the work. The image of Don Quijote "tilting at windmills" is part of Western cultural heritage.

How does one explain why the windmill adventure, which takes but a single page out of over a thousand to describe, and which takes place in chapter 8 out of a total of 126, with about 95 percent of the work yet to follow, should be chosen to epitomize the novel? Other episodes (for instance, the penance in Sierra Morena, the enchantment of Dulcinea, the cave of Montesinos) may be more important in the course of the story. Don Quijote evolves with the course of events and eventually becomes a very different person from what he is when he attacks the windmills. Why then is quixotism defined as tilting at windmills?[22]

The answer, I believe, has two parts. First, there is the truly singular nature of the episode. It is the only adventure Don Quijote ever has in which no other human being is involved; the encounter is strictly between man and machine.[23] This singularity is compounded by the size differential: Don Quijote never before or after contends with anything as large as the windmills.[24] The visual potential of a small, impotent, and imperti-

22. It is true, but insufficient, to say, as Martín de Riquer does (*Don Quijote*, p. 88, note), that this episode is an accurate parody of the knight-versus-giant motif so common in romances of chivalry. It is only necessary to observe Alonso Fernández de Avellaneda's more "realistic" giant adventure in his *Don Quijote* (chapters 12 and 34) in order to realize that the mere evocation, no matter how cleverly done, of chivalric giants is not in itself enough to elevate an adventure to the classic status enjoyed by that of the windmills.

23. See the provocative article by Robert Plank, "Quixote's Mills," in which it is suggested (pp. 69–70) that this adventure represents one of the first and greatest classic science-fiction encounters between man and new technology (windmills being a comparatively recent addition to the scene in La Mancha in the late sixteenth century).

24. The corresponding adventure in part II, that of the water mill, is not really parallel. Don Quijote never actually attacks or even comes into contact with the water mill; he is rescued from the river by some millers. See the brief discussion by Juan Bautista Avalle-Arce, *Don Quijote como forma de vida*, p. 202, and the extended comparison by Carlota B. Cannon, "Transformación y cambio de Don Quijote," pp. 193–202.

nent man doing battle with a huge, impersonal, and invincible machine is immense, as any survey of graphic interpretations of *Don Quijote* readily demonstrates.

A second factor seems to be precisely that this adventure takes place very early in the novel. It is nearly axiomatic that readers seize on their early impression of a literary character and maintain that impression throughout the work, even though the character may evolve away from what he or she was when that original impression was made. Elsewhere I have discussed briefly how this process, which we might call the windmill principle, works in the cases of *Lazarillo de Tormes* and *Don Quijote*[25] and have studied the matter in more detail with respect to the former.[26] To no small extent, this book is an attempt to resolve the question in Cervantes's novel.

My thesis is that Alonso Quijano recognizes the futility and mediocrity of his life and takes the radical step of attempting to bring meaning to his existence, or at least to escape the reality of a man who has nearly reached the critical age of fifty without having ever really done anything of worth, by attempting to live life according to a set of ideal standards, those of knight-errantry. As Don Quijote, he sets out with the highest possible enthusiasm, speaking and acting his part enthusiastically, directing his own life and that of others. But, slowly, he begins to make concessions to physical and psychological reality, being distracted from his original proposal by Sancho Panza, lying, acting inauthentically, and losing his original spirit. In the latter half of part I, the priest, the barber, Dorotea, and her friends usurp Don Quijote's rhetoric and his powers, reducing him to the status of a mere pawn or, worse yet, a slapstick buffoon. After his dehumanizing experience with Eugenio and his painful defeat in the encounter with the penitents, for which he offers no excuse, he surrenders to the superior forces of conformity and withdraws in shame from his world of chivalry.

Don Quijote's attention to chivalric ideals undergoes a profound evolution in part I. His career might be summarized thus:

25. Howard Mancing, "A Note on the Formation of Character Image in the Classic Spanish Novel," pp. 528–31.

26. Howard Mancing, "The Deceptiveness of *Lazarillo de Tormes*," pp. 426–32.

the initial enthusiasm (chaps. 1–10), the embarrassing pastoral interlude (chaps. 11–14), a partial but incomplete recovery (chaps. 15–22), the withdrawal to Sierra Morena (chaps. 23–28), the excitement of the Princess Micomicona adventure (chaps. 29–31), the diastrous eclipse at the inn (chaps. 32–46), and the pathetic return home (chaps. 47–52).[27] The trajectory this summary suggests is shown in Figure 3.1a. Or, reduced to the simplest possible terms, Don Quijote's trajectory as a knight-errant in part I is as shown in Figure 3.1b.

3.6 The Critics and Part I

Salvador de Madariaga's *Guía del lector del "Quijote"* (1926), which he rewrote in English with the title *Don Quixote: An Introductory Essay in Psychology* (1961), is a classic of Cervantine criticism.[28] It is in this work that Madariaga develops the idea of

Figure 3.1a.   Don Quijote's Career as a Knight-Errant (Part I)

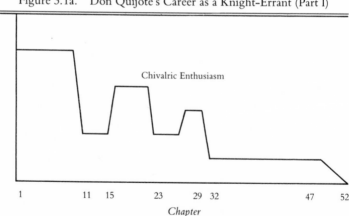

27. Alexander A. Parker divides part I into five subdivisions: chapters 1–5, 6–22, 23–28, 29–46, and 47–52; "Fielding and the Structure of *Don Quixote*," p. 9. Although our purposes are quite different, the similarity between Parker's subdivisions and mine is noteworthy.

28. In the prologue to the recent reedition of Salvador de Madariaga's *Guía del lector del "Quijote"* as number 14 in the popular series "Selecciones Austral," Luis María Ansón correctly calls it (p. 14) "uno de los libros claves [key books] de la literatura cervantina." My references in the text are to the English version published by the Oxford University Press in 1961.

Figure 3.1b. A Simplified Version of Don Quijote's Career as a
Knight-Errant (Part I)

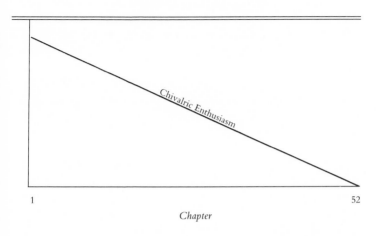

1

Chivalric Enthusiasm

52

Chapter

the "Sanchification" and general decline of Don Quijote and the
"Quixotization" and general rise of Sancho Panza. Rejecting
the "false and superficial antithesis" in which Don Quijote
represents "valour–faith–idealism–utopia–liberalism–progress"
and Sancho "cowardice–skepticism–realism–practical-sense–reaction" (pp. 107–8), Madariaga suggests that from the very beginning Don Quijote is plagued by doubt, "this inner enemy"
(p. 114), and makes tacit concessions to reality, but that only in
part II, with the "enchantment" of Dulcinea (II, 10), does Don
Quijote begin to lose his characteristic vitality. This adventure
"initiates a new phase" in the work, which Madariaga describes
thus:

> With Don Quixote depressed and humiliated, and Sancho
> strengthened and (in his own eyes) exalted, the relationship
> between the two has changed. It is no longer as before that of
> the knight above over the squire below, but that of the influ-
> ence now of Don Quixote on Sancho, now of Sancho on Don
> Quixote. In this phase the curves of the spiritual evolution of
> master and man are intertwined. But the general tendency is
> for Sancho to rise and Don Quixote to fall. (p. 166)

Although there are certain conceptual inconsistencies in Ma-

dariaga's presentation of his thesis,[29] the trajectories he suggests
for knight and squire are essentially as illustrated in Figure 3.2.

Madariaga's most important contribution to *Quijote* criticism
is his presentation of Don Quijote's decline in part II from the
psychology that characterized him in part I. Directly under Ma-

Figure 3.2.   Madariaga's Outline of the Spiritual Evolution of
Don Quijote and Sancho Panza

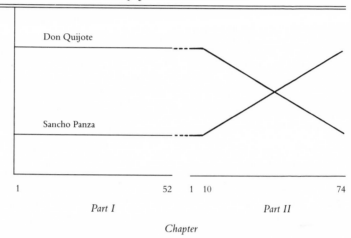

29. Though he states that the scene with Dulcinea begins a new phase
in the novel that suggests the beginning of the respective rise and fall
of the trajectories of Sancho and Don Quijote, Madariaga (*Don Quixote: Psychology*, p. 145) also states that the same scene represents the
point where "the two curves cross," implying that their ascending and
descending paths began somewhat earlier. Similarly, Madariaga states
that Don Quijote's melancholy spirit during his enchantment at the end
of part I "already forbodes" (p. 147) his decline in part II. And, for
some reason, Madariaga calls the last third of the first part of the novel
and the first third of the second part "the height of his splendour [in
which] Don Quixote lives on his own faith" (p. 117). Though he seems
to equivocate somewhat with these suggestions of an earlier beginning
to Don Quijote's descent, I think that ultimately, as suggested in the
text, Madariaga prefers to see the scene in II, 10, as the moment when
Don Quijote begins to decline: "The adventure . . . through which the
spirit of Don Quixote . . . enters finally on its decline" (p. 150).

dariaga's influence are scores of modern readers who assert as commonly accepted truths that Don Quijote and Sancho Panza remain unchanged throughout the first part of the novel[30] or that the enchantment of Dulcinea in II, 10, marks the beginning of a new phase in the work.[31]

For Juan Bautista Avalle-Arce, Don Quijote's decline in part II only begins after the knight-errant reaches a height in the adventure of the lions (chapter 17). In contrast with the protagonist of the first part, who "estaba en lo que se podría llamar el ciclo asencional de su vida" ("was in what might be called the ascending cycle of his life"), the Don Quijote of part II:

> está dilatada al máximo y ocupa, en forma física o espiritual, todos los episodios del libro. Ya hemos visto cómo en la primera parte don Quijote está ausente de todos los capítulos centrales en que se narran las dos historias intercaladas. En la segunda parte don Quijote llega a su plenitud vital, simbolizada, si se quiere, en el hecho de llamarse a sí mismo el Caballero de los Leones. Pero alcanzado el punto de plenitud toda vida se viene abajo con mayor o menor velocidad, y este

30. See, for example, Franklin O. Brantley ("Sancho's Ascent to the Spheres," p. 37), "Don Quijote and Sancho evince no change of character in Part One of the Cervantes masterpiece"; Church (*The Knight of La Mancha*, p. 68), "The Don Quixote who returns to his village is essentially the same Don Quixote who left—only a little more distracted, a little more weary"; and Ruth S. El Saffar (*Novel to Romance: A Study of Cervantes's "Novelas ejemplares,"* p. 24), "There is no indication at the end of Part I that a development has taken place."

31. See, for example, Luis Rosales (*Cervantes y la libertad*, 2: 128–29), "En efecto, en la aventura del *engaño buscado* [i.e., II, 10] cambia el tono de la novela" ("Indeed, in the adventure of the *sought-after trick*, the tone of the novel changes"); Riquer (*Don Quijote*, p. 642, note), "Este episodio señala decididamente una nueva fase de la locura de don Quijote, insinuada en algunos episodios de la primera parte" ("This episode decidedly indicates a new phase in Don Quixote's madness, suggested in some episodes of the first part"); and Guillermo Díaz-Plaja (*En torno a Cervantes*, p. 129), "La técnica del relato cervantino va a cambiar. A partir de este momento, Don Quijote deberá ser sorprendido por una situación previamente establecida, . . . Es decir, en torno al caballero van a organizarse, a partir de este capítulo, una serie de montajes escénicos" ("The technique of Cervantine narration is going to change. From this moment on, Don Quixote is to be surprised by a situation previously established . . . That is to say, there will be organized around the knight, from this chapter on, a series of scenic montages").

descenso remata con la muerte. Ni más ni menos ocurre en el *Quijote* de 1615: al momento de plenitud vital le sigue un lento descenso, marcado por lastimosos hitos.[32]

(is expanded to the maximum and occupies, in a physical or spiritual form, all the episodes of the book. We have already seen how in the first part Don Quijote is absent from all the central chapters in which the intercalated stories are related. In the second part Don Quijote achieves his vital fullness, symbolized, if you will, by the act of calling himself the Knight of the Lions. However, having reached the point of fullness, every life falls with greater or lesser velocity, and this descent ends in death. Neither more nor less takes place in the *Quijote* of 1615; a slow descent, characterized by painful landmarks, follows the moment of vital fullness.)

John J. Allen has presented the most coherent and convincing case for a Don Quijote who is essentially comic and ridiculous, consistently exposed by the narrator, other characters, and himself as a "vain and meddling man with whom one does not identify strongly" in part I, but who (presumably having undergone a significant change in the one-month interval between the two parts) becomes increasingly sympathetic as "an intelligent, well-intentioned, self-doubting man, the victim of his fellow man as well as of his own presumption," in part II.[33] Thus, Cervantes directs the reader to turn "from a systematically and painstakingly established attitude of derision, delighting in one deflation after another, to increased respect, sympathy, even admiration, in the progress of Part II."[34]

Before commenting further on this type of reading of the novel, I must refer to two other basic, and diametrically opposed, views of the book and its protagonist. Oscar Mandel has made a valuable contribution to Cervantine studies in dividing the critics of *Don Quijote* into two categories that he calls "soft" and "hard." "Soft" critics regard Don Quijote as "the hero as well as the protagonist of the novel, and the world of windmills and Yanguesans as the 'villain' or, at any rate, the butt of Cer-

32. Avalle-Arce, *Forma de vida*, p. 55.
33. Allen, *Hero or Fool*, 1:41, 45.
34. Ibid., 1:83.

vantes' real satire," while for "hard" critics, he "remains . . . , in spite of his nobility, the butt of the satire."[35]

The classic soft critic is Miguel de Unamuno, who calls his hero "Our Lord Don Quijote" and passionately defends the inspirational qualities of the character.[36] The view of W. H. Auden, for whom Don Quijote is an ironic Christ, is comparable.[37] Gerald Brenan identifies Don Quijote with Cervantes and sees the book as "twice over a tragedy" that depicts "the defeat of the man of noble feelings by the second-rate and vulgar" and simultaneously convinces us that "that defeat was right."[38]

While elements of the soft approach to the novel are seen in the great majority of contemporary critics and are dominant in the popular conception of Don Quijote, there is probably no important, serious, contemporary critic of the work who takes a consistently soft approach. Furthermore, the very softest critics have tended to be nonspecialists and often approach Cervantes from a modern perspective.[39] Their readings of *Don Quijote* are the easiest to dismiss. In almost every case, the Don Quijote they describe and defend is their own creation rather than the character found in the pages of Cervantes's novel. Unamuno specifically says that he rejects Cervantes's version of the Don Quijote story in favor of his own. This tendency in Cervantine criticism, which dates from the creation of the mythic Don Quijote by German and other romantic writers of around 1800,[40] can be insightful, fascinating, inspirational, and provocative; Unamuno's *Life of Don Quixote and Sancho* is a brilliant and beautiful work. But, at the same time, it is not real literary criticism; Unamuno's book ultimately tells us more about Unamuno than it does about *Don Quijote*.

Hard critics, on the other hand, tend to stress the seventeenth-

35. Mandel, "Function of the Norm," pp. 154–55.

36. Unamuno, *Our Lord*, p. 9.

37. W. H. Auden, "The Ironic Hero: Some Reflections on Don Quixote," pp. 73–81.

38. Gerald Brenan, *The Literature of the Spanish People*, p. 194.

39. J. M. Sobré, "Don Quijote, the Hero Upside-Down," p. 140, note 23.

40. See Anthony Close's excellent history of this trend in *The Romantic Approach to "Don Quixote."*

century reaction to the novel and Cervantes's repeated statements that he was writing to satirize the romances of chivalry. One of the best and most convincing critics of this type is P. E. Russell, who insists that there are "no grounds for suggesting that Cervantes himself thought of his book . . . as anything other than a funny book."[41] Anthony Close takes essentially the same approach.[42]

The dean of the hard faction that sees *Don Quijote* as strictly comic is Erich Auerbach, who, in his classic book *Mimesis*, concludes that "the whole book is a comedy in which well-founded reality holds madness up to ridicule."[43] Martín de Riquer, the most distinguished editor of the novel so far in the twentieth century, holds that Don Quijote is "rematadamente loco, desde el primer capítulo de la primera parte . . . hasta el último de la segunda" ("hopelessly mad, from the first chapter of the first part . . . to the last chapter of the second part") and that both parts "están escritas en actitud irónica y sin que el humorismo decaiga" ("are written in an ironic attitude without a loss of humor").[44] Daniel Eisenberg, since Clemencín unquestionably the most diligent and best-informed student of the romances of chivalry, suggests that "Cervantes' primary purpose in writing both parts of the *Quijote* is nothing more nor less than parody of the romances of chivalry" and that to share the hard reading of the novel, as he does, "implies accepting the book as a work of humor—no more, no less—written without further pretensions."[45]

Mandel does not introduce his hard–soft dichotomy without taking sides. He staunchly defends the hard position from the point of view that Don Quijote is at odds with the acceptable societal norm represented by the priest, the barber, and others: "In sum, Cervantes, writing as a champion of average reality, means us to respond to Don Quixote with *affectionate reprobation*,

41. P. E. Russell, "*Don Quixote* as a Funny Book," p. 324.
42. See Close's *Romantic Approach* and "Don Quixote as a Burlesque Hero: A Re-constructed Eighteenth-Century View," pp. 365–78.
43. Erich Auerbach, *Mimesis*, p. 305.
44. Riquer, *Don Quijote*, pp. xlii, lxxxi.
45. Daniel Eisenberg, "Cervantes' *Don Quijote* Once Again: An Answer to J. J. Allen," pp. 109, 110.

and he accomplishes this chiefly through the techniques of literal statement, an authorized norm, and conflict with an innocent norm."[46]

If the soft critics are easily criticized, the same is not true of the hard critics. The names cited in the preceding paragraphs are those of serious and well-trained literary scholars who represent a major critical attitude. And they are largely correct. There is no question that *Don Quijote* is an immensely funny book and that the protagonist is the appropriate object of much humor. Nor can one have any quarrel with those who want to determine what the work meant to its contemporary readers. This task is valid and valuable, but ultimately insufficient. As stated in section 1.2, the first step that must be taken in an attempt to comprehend a literary work from a past age is precisely that of trying to view it again, as clearly as possible, through the eyes of its contemporaries. But to stop at that point is, it seems to me, to deny the reality of our own times.[47]

Over three and a half centuries have passed since the publication of *Don Quijote*. To fail to see the universality of the novel in the light of the seventeenth-century scientific revolution, the Enlightenment of the eighteenth century, the positivism of the nineteenth century, or twentieth-century existentialism is to choose to blind ourselves; to fail to apply to the study of the works of Cervantes the techniques provided by modern psychology, linguistics, history, or science is absurd. For these reasons, I believe that the studies carried out by Madariaga, Avalle-Arce, Allen, and others who trace the evolution of character, style, theme, and narrative technique are those that contribute most to our reading of *Don Quijote*. For these reasons, I have consciously attempted to incorporate my own work into this tradition.

Not content, however, to leave anyone without some criticism, I must state that even the very best and most helpful readers of the novel have been partially blinded by the brilliance of

46. Mandel, "Function of the Norm," p. 163.
47. Robert Weimann has written perceptively on the need to confront and harmonize what he calls "the unresolved tension between past genesis and present meaning"; "Past Significance and Present Meaning in Literary History," p. 43.

the first half of part I and have failed to see how different the book becomes as it advances. Even the most perceptive modern readers and critics of *Don Quijote* have fallen victim to the windmill principle. One of the main purposes of my study has been to show that Don Quijote's consistent retreat from his original dedication to a world of chivalry is one of the most important and least acknowledged aspects of the first part of the novel. In general, part I has tended to be underestimated in comparison with part II.

Part II

Segunda Parte del Ingenioso Caballero don Quijote de la Mancha

Andaba ya en libros la historia
de vuestra merced (II, 3, 595)

(Your worship's history is
already in books, p. 437)

4

Knighthood Imposed

Y por ventura, . . . ¿promete el
autor segunda parte? (II, 4, 607)

(Does the author promise a
second part at all?, p. 445)

4.1 The Rhetoric of Pseudochivalry

In the prologue to the second part of his novel, Cervantes states that, in opposition to what is true of the inferior and apocryphal version published the year before, his continuation of the novel is (p. 577) "cortada del mismo artífice y del mesmo paño que la primera" ("Cut by the same craftsman and from the same cloth as the first," p. 417). As is often the case with Cervantes, this statement is true and false at the same time. The artisan ("artífice")—Cervantes—is literally the same person who presented part I, and he draws again on the material provided by Cide Hamete Benengeli, but both "author" and "editor" employ new procedures in part II (see section 5.4). The cloth ("paño") is also both the same and different. The Don Quijote and Sancho Panza whose lives are narrated in part II are the same ones who experienced the events in part I, but these characters too are quite different in personality from what they were previously; the Don Quijote and Sancho Panza of part II are not the same as they were in part I precisely because the decisive events of the first half of the novel have changed their lives.

I have not found it necessary to subdivide part II with the same exactness as was necessary with part I. In fact, the seventy-four chapters of the second part can all be summarized in only five sections:

1. Chapters 1–7: The third sally
2. Chapters 8–29: Pseudoadventures
3. Chapters 30–57: With the duke and duchess
4. Chapters 58–73: To Barcelona and back
5. Chapter 74: The death of Alonso Quijano el Bueno

The distribution of speeches among the various characters in part II, as shown in Table 4.1, is quite interesting. As we saw in part I, these figures do indeed reflect the relative importance of the characters in the novel. Don Quijote becomes almost a marginal figure during the stay at the palace of the duke and duchess. Overall, and most especially in chapters 30–57, Sancho Panza is at least as important as his master, if he does not in fact replace him as the most important character in the second part. Unlike part I, where Don Quijote and Sancho sometimes completely dominate the action, other characters are an ever-present and major factor in part II.

The distribution of Don Quijote's archaic speeches was a key to interpreting his character in part I. Figure 4.1 illustrates how radically and dramatically different the stylistic texture of part II really is. In part I, Don Quijote's speech is archaic fifty-four times, an average of 1.3 archaisms per chapter throughout that part of the novel. In part II, this is reduced to six times, an average of 0.1 per chapter. Archaism does not completely dis-

Table 4.1.   Distribution of Speeches (Part II)

Section	Don Quijote		Sancho		Others		Total
	No.	(%)	No.	(%)	No.	(%)	
1. Chaps. 1–7	63	(31)	61	(30)	82	(40)	206
2. Chaps. 8–29	220	(38)	176	(31)	177	(31)	573
3. Chaps. 30–57	96	(15)	215	(34)	330	(52)	641
4. Chaps. 58–73	122	(32)	98	(25)	164	(43)	384
5. Chap. 74	7	(58)	1	(8)	4	(33)	12
Total	508	(28)	551	(30)	757	(42)	1,816

Figure 4.1. Don Quijote's Archaic Speeches (Part II)

No. 2													
			X			XX		X	X X				

1	5	10	15	20	25	30	35	60	65	70

Chapter

appear from Don Quijote's speech, but it is so reduced in frequency as to be virtually meaningless.[1]

I charted the distribution of Don Quijote's use of six other chivalric motifs in section 1.4. As these motifs appear only slightly more than half as often in part II, it does not seem nec-

1. The decrease in Don Quijote's use of chivalric archaism in the second part of the novel has occasionally been commented on very briefly. John J. Allen (*Don Quixote: Hero or Fool?*, 1:57) points out that Don Quijote's decreased use of archaism in part II makes him appear less comic. Martín de Riquer ("Cervantes and the Romances of Chivalry," p. 913) states that in part II "it is no longer Cervantes who parodies the books of chivalry but the persons of his novel. Doubtless it is for this reason that the archaisms in Don Quixote's Castilian decrease considerably." Daniel Eisenberg ("Cervantes' *Don Quixote* Once Again: An Answer to J. J. Allen," p. 104, note 4) cites Riquer in order to criticize Allen and concludes that "the decrease in archaisms is explained by the diminished rôle of the narrator in relation to that of the characters." Riquer does not exactly say that the narrator is less important than the other characters or than he was in the first part; in fact, the narrative structure of the novel, especially the dialectic between Cervantes and Cide Hamete, is more important in part II than it was in part I (see section 5.4). At any rate, there is no reason to equate the relative importance of the narrator with this particular aspect of Don Quijote's style of speaking. It is both simpler and far more consistent with the character's presentation to relate the decrease in archaism in Don Quijote's speech to an evolution in his personality. Angel Rosenblat (*La lengua del "Quijote,"* p. 32) does precisely that when he observes briefly that in part II the archaic style appears very infrequently and then concludes that "Don Quijote se ha ido transformando" ("Don Quixote has been undergoing change").

essary to chart a separate graph for each one in Figure 4.2.[2] The number of times that Don Quijote uses these motifs (see Appendix B) is as follows: fame, six; chivalric mission, eleven; strength, six; order of chivalry, seventeen; chivalric onomastics, twenty-seven; and Dulcinea, twenty-seven. The heights reached in chapters 1, 23, and 26 are all due to the repetition of chivalric names when Don Quijote, pressured by the priest and the barber, talks about fictional knights-errant, when he describes his dream in the cave of Montesinos, and when he discusses the characters in the chivalric puppet show. The importance of Dulcinea throughout is due to her enchantment by Sancho in chapter 10; the repeated references to this incident are usually brought on by inquiries by other characters. In general, Don Quijote uses his chivalric motifs in response to others (for example, to Sansón Carrasco in chapter 14, to the duke and duchess in chapter 32) rather than on his own, as he does in the first part. The only notable progression in the frequency of use of these motifs (and archaism) is the decline from little to considerably less after chapter 32, when the powerful duke and duchess take complete control of events and relegate Don Quijote to secondary status.

Figure 4.2.   Don Quijote's Use of Chivalric Motifs (Part II)

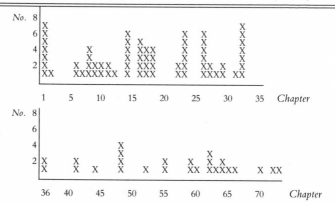

2. In Chapter 1, note 42, I cited José Antonio Maravall on the frequency with which Don Quijote appeals to the rules and regulations of the order of chivalry. Maravall adds, however, that as the book progresses Don Quijote makes increasingly fewer references to the rules of his profession; *Utopía y contrautopía en el "Quijote,"* p. 84.

The decline of Don Quijote's rhetoric of chivalry in part I was used to trace his spiritual decline in that part of the novel. Figures 4.1 and 4.2 suggest that there is virtually no framework for comparable psychological evolution in the second part. If speaking like a knight-errant is an external sign of believing oneself to be a knight-errant, or, at least, of consciously acting like one, then Don Quijote has no claim to chivalric status in part II. Don Quijote does not really decline as a knight-errant in part II; he hardly exists as a knight-errant at all.

4.2 Chapters 1–7: The Third Sally

As part I progressed, Don Quijote's chivalric gusto declined; when the knight met his definitive defeat in chapter 52, he returned home beaten and exhausted, his career as a knight-errant terminated. For about a month, he made no overt or covert preparations for a third sally, in contrast to his actions after the first sally when he seemed satisfied to remain at home but all the while was contacting Sancho Panza, preparing his armor, and arranging other details in order to set out again. He was now too different a man to rekindle his chivalric fantasy through the reading of romances of chivalry, even if he still had any of those books. The thoughts that went through his head during this period can in no conceivable manner be compared with the visions of fantasy that must have sustained Alonso Quijano in the weeks preceding his incarnation as Don Quijote. Several factors, however, combine to induce Don Quijote to make a third sally.

The first of these factors is the intervention, as usual, of the priest and the barber. Those who enjoy speculating on the chapters that Cervantes never wrote can imagine the activities of these two friends during the weeks after their return with Don Quijote. Telling and retelling their own glorious adventures and the comic antics of knight and squire, they undoubtedly spent many happy hours laughing and entertaining the local citizenry. Learning from the housekeeper and niece that the famous *hidalgo* is behaving quite rationally, they decide (II, 1, 579) to "visitarle y hacer experiencia de su mejoría" ("pay him a visit and test the improvement in his condition"), agreeing not to "tocarle en ningún punto de la andante caballería" ("touch on any matter connected with knight-errantry," p. 425). Indeed, they find that their friend speaks (p. 580) "con tanta discreción en todas las materias que se tocaron, que los dos esaminadores creyeron indubitadamente que estaba del todo bueno y en su entero juicio" ("with such good sense that the pair of examiners were fully convinced that he was quite recovered and in his full senses," p. 426). The priest, not willing to leave well enough alone (and miss a few laughs?), changes his mind and decides to test him, as he did earlier on the matter of the galley slaves, by discussing military matters (I, 30, 324)—"por ver lo que hacía o decía don Quijote" ("to see what would be said or done by Don Quixote," p. 228). Thus pressed—and the priest and the barber do not make any attempt to redirect the conversation once matters of war and chivalry are broached—Don Quijote defends, with considerable eloquence and logic,[3] his views on knight-errantry.

Several details of the conversation that takes place among the three men are of interest. For one thing, Don Quijote—perhaps resentfully recalling the barber's intervention during the fight with Eugenio—is consistently ironic or sarcastic in his relationship with the barber. The first time Maese Nicolás suggests indirectly (p. 581) that Don Quijote is about to make some "advertimientos impertinentes" ("impertinent suggestions"), the latter calls him "señor rapador" ("master shaver," p. 426), and surely there is at least a touch of irony intended in Don Quijote's statement (p. 582), "en fee de que sé que es hombre de bien el señor barbero" ("because I know the barber to be an honest fellow," p. 427). After the barber's offensively suggestive story of the madman of Seville, Don Quijote escalates his sarcasm, referring to Maese Nicolás as (p. 585) "señor rapista, señor rapista" ("master shaver, master shaver," p. 430); and (p. 587) "señor Bacía" ("Master Basin," p. 431).[4] Furthermore, although Don Quijote talks at some length about chivalry and knights-errant, he demonstrates a previously uncharacteristic reticence to carry

3. Note that when the barber questions Don Quijote about giants the latter cites the Bible and archaeological evidence in support of their existence. The priest has to concede, saying (p. 589), "Así es" ("That is true," p. 432).
4. Allen has pointed out that Don Quijote's new role as a conscious ironist early in part II is one of the most important differences in the opening pages of the two parts of the novel; *Hero or Fool*, 2:80–85.

the discussion too far (p. 582): "Y Dios me entiende, y no digo más . . . que otra vez digo que Dios me entiende" ("But God knows what I mean, and I say no more. . . . Once more I say, God knows what I mean," p. 427); and (p. 587) "Si puedo sentirme o no . . . yo me lo sé" ("As to whether I ought to be annoyed or not, I myself am the best judge," p. 431).

It is curious that before the subject of knights-errant is actually mentioned, the priest addresses his friend (p. 587) as "señor don Quijote" rather than as "señor don Alonso" or "señor Quijano."[5] Specifically, the priest (p. 589), "gustando de oírle decir tan grandes disparates" ("yielding to the enjoyment of hearing such nonsense," p. 432), continues prompting Don Quijote in his statements about famous fictional knights-errant.[6]

The commotion caused by the arrival of Sancho Panza, who, coincidentally, also chooses this same day to see his former master for the first time since their return, produces (II, 2, 592) more "grande gusto" ("great amusement," p. 434) for the priest and barber, who depart wishing they could hear, and thus enjoy, the conversation between Sancho and Don Quijote. Nothing indicates that Pero Pérez and Maese Nicolás have changed in any way: their concern for Don Quijote's well-being is second to the enjoyment they receive from his chivalric mania.

The nearly simultaneous introduction of Sansón Carrasco and of the printed version of the book entitled *El Ingenioso Hidalgo don Quijote de la Mancha* is a further inducement to Don Quijote to take up arms once again. The reader should immediately be able to judge the character of Sansón Carrasco when he is described as (II, 3, 597) as a "muy gran socarrón; . . . de condición maliciosa y amigo de donaires" ("a great joker . . . [with] a mischievous disposition and a love of fun and jokes," p. 438). The

5. In part II of Alonso Fernández de Avellaneda's *Don Quijote*, the protagonist is consistently called "señor Quijada" by Sancho Panza and other characters in the early part of the novel. Riquer (*Don Quijote*, p. 581, note 6) observes that referring to their friend as "Don Quijote" is not compatible with an authentic desire for his well-being.

6. While discussing this scene, Allen, a staunch supporter of Pero Pérez, concedes that the priest's motivation is "suspect"; Allen's statement (*Hero or Fool*, 2:80) that this is the "only time when [the priest] gratuitously indulges Don Quixote in his chivalric fantasies" is at least a great overstatement.

existence of Cide Hamete's text paradoxically confirms Don Quijote's heroic and chivalric status while it exposes his lack of heroism and chivalry. An omniscient enchanter has, as Don Quijote predicted, written and published, by magical means,[7] the history of his exploits, but because it is an accurate account of what happened to Don Quijote and Sancho Panza, it lacks the essential mythic quality of the romances of chivalry. When Don Quijote asks (II, 4, 607), rather timidly, "Y por ventura, . . . ¿promete el autor segunda parte?" ("Does the author promise a second part at all?," p. 445), he reveals that he has at this point made no plans for a third sally. He is asking, in effect, "What is expected of me?" Sansón tells him that the author is searching for further material to publish. Sancho, rather than Don Quijote, responds, stating:

> que yo y mi señor le daremos tanto ripio a la mano en materia de aventuras y de sucesos diferentes, que pueda componer no sólo segunda parte, sino ciento. . . . Lo que yo sé decir es que si mi señor tomase mi consejo, ya habíamos de estar en esas campañas deshaciendo agravios y enderezando tuertos, como es uso y costumbre de los buenos andantes caballeros. (pp. 607–8)

> (I and my master will give him enough material in the way of adventures and actions of all sorts that he can make up not only one second part, but a hundred. . . . All I say is, that if my master would take my advice, we would be out there now, redressing outrages and righting wrongs, as is the use and custom of good knights-errant.) (p. 445)

At this point Don Quijote hears the whinnies of Rocinante, a

---

7. Since, in the terms of the novel, only a month has passed since Don Quijote returned home, and in that time part I has been written and published in various editions and is being read all over Spain, the only way in which this could have been accomplished is by magic. Allen has observed (*Hero or Fool*, 1:79) that the ultimate irony in the multilevel play with reality in Cervantes's novel is that part I "is the only specific object in the phenomenal world of part II which exists literally, and lies ready at hand for our confirmation of its objective reality, yet it is precisely the presence of this book, *Don Quixote*, Part I, which violates the realistic terms of that world."

good omen, and, thus accosted from all sides, decides to go again in quest of adventures.

Without the intervention of the priest and the barber; Sancho Panza; Sansón Carrasco; *Don Quijote, Part I*; and Rocinante, would Don Quijote have made a third sally? Perhaps; or perhaps not. There is no textual evidence that suggests internal motivation on the part of Don Quijote. It must be considered at least very possible, if not probable, that left to his own devices he would have been content to stay quietly and safely at home, to remain a conventional *hidalgo* named Alonso Quijano who once had a very brief career as a knight-errant. In such a case, part II would never have been written. The accumulation of external pressure, however, is insurmountable. Alonso Quijano cannot ignore the fact that in the eyes of the world he is Don Quijote, comic madman, absurd *desfacedor de agravios*, ridiculous knight-errant. Don Quijote has, ironically, been too successful in his quest for literary fame.[8] If he once tried to make the real world a chivalric one against its will, the situation is now reversed, and the world imposes chivalry on a reluctant Don Quijote.

4.3 Chapters 8–29: Pseudoadventures

Chapters 8–29 of part II of *Don Quijote* correspond to chapters 15–22 of part I: they contain the most interesting adventures and episodes in the second half of the novel, and they most clearly establish the personalities of Don Quijote and Sancho Panza. At the same time, this section is radically different from the corresponding section of the first part where Don Quijote and Sancho absolutely dominated the scene and where the action was fast-paced (see section 2.4). Now the relative importance of Don Quijote, Sancho, and other characters is more nearly equal[9] and

8. Mia I. Gerhardt, *Don Quijote, la vie et les livres*, p. 47: "Dans la IIe Partie, un aspect nouveau et surprenant s'ajoute au personnage de Don Quichotte. C'est que son voeu s'est réalisé: il est devenu, comme il s'y était toujours attendu, un héros de roman" ("In the second part, a new and surprising aspect is added to the character of Don Quijote. His wish is realized: he has become, as he had always hoped, a hero of a novel").

9. The frequency of speech illustrates this fact: Don Quijote speaks 219 times; Sancho, 176 times; all other characters combined, 178 times.

the tempo is far more reposed. There is also a major difference in Don Quijote himself. Whereas in part I he still maintained his chivalric vision to a large degree, speaking fairly frequently in archaism, willfully transforming reality, boasting of his strength and achievements, now he almost never uses archaism (three times in twenty-two chapters), transforms reality exactly once, and restrains his prideful boasting. Don Quijote has become a more profoundly human and sympathetic person but is a poor imitation of his once chivalric self.

The first episode of Don Quijote's third and last sally is the "enchantment" of Dulcinea by Sancho. This is the scene that for Salvador de Madariaga and many others begins a new phase in the novel (see section 3.6). But just how new, really, are the events of this scene? Don Quijote sees only reality, as he did in part I in the adventures of the Yanguesans and the galley slaves; or as chivalric "reality" was presented to him by the Princess Micomicona when she described her plight, and by the priest and the barber when they convinced Don Quijote that he was enchanted; and as he did with many secondary characters (the goatherds, Cardenio, the captive and Zoraida, the canon of Toledo, and so on).[10] Don Quijote has previously seen prosaically real and familiar people presented as chivalric personages, especially when what looked like the priest and the barber were really malicious enchanters. Sancho lies to Don Quijote in order to avoid major problems for himself, as he did when he tied Rocinante's feet, one of the most important of the many details that anticipate some aspects of this episode (see section 5.2), or when he invented the scene of his visit to Dulcinea. Sancho does not actually refer to enchanters or enchantment in Don Quijote's presence before his master does, but, as he had anticipated, merely by insisting that he, master Reality Instructor, sees something other than what Don Quijote perceives, the latter will conclude that enchanters have intervened. Sancho's subtle insinuation of enchantment is therefore little more than a refinement of the excuse of enchantment that Dorotea used so often

10. Erich Auerbach's famous statement that "for once Don Quijote sees nothing except the actual reality" (*Mimesis*, p. 297) is, quite simply, in error.

in the inn or of the enchantment of Don Quijote by the priest and the barber.

The novelty of the scene, then, is strictly one of degree. Nothing—literally nothing—is formally original in the enchantment of Dulcinea. The events of II, 10, which are undoubtedly among the most important in the novel and are presented with unquestionable narrative brilliance, do not begin a new phase of the novel at all.[11]

Don Quijote's attitudes and actions early in this sally are curious and quite interesting. Whereas both of his previous departures were unannounced, occurred at dawn, and had no fixed destination, this time Don Quijote and Sancho inform their households, are accompanied by Sansón Carrasco, depart at nightfall, and head directly for El Toboso (II, 7, 630). Other characters, especially Sansón Carrasco, are involved because Don Quijote is no longer an enthusiastic knight-errant in spite of popular opinion but rather a reluctant one because of it. The early morning departures of part I symbolically present the knight riding optimistically into a new day. The departure at day's end that begins the third sally means that Don Quijote rides into the night, a symbol of his inevitable eclipse and eventual death. Furthermore, it is possible that Don Quijote calculated El Toboso at about a day's ride from his own village and preferred to arrive there at night rather than during the day, for reasons discussed later. Don Quijote's reason for going to El Toboso is rooted in events that took place in part I: Sancho had told him (I, 31, 338), that he should proceed "luego luego en camino del Toboso, si otra cosa de más importancia no le sucediese, porque tenía gran deseo de ver a vuestra merced" ("at once for El Toboso, unless something of greater importance should happen, for she [Dulcinea] had a great desire to see your worship," p. 238). Sancho, in turn, was merely following the instructions of the priest and the barber—the instigators again—who had told him to tell his master that Dulcinea had com-

11. It is precisely here that Salvador de Madariaga is least successful in the presentation of his thesis. While holding that II, 10, begins a new phase in the novel, he must acknowledge that events in the last half of part I already introduce aspects of the techniques used in this chapter. See Chapter 3, note 29.

manded that he (I, 27, 283) "luego al momento se viniese a ver con ella" ("come see her at once," p. 196).[12] They do in fact arrive at El Toboso the next day at twilight and, on Don Quijote's order, wait in a nearby thicket so that they can (II, 8, 637) "entrar en la ciudad entrada la noche" ("enter the city at nightfall," p. 468), an act completely incomprehensible unless interpreted as an accommodation on the part of Don Quijote with the reality of Dulcinea's nonexistence.[13]

Once in the darkened city, the charade of searching for Dulcinea's palace is somewhat reminiscent, especially on Don Quijote's part, of the game that knight and squire played in I, 31 (see section 3.1). Both Don Quijote and Sancho Panza are relieved when the latter finally comes up with a solution: Don Quijote should withdraw and wait outside the city for Sancho to bring news of the lady. Don Quijote says (II, 9, 641–42), "Has dicho, Sancho . . . , mil sentencias encerradas en el círculo de breves palabras: el consejo que ahora me has dado le apetezco y recibo de bonísima gana" ("Sancho, you have delivered a thousand sentences condensed in the compass of a few words. I thank you for the advice you have given me and take it most gladly," p. 471). As he dispatches his squire on this second visit to Dulcinea, Don Quijote prompts him on the sort of response with which he is to return.

> Ten memoria, y no se te pase della cómo te recibe: si muda las colores el tiempo que la estuvieres dando mi embajada; si se desasosiega y turba oyendo mi nombre; si no cabe en la almohada, si acaso la hallas sentada en el estrado rico de su autoridad; y si está en pie, mírala si se pone ahora sobre el uno, ahora sobre el otro pie; si te repite la respuesta que te diere dos o tres veces; si la muda de blanda en áspera, de aceda en amorosa; si levanta la mano al cabello para componerle, aunque no esté desordenado; finalmente, hijo, mira todas sus acciones y movimientos; porque si tú me los relatares como ellos fue-

12. Juan Bautista Avalle-Arce and Edward C. Riley discuss this causal sequence as a key to the Cervantine theme of the interrelations between intentions and consequences in the novel; "*Don Quijote*," p. 63.

13. See Carroll B. Johnson, "A Second Look at Dulcinea's Ass: *Don Quijote*, II. 10," pp. 193–94.

ron, sacaré yo lo que ella tiene escondido en lo secreto de su corazón acerca de lo que al *fecho* de mis amores toca. (II, 10, 643–44)

(Note and let it not escape your memory, how she receives you, if she changes color while you deliver my message, if she is agitated and disturbed at hearing my name, if she cannot rest upon her cushion, should you find her seated in the sumptuous state chamber proper to her rank. Should she be standing, observe if she rests now on one foot and now on the other, if she repeats her reply two or three times, if she passes from gentleness to austerity, from asperity to tenderness, or if she raises her hand to smooth her hair though it be not disarranged.

In short, my son, observe all her actions and motions, for if you report them to me as they were, I will divine what she hides in the recesses of her heart as regards my love.) (p. 472)

What Don Quijote does here is provide Sancho with the script for an improved version of the pseudovisit described in I, 31.[14] Unfortunately for the knight, his messenger fails to take the hints so abundantly provided and invents a daring and original scenario of his own that has far-reaching consequences.

When Sancho returns, Don Quijote is ready to reenact the scene from I, 31, but with the improvements that he assumes his squire has incorporated. Sancho's announcement that Dulcinea herself, accompanied by two maidens, is actually coming to see Don Quijote evokes the knight's very revealing and quite stunned incredulity (p. 647): "¡Santo Dios! ¿Qué es lo que dices, Sancho amigo? . . . Mira no me engañes" ("Holy God! What are you saying, Sancho, my friend? . . . Take care lest you deceive me," p. 474). Don Quijote's hesitation and doubt, his inability to turn any unexpected event into a chivalric episode, and his anticipation of being deceived underscore the inauthenticity of his chivalric career in part II.

By misdirecting his master's attention to the animals ridden by the three girls, Sancho makes Don Quijote doubt the empirical evidence of his own visual perception. His statement— "Pues yo te digo, Sancho amigo . . . que es tan verdad que son

14. Ibid., p. 195.

borricos, o borricas, como yo soy don Quijote y tú Sancho
Panza" ("Well, I can only say, Sancho my friend . . . that it is as
plain they are jackasses—or jennies—as that I am Don Quixote
and you Sancho Panza")—has the potential of destroying Sancho's carefully prepared deceit, but when Don Quijote adds (p.
648) "a lo menos, a mí tales me parecen" ("At any rate they
seem to be so," p. 475), he has already begun to concede; by the
time Sancho finishes addressing the peasant girl "Reina y princesa y duquesa de la hermosura" ("Queen and princess and
duchess of beauty"), Don Quijote is completely at the mercy of
his squire.[15] Don Quijote begins to grow accustomed to this unexpected, but thoroughly acceptable, turn of events, gloating
over his status as a martyr (p. 651): "yo nací para ejemplo de
desdichados" ("I was born to be an example of misfortune," p.
477); and (p. 652) "Ahora torno a decir, y diré mil veces, que
soy el más desdichado de los hombres" ("Once more I will say,
and will say a thousand times, I am the most unfortunate of
men," p. 478). As Don Quijote and Sancho head away from El
Toboso, the former is described (II, 11, 653) as "pensativo
además" ("dejected beyond measure," p. 478), and these thoughts,
as he expresses them to his companion (p. 654)—"yo solo tengo
la culpa" ("I am alone to blame") and "contra mí solo" ("against
me alone," pp. 478, 479)—continue the melancholy tone on
which the previous chapter ended.

The meeting with the company of actors brings Don Quijote
symbolically face to face with Death (p. 655): "La primera figura
que se ofreció a los ojos de don Quijote fue la de la misma
Muerte, con rostro humano" ("The first figure Don Quixote's
eyes lit upon was that of Death itself with a human face," p.
480).[16] But whereas in part I (I, 8, 93) Don Quijote had no need

15. Howard Mancing, "Dulcinea's Ass: A Note on *Don Quijote*, Part
II, Chapter 10," p. 75.
16. There exists, unfortunately, no consistent study of the substruc-
ture of imagery and symbolism that informs *Don Quijote*: the figure of
Death in the actors' cart, the lion (pride), the ass (Saint Francis's
"brother ass," the pleasures of the body, especially in the figure of Sancho Panza), Sansón Carrasco's mirrors (reality) and moons (death), the
sea in Barcelona (death), and many more (see also Chapter 2, note 15).
As first steps toward such a study, see Pierre Ullman's "An Emblematic

to hear factual explanations from his potential adversaries—
"Para conmigo no hay palabras blandas; que ya yo os conozco,
fementida canalla" ("No soft words with me, for I know you,
lying rabble," p. 62)—now he patiently listens to a lengthy description of the facts and is satisfied with reality. Early in part I
(I, 8, 93), his own will was supreme: "lo que yo digo es verdad"
("What I say is the truth," p. 62). Now nothing is certain (p.
656): "y ahora digo que es menester tocar las apariencias con la
mano para dar lugar al desengaño" ("but I declare one must
touch with the hand what appears to the eye, if illusions are to
be avoided," p. 480). After Don Quijote and Rocinante are ridiculed by the jester and take a spill, and Sancho's ass is briefly
stolen, the knight must face the entire group, armed with
stones, and he pauses (p. 658), considering "de qué modo los
acometería con menos peligro de su persona" ("in what way he
could attack them with the least danger to himself," p. 482). A
knight-errant worried about the odds against him? A knight-
errant concerned for his own personal safety? The Don Quijote
of the earlier chapters of part I would never have hesitated, but
the Don Quijote of part II eagerly accepts Sancho's reminder
that these people are not knights and lets his humiliation go
unavenged (p. 659): "dejemos estas fantasmas y volvamos a buscar mejores y más calificadas aventuras" ("let us leave these
phantoms alone and turn to the pursuit of better and worthier
adventures," p. 482).

It is only necessary to juxtapose an early chapter, such as I, 4,
or I, 8, with this one to see that Don Quijote does not begin to
change in part II. The change is of major proportions and has
already taken place, as I have outlined in Chapters 1–3, in part I
of the novel.

The Caballero de los Espejos (that is, Sansón Carrasco) is the
first properly armed and dressed knight-errant whom Don Quijote meets. Throughout the night preceding their battle, Don
Quijote repeatedly demonstrates that strange reluctance observed earlier in his conversation with the priest and the barber.

Interpretation of Sansón Carrasco's Disguises," pp. 223–38; and Francisco Márquez Villanueva's "La locura emblemática en la segunda parte
del *Quijote*," pp. 87–112.

When he hears the other knight boast of a victory over all the knights of La Mancha, Don Quijote says (II, 12, 665), "Eso no" ("Not so"), but, rather than confronting his adversary on this matter, he merely adds, "Pero escuchemos: quizá se declarará más" ("But let us listen, perhaps he will tell us more about himself," p. 487). Later when they discuss the alleged battle (II, 14, 675), Don Quijote "estuvo mil veces por decirle que mentía, y ya tuvo el mentís en el pico de la lengua; pero reportóse lo mejor que pudo" ("was a thousand times on the point of telling him he lied, and had the words already on the tip of his tongue. But he restrained himself as well as he could," p. 494) and simply suggests "sosegadamente" ("quietly") that he disagrees. Don Quijote's victory in tnis case is absolute and authentic (the fact that his opponent was not really ready hardly matters).

According to the narration, Don Quijote's pride is boundless (II, 15, 685): "En estremo contento, ufano y vanglorioso iba don Quijote por haber alcanzado vitoria de tan valiente caballero como él se imaginaba que era el de los Espejos" ("Don Quixote went off satisfied, elated, and vainglorious in the highest degree at having won a victory over such a valiant knight as he imagined the Knight of the Mirrors to be," p. 501); and (II, 16, 687) "Con la alegría, contento y ufanidad que se ha dicho seguía don Quijote su jornada, imaginándose por la pasada vitoria ser el caballero andante más valiente que tenía en aquella edad el mundo" ("Don Quixote pursued his journey with the high spirits, satisfaction, and complacency already described, imagining himself the most valorous knight-errant of the age because of his recent victory," p. 503). But whereas in part I, following his comparable victory over the Biscayan, Don Quijote's pride was evident in his words (I, 10, 106)—"Pero dime por tu vida: ¿has visto más valeroso caballero que yo en todo lo descubierto de la tierra?" ("But tell me on your life, have you seen a more valiant knight than I in all the known world?," p. 70)—now he only talks calmly with his squire about whether or not his defeated opponent was in fact his friend Sansón Carrasco. Very shortly afterward, there is a reference (p. 693) to Don Quijote's "profunda malencolía" ("profound melancholy," p. 508) which rings somewhat truer than the statements about his pride. As we have seen before (section 2.4), what is said about Don Quijote and what he actually does and says are sometimes in conflict.[17] Cide Hamete Benengeli seems to be a better historian than psychologist: his narration of events is generally quite acceptable, but his interpretation of these events or of the characters' motives or psychological states is frequently questionable (see section 5.4).

The most interesting aspect of the relationship between Don Quijote and Don Diego de Miranda is the former's very lucid awareness that his appearance and actions are unusual. Don Quijote notices that his new traveling companion is staring at him and anticipates his feelings, saying (p. 690) "Esta figura que vuesa merced en mí ha visto, por ser tan nueva y tan fuera de las que comúnmente se usan, no me maravillaría yo de que le hubiese maravillado" ("The appearance I present to your worship being so strange and so out of the common, I should not be surprised if it filled you with wonder") and referring (p. 691) to "la amarillez de mi rostro" ("the sallowness of my complexion") and "mi atenuada flaqueza" ("my gaunt leanness," p. 506). Later, after the adventure with the lion, Don Quijote again correctly anticipates his companion's feelings (II, 17, 705): "¿Quién duda, señor don Diego de Miranda, que vuestra merced no me tenga en su opinión por un hombre disparatado y loco? Y no sería mucho que así fuese, porque mis obras no pueden dar testimonio de otra cosa" ("No doubt, Señor Don Diego de Miranda, you look on me as a fool and a madman. It would be no wonder if you did, for my deeds bear witness to nothing else," p. 517). No one in a romance of chivalry would think that a knight-errant looked strange or acted like a madman. The Don Quijote of the early chapters of part I, thoroughly divorced from reality, would never have articulated such apprehensions.

The adventure with the lion is one that has frequently evoked the highest admiration for the protagonist.[18] This truly singular

17. Arturo Serrano-Plaja has also noted that Cide Hamete's statements are not always consistent with Don Quijote's words; *"Magic" Realism in Cervantes: "Don Quixote" as Seen through "Tom Sawyer" and "The Idiot,"* p. 149.
18. Juan Bautista Avalle-Arce calls it Don Quijote's moment of "plenitud vital" ("vital fullness"); *Don Quijote como forma de vida*, p. 55. For Thomas Mann, it is "the climax of Don Quixote's 'exploits' and in all seriousness the climax of the novel"; "Voyage with Don Quixote,"

episode is certainly the occasion on which Don Quijote faces the greatest potential danger.[19] We can assume that Don Quijote undertakes the adventure, at least in some large measure, in order to recover some of the heroic status that he ascribed to himself in his talk with Don Diego shortly before being made to look so ridiculous by the curds oozing from his helmet. The fact that Don Quijote pays in cash for his adventure is a novelty. This behavior and his previously cited remarks to Don Diego about the obvious madness of his deed undercut somewhat the bravery that he displays.[20]

Don Quijote and Sancho spend four restful and placid days at the home of Don Diego de Miranda and, after the wedding of Basilio and Quiteria, three more days visiting with the newlyweds, both strangely unchivalric actions with no parallel in the first part of the novel. At the bountiful and joyous wedding celebration provided by the unfortunate but wealthy Camacho, Don Quijote is essentially a spectator, as he was during the burial of Grisóstomo in part I. Just as Don Quijote acted in Marcela's defense at the end of her dramatic speech in part I, he now steps in to defend the newly wedded couple after the unexpected

---

p. 452. For Theodore Holmes, however, the scene is "simply a circus act without noble intent"; "Don Quixote and Modern Man," p. 53.

19. The lion's actions in remaining in his cage, not unlike those of the caged Don Quijote in I, 47–49, are really quite consistent with the psychology of captive animals, who often prefer the safety of their confinement to the dangers of "freedom."

20. One is tempted to interpret Don Quijote's enigmatic smile and famous line (p. 699) "¿Leoncitos a mí? ¿A mí leoncitos, y a tales horas?" ("Lion whelps against me? Lion whelps against me? And at such a time!," p. 512) as bordering on hysteria. Furthermore, there is a temptation to suggest that Don Quijote's statement (p. 701)—"Retírate, Sancho, y déjame; y si aquí muriere, ya sabes nuestro antiguo concierto: acudirás a Dulcinea, y no te digo más" ("Retire, Sancho, and leave me. If I should die here you know our old agreement. You will hasten to Dulcinea—I say no more," p. 514; the reference is to what Don Quijote told Sancho in I, 20, the last time he mentioned his own possible death)—implies not only a willingness to face potential death but even a suicide wish. I believe, however, that it would be going too far to interpret this episode as a desire on Don Quijote's part to end the chivalric masquerade that he is being forced to maintain by purposefully undertaking an enterprise with potentially fatal results.

denouement of the wedding.[21] His threatening words and gestures inspire fear (II, 21, 741) in "todos los que no le conocían"
("all those who do not know him"), but the "persuasiones" of
the priest who performed the ceremony, "que era varón prudente y bien intencionado" ("a wise and kindly disposed man,"
p. 542) seem to do most to calm Camacho's just ire.

The episode of the cave of Montesinos has probably evoked
more critical commentary than any single event in the novel.
The absurdly comic, realistic, and unchivalric details that characterize Don Quijote's dream-vision reveal the sad truth of his
basically prosaic reality.[22] As Juan Bautista Avalle-Arce says,
"Tiene que ser evidente para todos el hecho de que este hombre
ha reconocido, desde mucho antes de la aventura de la cueva de
Montesinos, que su ideal de vida era total y trágicamente inade-
cuado para vivir en este mundo" ("It has to be evident to everyone that this man has recognized, long before the adventure of
the cave of Montesinos, that his ideal of life was totally and tragically inadequate in order to live in this world").[23] The subsequent echoes of this episode underscore its pathetic tone. By
asking Maese Pedro's divining monkey (II, 25, 776–77) and later
the enchanted head (II, 62, 1061) about what happened to him in
the cave, Don Quijote indicates that he needs help in maintain-
ing a semblance of his chivalric vision. Most revealing of all, of
course, is the sad bargain he attempts to strike with Sancho after
the ride on Clavileño (II, 41, 895): "Sancho, pues vos queréis
que se os crea lo que habéis visto en el cielo, yo quiero que vos
me creáis a mí lo que vi en la cueva de Montesinos. Y no os digo

21. Basilio's feigned suicide for love recalls not only the genuine
death for love, probably a suicide, of Grisóstomo but also the inaction
of Cardenio as he watched the marriage of Luscinda and Fernando.
Basilio's *industria* in interrupting the wedding and winning the hand of
the woman he loves is the obvious antidote to Cardenio's *cobardía*.

22. See Gerald Brenan, *The Literature of the Spanish People*, p. 189.

23. Avalle-Arce, *Forma de vida*, p. 211. It would seem that Avalle-
Arce's assertion (p. 205) that Don Quijote arrives at the cave "con la
voluntad vencida y en bancarrota" ("with his will defeated and bank-
rupt") and his statement cited in the text support my thesis of a Don
Quijote already totally changed more than Avalle-Arce's own previously cited, Madariaga-like position that there is a slow descent following II, 17 (see section 3.6).

más" ("Sancho, as you would have us believe what you saw in heaven, I require you to believe me as to what I saw in the cave of Montesinos. I say no more," p. 653). The glorious deeds of chivalry have become mere bargaining units to be traded for insubstantial and hypocritical reinforcement. One is reminded of the soldier cited in the prologue to *Lazarillo de Tormes* who generously rewards the *truhán* for praising his phony exploits, which evokes the author's cynical comment, "¿qué hiciera si fuera verdad?" ("What would he have done if the praise had been justified?").[24]

When they arrive at an inn, the narration records (II, 24, 768) that Sancho is glad to see that "su señor la juzgó por verdadera venta, y no por castillo, como solía" ("his master took it for a real inn, and not for a castle, as he usually did," p. 562). But it has been about six weeks since Don Quijote last referred to an inn as a castle, and during this third sally, there has not yet been an occasion when he transformed reality in the slightest. The first thing that Don Quijote does at the inn is to locate the man he had met on the road carrying some lances and shields who had promised an interesting story. In order to get more quickly to the tale, Don Quijote offers to help the man care for his mount in the stable, which he does by (II, 25, 769) "ahechándole la cebada y limpiando el pesebre" ("sifting the barley for him and cleaning out the feedbox," p. 563). This generous "humildad" ("humility") on Don Quijote's part—the knight-errant as stable boy—is as out of keeping with the station of a knight-errant as were the services he rendered to the ailing Sancho in the inn of Juan Palomeque (see section 2.4).

Don Quijote's interruption of Maese Pedro's puppet show and his destruction of the puppets seem to represent a return to fantasy on the part of the knight. His excuse after he destroys the spectacle is (II, 26, 785): "Real y verdaderamente os digo, señores que me oís, que a mí me pareció todo lo que aquí ha pasado que pasaba al pie de la letra: que Melisendra era Melisendra, don Gaiferos don Gaiferos, Marsilio Marsilio, y Carlomagno Carlomagno" ("In very truth I assure you gentlemen now listening to me that everything that has taken place here seemed

24. *Lazarillo de Tormes*, p. 89; *Two Spanish Picaresque Novels*, p. 23.

to me to take place literally. Melisendra was Melisendra, Don Gaiferos Don Gaiferos, Marsilio Marsilio, and Charlemagne Charlemagne," p. 575). This version of being swept away by the illusion of adventure, however, is not consistent with the actual sequence of events. Don Quijote knows that he is watching a puppet show: he has interrupted the presentation on two occasions to discuss matters of style and verisimilitude with the puppeteer and his assistant. There is no question that he has been perceiving the scene from an objective and critical point of view. His destructive intervention comes approximately *one-half minute* (the amount of time I estimate that it takes the narrating assistant to pronounce exactly fifty-six words) after the end of his last discussion with Maese Pedro. It is simply not acceptable that the new Don Quijote of the third sally could be deceived by the illusion of reality in such a brief period.[25] Rather, I suggest that Don Quijote, reacting somewhat petulantly to the rebuke that the puppeteer just delivered (p. 782)—"No mire vuesa merced en niñerías, señor don Quijote" ("Don't pay attention to trifles, Señor Don Quixote," p. 572)—and having some general misgivings about Maese Pedro, who is, after all, Ginés de Pasamonte (and Don Quijote must wonder about the identity of this familiar-looking man with the eye patch who lavishes so much—sarcastic?—praise on him), simply decides to get even in a very elemental way permitted only, as he has seen on previous occasions, to him. After all, he can always blame enchanters and then pay for the damage he causes. In fact, Don Quijote says that his intentions were good but

> si me ha salido al revés, no es culpa mía, sino de los malos que me persiguen; y, con todo esto, deste mi yerro, aunque no ha procedido de malicia, quiero yo mismo condenarme en costas:

25. It does not seem reasonable to hold that Don Quijote, who is obviously so familiar with the characters and stories of the Spanish *Romancero* on other occasions, is here alone in his ignorance of the outcome of the legend of Gaiferos and Melisendra and/or that he believes that he is watching living—and therefore alterable—history in the making. For such readings, see George Haley, "The Narrator in *Don Quijote*: Maese Pedro's Puppet Show," pp. 154–55; and Ruth S. El Saffar, *Distance and Control in "Don Quixote." A Study in Narrative Technique*, p. 133.

vea maese Pedro lo que quiere por las figuras deshechas, que
yo me ofrezco a pagárselo luego, en buena y corriente moneda
castellana. (p. 785)

(If the exact opposite has occurred, the fault is not mine, but
that of the wicked beings who persecute me. Nevertheless, I
am willing to shoulder the expenses of this error of mine,
though no ill will lay behind it. Let Master Pedro see what he
wants for the spoiled figures, for I agree to pay it at once in
good Castilian currency.) (p. 575)[26]

Later (p. 787), Don Quijote, "que era liberal en todo estremo"
("for he was the height of generosity," p. 576), pays for dinner,
gives some money to the man who had told about the braying,
and has Sancho pay the innkeeper. This generosity stands in
stark contrast to his pronouncements on the rules of chivalry
when Juan Palomeque requested payment in I, 17:

que yo no puedo contravenir a la orden de los caballeros andantes, de los cuales sé cierto, sin que hasta ahora haya leído
cosa en contrario, que jamás pagaron posada ni otra cosa en
venta donde estuviesen, porque se les debe de fuero y de derecho cualquier buen acogimiento que se les hiciere. (p. 169)

(I cannot contravene the rule of knights-errant, of whom I
know as a fact (and up to the present have read nothing to the
contrary) that they never paid for lodging or anything else in
any inn where they might be. For any hospitality offered them
is their due by law and right.) (p. 115)

In I, 18, after leaving the inn where he refused to pay, the
knight saw two clouds of dust that he assumed were raised by
two armies. As the two herds of sheep grew closer, Don Quijote actually seemed to hear (p. 179) "el relinchar de los caballos,
el tocar de los clarines, el ruido de los atambores" ("the neighing

26. John G. Weiger (*The Individuated Self: Cervantes and the Emergence
of the Individual*, pp. 13–15) has similar misgivings about Don Quijote's
supposed illusion in this episode, suggesting that the knight-errant recognizes the galley slave from part I and wishes to "settle an old score";
his payment for the damage he creates provides proof of his "rational
behavior."

of the steeds, the braying of the trumpets, the roll of the drums,"
p. 121). This time, after leaving the inn where he paid so freely
and after traveling for two uneventful days, Don Quijote hears
(II, 27, 790) a potentially chivalric "gran rumor de atambores,
de trompetas y arcabuces" ("great noise of drums, trumpets, and
musket shots," p. 578). But now, although the circumstances are
more suggestive than on the previous occasion, there is no
imaginative flight of fantasy; Don Quijote's reaction is perfectly
realistic (p. 790): "Al principio pensó que algún tercio de soldados pasaba por aquella parte" ("At first he imagined some regi-
ment of soldiers was passing that way," p. 578).

Rather than choose to support the side that seemed to have
the most right in a real battle, as he did in the adventure of the
sheep-armies in I, 18, and as a knight-errant should have done,[27]
Don Quijote unleashes his rhetoric and delivers an intelligent
speech on the concept of a just war. He might have been able to
talk the antagonists out of their rancor and to forestall the proposed battle had Sancho not intervened with his own display of
braying abilities. When one of the insulted villagers strikes Sancho for his impertinence, Don Quijote is unwilling to face so
many well-armed opponents in order to defend his squire in distress:

> antes, viendo que llovía sobre él un nublado de piedras, y que
> le amenazaban mil encaradas ballestas y no menos cantidad de
> arcabuces, volvió las riendas a Rocinante, y a todo lo que su
> galope pudo, se salió de entre ellos, encomendándose de todo
> corazón a Dios, que de aquel peligro le librase, temiendo a
> cada paso no le entrase alguna bala por las espaldas y le saliese
> al pecho; y a cada punto recogía el aliento, por ver si le faltaba.
> (p. 794)

> (Far from it, finding a shower of stones rained upon him, and
> crossbows and muskets unnumbered leveled at him, he
> turned Rocinante around, and as fast as his gallop could take
> him, he left them behind, commending himself to God with
> all his heart to deliver him out of this peril, in dread every
> step that some bullet would hit his back and come out

27. See Eisenberg, *"Don Quijote* Once Again," p. 107.

through his breast. Every minute he took a deep breath to see
whether he still could.) (p. 581)[28]

Self-preservation is Don Quijote's only concern; breathtak-
ing, palpable fear is what he experiences as he flees. Don Quijote echoes his squire's words (I, 23, 233)—"Señor . . . , que el
retirar no es huir" ("Señor . . . , to retire is not to flee," p. 160)—
as he rationalizes his flight (II, 28, 795): "No huye el que se re-
tira" ("He who retires does not run away," p. 582). Sancho recalls Don Quijote's comparable action in the first part when he
mentions (p. 796) "los manteamientos de marras" ("blanketings
like the other day," p. 583) and decides for the first time on this
sally that it might be time to "volverme a mi casa, y a mi mujer,
y a mis hijos" ("go home to my wife and children").

It is against this background of Sancho's discouragement and
Don Quijote's humiliating display of cowardice that the latter
undertakes his only adventure in part II, that of the enchanted
boat (II, 29, 804–6), that has a structure comparable to that described as typical of part I (see section 3.5).

    1. Reality is stated: "descubrieron unas grandes aceñas que
en la mitad del río estaban" ("They now came in sight of some
large water mills that stood in the middle of the river," p.
588).
    2. Don Quijote transforms reality: "la ciudad, castillo o for-
taleza donde debe de estar algún caballero oprimido, o alguna
reina, infanta o princesa malparada, para cuyo socorro soy
aquí traído" ("the castle or fortress where there is, no doubt,
some oppressed knight or ill-used queen or infanta or princess, in whose aid I am brought here").
    3. Sancho points out reality: "¿Qué diablos de ciudad, for-
taleza o castillo dice vuesa merced, señor? . . . ¿No echa de
ver que aquéllas son aceñas que están en el río, donde se muele
el trigo?" ("What city, fortress, or castle is your worship talking about, señor? . . . Don't you see that those are mills
moored in the river to grind wheat?").
    4. Don Quijote rejects Sancho's interpretation: "Calla, San-
cho . . . ; que aunque parecen aceñas, no lo son" ("Hold your

28. Particularly noteworthy here is the fact that Don Quijote commends himself to God and not to Dulcinea.

peace, Sancho. . . . Though they look like mills, they are not").[29]

5. Don Quijote undertakes the adventure: "echó mano a su espada y comenzó a esgrimirla en el aire" ("he drew his sword and began making passes in the air").

6. Don Quijote cites one of his chivalric motifs: "el valor de mi brazo" ("the might of my arm").

7. The results are unfortunate: "trastornar el barco y dar con don Quijote y con Sancho al través en el agua" ("upsetting the boat and throwing Don Quixote and Sancho into the water," p. 589).

8. Don Quijote blames enchanters: "Y en esta aventura se deben de haber encontrado dos valientes enchantadores, y el uno estorba lo que el otro intenta: el uno me deparó el barco, y el otro dio conmigo al través" ("In this adventure two mighty enchanters must have encountered one another, and one frustrates what the other attempts; one provided the boat for me, and the other overturned me," p. 590).

Missing only are the invocation of Dulcinea and the use of archaism. Again, as is now his nonchivalric custom, Don Quijote willingly pays for the damage he has caused.

In I, 8, after attacking the windmills and first blaming his failure on the intervention of enchanters, Don Quijote's spirit was optimistic (p. 90): "mas al cabo al cabo, han de poder poco sus malas artes contra la bondad de mi espada" ("But in the end his wicked arts will avail but little against my good sword," p. 60). Now he admits his complete helplessness (p. 806): "Dios lo remedie; que todo este mundo es máquinas y trazas, contrarias unas de otras. Yo no puedo más" ("God help us; this world is all machinations and schemes at cross purposes one with the other. I can do no more," p. 590). The highly meaningful "Yo no puedo más," which also evokes the famous line, "Yo valgo por ciento" of I, 15, 148 ("I count for one hundred," p. 100), are virtually the knight's last words in this section, Don Quijote's final statement before the chance meeting with the duke and duchess that so radically changes the course of events. These

29. Don Quijote's statement that they "parecen aceñas" ("look like water mills") indicates that he perceives quite fully the reality of the situation, precisely the opposite of the case of the windmills in I, 8.

words capture, as well as any others, the pathetic essence of Don Quijote in part II.[30]

4.4 Chapters 30–57: With the Duke and Duchess

In part I of *Don Quijote*, the second stay in Juan Palomeque's inn is the low point for the protagonist. Left alone, ignored, laughed at, and finally put on display in an ox cart, Don Quijote is diminished in importance and in stature as a knight-errant. The long stay in the castle of the duke and duchess is a comparable episode in part II. Don Quijote is scratched by cats and pinched by women, constantly laughed at and deceived by his hosts and their household, and left alone to contemplate his material and spiritual poverty as Sancho Panza rides off in glory to be a just and wise ruler of an *ínsula*. The frequency of speech reflects the prominence of the various characters. The ducal pair and other characters who generally control the action speak 330 times in these twenty-eight chapters; Sancho Panza, loquacious as never before, speaks 215 times; Don Quijote speaks only 96 times, using archaism on only three occasions.

The duke and duchess, avid readers of romances of chivalry and of part I of *Don Quijote*, readily greet the famous knight and prepare a proper reception for him at their palace. Whether inspired by readings in the literature of chivalry or by Don Quijote's scenario from I, 21, they prepare a sumptuous greeting for their guest. Two maidens place (II, 31, 813) "un gran manto de finísima escarlata" ("a big cloak of the finest scarlet cloth") on Don Quijote's shoulders, and everyone shouts: "¡Bien sea venido la flor y la nata de los caballeros andantes!" ("Welcome, flower and cream of knight-errantry," p. 595).[31] Don Quijote is

30. Ruth S. El Saffar has written perceptively on Don Quijote's actions in the first half of part II, pointing out how he is "prone to contemplation and melancholy, slow to jump into his knightly image, and sensitive to his bodily hunger and fatigue as never in part I. . . . Don Quixote often looks on in amazement at the world which reflects back on him more than he had intended, and much that he does not recognize as his"; "Cervantes and the Games of Illusion," p. 148. See also El Saffar's discussion on pp. 147–52.

31. In his summary of the life of a typical knight-errant, Don Quijote had said that after gaining fame the knight is received by a king

amazed by this reception, and the comment is added that "aquél fue el primer día que de todo en todo conoció y creyó ser caballero andante verdadero, y no fantástico, viéndose tratar del mesmo modo que él había leído se trataban los tales caballeros en los pasados siglos" ("this was the first time that he thoroughly felt and believed himself to be a knight-errant and not an imaginary one, now that he saw himself treated in the same way as he had read of such knights being treated in days of yore").

If in fact this is the first day in his life in which Don Quijote honestly and truly believes himself to be a genuine knight-errant, and if he has previously been conscious that he was not actually a knight, then the thesis that I have attempted to sustain throughout this work, along with most other readings of the novel, is invalid. The overwhelming impression on the reader, however, is that Don Quijote is most consciously chivalric at the beginning of his career. If one has to choose between the validity of this single statement and the cumulative evidence of the previous eight hundred pages of text, there is no alternative but to opt for the latter. What this statement illustrates, as well as any in the novel, is the unreliability of the narrator, specifically of Cide Hamete Benengeli (see section 5.4). The statement might mean simply that Don Quijote believes that he is being honored as a knight-errant more authentically than ever before, but accepting it as a literal truth can only lead to confusion.[32]

---

who says (I, 21, 214), "¡Ea, sus! ¡Salgan mis caballeros, cuantos en mi corte están, a recebir a la flor de la caballería, que allí viene!" ("What ho! Forth all ye, the knights of my court, to receive the flower of chivalry who cometh hither!," p. 146), and then in the palace, the hero is brought "un rico manto de escarlata, con que se cubra" ("a rich mantle of scarlet wherewith to robe himself," p. 147).

32. Several critics have cited these words as a high point in Don Quijote's chivalric madness, often in conflict with their own previous statements about the protagonist. The most interesting reactions come, as one might expect, from those who see Don Quijote as playing or acting throughout the novel. Serrano-Plaja (*"Magic" Realism*, p. 165) triumphantly stresses the literal truth of these words: "So for once, as if in passing, the historian tells us everything: before now Don Quixote had never believed he was a knight-errant in fact, but only in imagination. But is this very thing not what we clearly and simply call playing? Could it be stated more plainly that, until now at least, Don Quixote has been playing the part of a knight, just as he was playing at being in

What is more, Don Quijote's own words almost immediately after this comment suggest his complete consciousness of his own nonchivalric reality. After Sancho's exchange with Doña Rodríguez, the knight takes his squire aside and counsels him to restrain his tongue (p. 816): "¿No adviertes, angustiado de ti, y malaventurado de mí, que si veen que tú eres un grosero villano, o un mentecato gracioso, pensarán que yo soy algún echacuervos, o algún caballero de mohatra" ("Do you not see—miserable wretch that you are, and unlucky mortal that I am!—that if they perceive you to be a coarse clown or an amusing simpleton, they will think I am some imposter or swindler?," p. 597).[33] This warning and Sancho's response that "nunca por él se descubriría quién ellos eran" ("He would never do anything to embarrass them") are virtual admissions that both are quite aware of reality.

In spite of Sancho's reassurances, when the squire offers to tell a story that will be analogous to Don Quijote's actions, the knight trembles (p. 817), "creyendo sin duda alguna que había de decir alguna necedad" ("convinced that he was about to say

---

love?" Mark Van Doren, the original and still the best proponent of the "Don Quijote actor" reading of the novel, expresses doubt concerning the reliability of the statement; *Don Quixote's Profession*, p. 59. Gonzalo Torrente Ballester provides a careful discussion of the implications involved in either accepting or rejecting Cide Hamete Benengeli's comment; *El "Quijote" como juego*, pp. 206–7.

33. From the beginning of the second part, Don Quijote has been afraid of what Sancho might say. When Sancho burst in upon the conversation that his master was sustaining with the priest and the barber, Don Quijote was (II, 2, 592) "temeroso que Sancho se descosiese y desbuchase algún montón de maliciosas necedades, y tocase en puntos que no le estarían bien a su crédito" ("uneasy that Sancho might blab and blurt out a whole heap of mischievous stupidities and touch on points that might not be altogether to his credit," p. 434). When he first sent his squire to approach the duchess, Don Quijote warned him (II, 30, 808), "Y mira, Sancho, cómo hablas" ("and mind, Sancho, how you speak," p. 591). Then Don Quijote apologized to the duchess, saying (p. 811) that she must believe that "no tuvo caballero andante en el mundo escudero más hablador" ("never had knight-errant in this world a more talkative squire"). When the lady described Sancho as "gracioso y donairoso . . . [y] discreto" ("droll and witty . . . [and] shrewd"), Don Quijote could only add, "Y hablador" ("and talkative," p. 594).

something foolish," p. 598). The story absolutely mortifies Don Quijote and provides laughter for the duke and duchess. The insults of the serious clergyman—to which Don Quijote responds with genuine nobility—and the embarrassment of the lathering of his beard also make the dinner quite uncomfortable and unpleasant for Don Quijote.

The duchess, who seems more astute than her husband and who seems to take the initiative in more matters,[34] particularly enjoys hearing Sancho talk (II, 32, 825), "y en su opinión le tenía por más gracioso y por más loco que a su amo" ("and in her own mind she set him down as funnier and madder than his master," p. 604). So it is Sancho who is prompted as court jester by the duchess and her retinue, Sancho who is assigned the major role in the disenchantment of Dulcinea, Sancho who banters with the Countess Trifaldi and is the center of attention before and after the ride on Clavileño, and, finally, Sancho who leaves in glory to be a governor. Don Quijote goes off to take a nap or stands by comparatively inactive and silent, allowing his squire to occupy center stage.

Sancho may not have been motivated solely by the desire to become wealthy by governing an *ínsula*, and certainly by the end of his first sally with Don Quijote he had begun to enjoy the quest for adventures and fame for its own sake, as his words to his wife in I, 52, reveal. Still, there is no question that Don Quijote's promise to bestow an *ínsula* on his loyal squire has been a constant factor in the novel. Now, however, when the long-awaited governorship arrives, it is not won by the strong right arm of the knight-errant but casually awarded as an impromptu gesture by the idle, wealthy duke (II, 32, 823): "que yo, en nombre del señor don Quijote, os mando el gobierno de una que tengo de nones, de no pequeña calidad" ("for in the name of Señor Don Quixote I confer upon you the government of one of no small importance that I have at my disposal," p. 602). As Sancho is about to depart in order to take possession of his new office, his master takes him aside and lectures him on

34. The duchess speaks fifty-two times in the novel; the duke, thirty-seven times.

the moral and physical attributes of a good governor. The apparent generosity and nobility of this speech are undercut by inconsistency and absurdity,[35] but even the effort is remarkable considering the dejection, envy, and jealousy (not to mention the sarcasm, or at least irony) with which Don Quijote prefaces his advice.

> Infinitas gracias doy al cielo, Sancho amigo, de que antes y primero que yo haya encontrado con alguna buena dicha, te haya salido a ti a recebir y a encontrar la buena ventura. Yo, que en mi buena suerte te tenía librada la paga de tus servicios, me veo en los principios de aventajarme, y tú, antes de tiempo, contra la ley del razonable discurso, te vees premiado de tus deseos. (II, 42, 897)

> (I give infinite thanks to heaven, friend Sancho, that, before I have met with any good luck, fortune has come forward to meet you. I, who counted upon my good fortune to repay you for your services find myself still waiting for the advancement, while you, before the time and contrary to all reasonable expectation, see yourself blessed in the fulfillment of your desires.) (p. 654)

As soon as Sancho departs, Don Quijote experiences remorse and loneliness ("sintió su soledad," II, 44, 909) and would gladly revoke the governorship if possible in order to have his friend with him again. The duchess notices Don Quijote's melancholy and guesses the cause. Don Quijote attempts to hide the truth with an unconvincing lie (p. 909): "Verdad es, señora mía . . . , que siento la ausencia de Sancho; pero no es ésa la causa principal que me hace parecer que estoy triste" ("The truth is, señora . . . , that I do feel the loss of Sancho. But that is not the main cause of my looking sad," p. 664). It is worth noting that the knight offers no alternative explanation for his admitted dejection.[36] When Don Quijote rejects the duchess's offer of four

35. See Arthur Efron, *Don Quixote and the Dulcineated World*, pp. 15–16, 87–90; and Helena Percas de Ponseti, "Los consejos de Don Quixote a Sancho," pp. 194–236.
36. Only Efron seems to accept Don Quijote's statement as the literal truth; *Don Quixote and the Dulcineated World*, pp. 93–94.

maidens to serve him[37] and retires alone to his room, one of the saddest scenes in the novel takes place.

> Cerró tras sí la puerta, y a la luz de dos velas de cera se desnudó, y al descalzarse—¡oh desgracia indigna de tal persona!—se le soltaron, no suspiros, ni otra cosa, que desacreditasen la limpieza de su policía, sino hasta dos docenas de puntos de una media, que quedó hecha celosía. Afligióse en estremo el buen señor, y diera él por tener allí un adarme de seda verde una onza de plata; digo seda verde porque las medias eran verdes. (p. 911)

> (He locked the door behind him, and by the light of two wax candles undressed himself, but as he was taking off his stockings—O disaster unworthy of such a personage!—there came a burst, not of sighs or anything belying his delicacy or good breeding, but of some two dozen stitches in one of his stockings that made it look like a window lattice. The worthy gentleman was distressed beyond measure, and at that moment he would have given an ounce of silver to have had a bit of green silk thread there; I say green silk, because the stockings were green.) (p. 665)[38]

This juxtaposition in chapters 44 and 45 of *Don Quijote*—alone, melancholy, and with holes in his stockings—and of Sancho Panza—received in Barataria (p. 917) "con mucha pompa," given the keys to the city, and proclaimed perpetual governor—can serve as an emblem for all of part II of Cervantes's novel.

In the ten chapters (45–54) in which Don Quijote and Sancho are separated, the knight speaks a total of sixteen times, being

37. This rejection is not in keeping with standard practices of knighthood according to the romances of chivalry; see Diego Clemencín, ed., *Don Quijote*, p. 1767, note 18.

38. Before leaving on the third sally, Sancho had told Don Quijote (II, 2, 594) that, among other things said about him, he had been compared to "aquellos hidalgos escuderiles que dan humo a los zapatos y toman los puntos de las medias negras con seda verde" ("poor hidalgos who polish their own shoes and darn their black stockings with green silk"). Don Quijote's response was: "Eso . . . no tiene que ver conmigo, pues ando siempre bien vestido, y jamás remendado" ("That . . . does not apply to me, for I am always well dressed and never patched," p. 436).

absent or silent in seven chapters. Sancho, in comparison, speaks eighty-two times in six of the chapters. Don Quijote is badly scratched in the face by some cats (chapter 46) when a joke gets out of hand and is forced to spend several days in bed. Later, he cringes in fear (rather than coming to the rescue) as the duchess and Altisidora first beat Doña Rodríguez and then pinch the erstwhile knight-errant (II, 48, 945–46).

Finally reunited, Don Quijote and Sancho depart from the ducal palace and continue toward Zaragoza. Don Quijote's first words put the whole long visit with the duke and duchess into perspective and express one of his noblest thoughts (II, 58, 1015): "La libertad, Sancho, es uno de los más preciosos dones que a los hombres dieron los cielos" ("Freedom, Sancho, is one of the most precious gifts that heaven has bestowed upon men," p. 741).

4.5 Chapters 58–73: To Barcelona and Back

While Don Quijote was with the duke and duchess, he did not initiate anything but rather merely accepted what was arranged for him. He reacted very phlegmatically to the adventure of the Countess Trifaldi. He would have left without taking action in the matter of Doña Rodríguez and her daughter had they not forced his hand by daringly appealing to him in the presence of the duke. He allowed his host to take care of all matters in the challenge concerning the marriage of the genuinely distressed daughter of the *dueña*.

We are told that, on leaving the ducal palace, Don Quijote is ready to return to his chivalric pursuits (II, 58, 1015): "los espíritus se le renovaban para proseguir de nuevo el asumpto de sus caballerías" ("he felt . . . ready to take up the pursuit of chivalry once more with renewed vigor," p. 741). But the fact is that in the remainder of the novel Don Quijote exhibits no more willingness to see the world in terms of chivalric standards than he had while with the duke and duchess. If in I, 52, a statue of the Virgin could be perceived as a maiden in distress, in II, 58, the four chivalric religious figures are mere statues for Don Quijote. Interestingly, the very chivalric Santiago suffers in comparison with the pacific Saint Paul in Don Quijote's disquisition about the four saints (pp. 1017–19). Equally interesting is his admission of failure, or, at least, of confusion and self-doubt, in comparison with the obvious accomplishments of the saintly knights (p. 1018): "Ellos conquistaron el cielo a fuerza de brazos, . . . y yo hasta agora no sé lo que conquisto a fuerza de mis trabajos" ("They won heaven by force of arms . . . and I, so far, know not what I have won by dint of my sufferings," p. 743).

Following the meeting between the feigned knight-errant and the feigned shepherds of the New Arcadia (reminiscent of Grisóstomo and friends in I, 13–14), where Sancho mortifies his master after the latter delivers a postdinner speech (recall the Golden Age and arms-and-letters speeches), Don Quijote defends the beauty of the pseudoshepherdesses against all who pass by on the road. It might have been interesting had some merchants from Toledo happened by and been challenged by Don Quijote, for surely the events of I, 4, would not have been repeated. As it is, Don Quijote merely shouts his challenge to the wind, rather as though he had no interest in actually confronting anyone. When a herd of bulls comes along, there is no time for a statement of principles and a challenge: Don Quijote merely gets trampled. The knight's rhetoric recalls his actions in part I (II, 59, 1026): insults—"¡Ea, canalla . . . ! Confesad, malandrines, . . . ¡Deteneos y esperad, canalla malandrina" ("Rabble! . . . Confess at once, scoundrels, . . . Stop! Wait! Ye wicked rabble"); challenge— "si no, conmigo sois en batalla" ("else ye have to deal with me in combat"); and persistence—"que un solo caballero os espera" ("a single knight awaits you," p. 749). But Don Quijote is more sympathetic and less deserving of his humiliation than in comparable scenes from early in the novel.

The interlude with Roque Guinart again puts Don Quijote in an unfavorable light. The bandits lead a genuinely adventuresome and dangerous life, in comparison with Don Quijote's ineffectiveness. When a maiden in distress, Claudia Jerónima, appeals for help, Don Quijote's offer of assistance is ignored by the bandit chief, who undertakes the deed himself. Don Quijote, supposedly a knight-errant whose life is constantly in danger, delivers to the bandits (II, 60, 1045) "una plática en que les per-suadía dejasen aquel modo de vivir tan peligroso así para el alma como para el cuerpo" ("a speech . . . in which he urged them to give up a mode of life so full of peril, as well to the soul as to the body," p. 762).

By the time he arrives in Barcelona, Don Quijote acts more like a celebrity tourist than a knight-errant. He rides along the beach and through the streets of the city in the company of a prominent local citizen, Don Antonio Moreno. A dinner and a dance are celebrated, and an exhibition of an enchanted talking head is arranged, all in the knight's honor. At the dinner, Don Quijote is, according to the narration, treated like a knight-er-rant. He reacts, it is said (II, 62, 1054), by becoming "hueco y pomposo, no cabía en sí de contento" ("puffed up and conceited as a result, could not contain himself for satisfaction," p. 768). None of Don Quijote's words or acts, however, confirms this statement. At the soiree, two ladies, described (p. 1068) as "de gusto pícaro y burlonas" ("of a mischievous and joke-loving turn") dance repeatedly with Don Quijote, "largo, tendido, flaco, amarillo, estrecho en el vestido, desairado, y sobre todo, no nada ligero" ("long, lank, lean, and sallow in his tight-fitting clothes, ungainly, and above all anything but agile," p. 771), un-til he sits "en mitad de la sala, en el suelo, molido y quebrantado de tan bailador ejercicio" ("in the middle of the room, tired out and broken down by all this exertion in the dance," p. 772). He visits a printing press and a ship, where he witnesses an exciting sea capture. Chivalry and knight-errantry may be referred to occasionally, but they are clearly not vital factors in Don Qui-jote's existence.

But the world of chivalry is brought back again to Don Qui-jote with the arrival of the Caballero de la Blanca Luna, alias Sansón Carrasco. Don Quijote responds to the knight's arrogant challenge (II, 64, 1078) "con reposo y ademán severo" ("with calm dignity") defending his lady thus: "yo osaré jurar que jamás habéis visto a la ilustre Dulcinea; . . . y así, no diciéndoos que mentís, sino que no acertáis en lo propuesto" ("I will ven-ture to swear thou hast never seen the illustrious Dulcinea; . . . and so, not saying thou liest, but merely that thou art not correct in what thou sayest," p. 786).[39] His defeat is absolute; no excuse is offered; death is welcomed in his moving words that echo within his helmet "como si hablara dentro de una tumba" ("as if he were speaking out of a tomb"):

> Dulcinea del Toboso es la más hermosa mujer del mundo, y yo el más desdichado caballero de la tierra, y no es bien que mi flaqueza defraude esta verdad. Aprieta, caballero, la lanza, y quítame la vida, pues me has quitado la honra. (p. 1079)

> (Dulcinea del Toboso is the fairest woman in the world, and I the most unfortunate knight on earth. It is not fitting that this truth should suffer by my feebleness; drive thy lance home, sir knight, and take my life, since thou hast taken away my honor.) (p. 787)

Cide Hamete uses one of his rare similes to describe Don Quijote's dejection on the way home from Barcelona (II, 67, 1091): "Si muchos pensamientos fatigaban a don Quijote antes de ser derribado, muchos más le fatigaron después de caído. . . .como moscas a la miel, le acudían y picaban pensamientos" ("If a multitude of reflections troubled Don Quixote before he was knocked off his horse, a great many more harassed him after his fall. . . . like flies to honey, thoughts came crowding upon him and stinging him," p. 796). Once again, the illustrious historian's word is not to be taken literally. There is no evidence in anything that Don Quijote does or says that suggests that his defeat has been a crucial factor in his withdrawal from action to thoughtfulness. Don Quijote's pensiveness started early in part II and was mentioned with increasing frequency through the stay at the ducal palace and afterward.

The references to the thoughts of the knight are all significant. They appear after the enchantment of Dulcinea (II, 11, 653)— "Pensativo además iba don Quijote" ("Dejected beyond measure, Don Quixote pursued his journey," p. 478); after the adventure of the enchanted boat (II, 30, 807)—"sepultado en los pensamientos de sus amores" ("absorbed in thoughts of love,"

---

39. Recall Don Quijote's words to the Toledan merchants (I, 4, 61): "La importancia está en que sin verla lo habéis de creer" ("The essential point is that without seeing her ye must believe," p. 42).

p. 590); after discovering the holes in his stockings and hearing Altisidora's love lament (II, 46, 924)—"Dejamos al gran don Quijote envuelto en los pensamientos . . . Acostóse con ellos y, como si fueran pulgas, no le dejaron dormir ni sosegar un punto" ("We left Don Quixote wrapped up in his reflections. . . . He went to bed with them, and like flies they would not let him sleep or get a moment's rest," p. 675); after being pinched by the duchess and Altisidora (II, 48, 946)—"doloroso y pellizcado, confuso y pensativo" ("sorely pinched, puzzled, and dejected," p. 690); after being trampled by bulls and while contemplating (literally?) suicide (II, 59, 1027–28)—"y déjame morir a mí a manos de mis pensamientos y a fuerzas de mis desgracias" ("leave me to die from my worries and the pressures of my misfortunes," p. 750); after he is surprised and taken prisoner by the Catalan bandits (II, 60, 1040)—"armado y pensativo, con la más triste y melancólica figura que pudiera formar la misma tristeza" ("in armor and dejected, with the saddest and most melancholy face that sadness itself could produce," p. 758); after his defeat by the Caballero de la Blanca Luna (II, 65, 1082)—"Seis días estuvo don Quijote en el lecho, marrido, triste, pensativo y malacondicionado, yendo y vinendo con la imaginación en el desdichado suceso de su vencimiento" ("Six days did Don Quixote keep to his bed, sick, melancholy, moody, and out of sorts, brooding over the unhappy event of his defeat," p. 789); and once more subsequent to Cide Hamete's statement on the way home (II, 68, 1099–1100)—"daré rienda a mis pensamientos, y los desfogaré en un madrigalete" ("I will give free rein to my troubled thoughts and seek a release for them in a little madrigal," p. 802). Admittedly, the words *pensamiento* or *pensativo* do not need to be present in narration for the reader to perceive the thoughtfulness of the character, but overall it seems clear that there is no textual support for the historian's statement.

The trampling by the pigs is completely gratuitous.[40] A short

40. Allen calls the part of the novel between the trampling by the bulls (II, 58) and the trampling by the pigs (II, 68) "the crucial section of the novel" and Don Quijote's "finest hour," in which his seven defeats or humiliations are unjustified, with the result that "the sensitive reader suffers with a man at whom he has repeatedly laughed for some eight hundred pages"; *Hero or Fool*, 1:47. The very scenes that for Allen

while before, Don Quijote had run after the bulls shouting semicoherently about revenge, but now he accepts this swinish affront as (II, 68, 1099) "pena de mi pecado, y justo castigo del cielo" ("the penalty of my sin; and it is the righteous chastisement of heaven," p. 802). The pair of travelers is then returned to the ducal palace for a final episode in the tiresome Altisidora affair and for a few more laughs at the expense of Sancho Panza.

By the time they arrive home at their village, it is a triumphant and eloquent Sancho who delivers a speech and a spiritually exhausted Don Quijote who mutters (II, 72, 1126), "Déjate desas sandeces" ("Leave off this foolishness," p. 821). Just as at the end of part I, Sancho and his wife provide the main interest. Don Quijote, after a brief conversation with his friends, announces to the housekeeper and niece (II, 72, 1131), "yo sé bien lo que me cumple. Llevadme al lecho" ("I know very well what my duty is; help me to bed," p. 825). Don Quijote's last act, again, is to go to bed.

---

represent Don Quijote's *via crucis* are for Carlos Varo further examples (see Chapter 3, note 19) of Cervantes's bad taste; *Génesis y evolución del "Quijote,"* pp. 512–14, 526.

5

Knighthood Denied

Ya yo no soy don Quijote de la Mancha,
sino Alonso Quijano, a quien mis costumbres
me dieron renombre de *Bueno* (II, 74, 1133)

(I am no longer Don Quixote of La Mancha,
but Alonso Quixano, whose way of life won
for him the name of Good, p. 826)

5.1 The Pattern of Pseudoadventure

There is no elaborate pattern to Don Quijote's adventures in part II as there was in part I. Don Quijote is not prone to transforming reality; Sancho Panza does not have to act as Reality Instructor; Don Quijote does not often employ his rhetoric of chivalry; he does not attack and suffer ill consequences; he does not need to blame his failures on the intervention of enchanters. In fact, the very use of the word *adventure* becomes problematic during Don Quijote's third sally.[1]

1. Richard L. Predmore's discussion of Don Quijote's adventures in part II in the same terms he used when discussing those of part I (*The World of Don Quixote*, pp. 23–27) is not very satisfactory from several points of view. After listing ten episodes as adventures, Predmore goes on to discuss nearly all of them in terms of having only the appearance of adventures, of being dreams, of being contrived, of being "sham adventures." Three of the four "successes"—Predmore does not call them victories—that he discusses (lions, Clavileño, Tosilos) never even reach the point of physical contact between Don Quijote and his opponents (p. 26). Luis Morales Oliver's long list of adventures in the second part (*Sinópsis de "Don Quijote,"* pp. 21–23) is so all-inclusive that it borders on the meaningless. Colbert I. Nepaulsingh's list of fourteen principal adventures in the second part, which is symmetrical to the adventures in part I ("Cervantes, *Don Quijote*: The Unity of the Action," p. 244), likewise seems forced.

167

The events in the second part of the novel do, however, tend to follow two basic, simple patterns. What usually happens is that Don Quijote and all who surround him perceive reality just as it is and act in full accord with that reality. Such is the case with the encounter with the troupe of actors, all the events involving Don Diego de Miranda (including the adventure with the lion), the wedding of Basilio and Quiteria, Maese Pedro's puppet show,[2] the braying episode, and everything that takes place after Don Quijote and Sancho depart from the duke's palace (with the exceptions of the interventions of Sansón Carrasco and the ducal pair).

The second type of event is the pseudoadventure arranged by others. Included in this category are the enchantment of Dulcinea by Sancho (here Reality Instructor turned Fantasy Instructor), the two chivalric battles that Don Quijote has with Sansón Carrasco, and everything that happens at the palace of the duke and duchess: the speech by Merlin, the Countess Trifaldi–Clavileño adventure, the Altisidora affair (including the bag of cats), and the battle arranged with the lackey Tosilos.

The only genuine exception is the adventure of the enchanted boat (discussed in section 4.3), which might be explained, at least in part, as an attempt by Don Quijote to compensate for his cowardly actions shortly before when he abandoned Sancho to an angry mob. Don Quijote's rhetoric and actions in the scene of the bulls (see section 4.5) are also somewhat reminiscent of those in part I. The dream in the cave of Montesinos is, of course, a unique event that falls into no category; Don Quijote's dream in part I—the wineskins—was not so thoroughly undercut by nonchivalric reality.

Another interesting feature of the events of part II is their lack of substance and/or resolution.[3] Whereas in part I Don Quijote's adventures tended to result either in an outright victory (as over

2. I do not believe that Don Quijote transforms reality when he attacks the puppets; see section 4.3.

3. Luis Rosales calls the adventures of part I "de acontecimiento" ("of happening") and those of part II "vacíos" ("empty"); *Cervantes y la libertad*, 2:27. Theodore Holmes calls the latter "parodies of adventures" and states that Don Quijote is now "an entertainer . . . a pawn in the hands of others"; "Don Quixote and Modern Man," p. 51.

the Biscayan or the knight wearing Mambrino's helmet) or a setback for which there was a good excuse (as when Rocinante fell or enchanters intervened), those in part II are often less conclusive. The enchantment of Dulcinea lasts throughout some sixty-two chapters until Sancho finally disenchants (?) her; Don Quijote accepts an excuse not to take action when confronted by the actors; there is no encounter between Don Quijote and the lion; the events of the cave of Montesinos are a dream; Don Quijote flees from combat in the braying affair; he concludes the Trifaldi charade merely by undertaking it; the Altisidora affair is carried on *ad nauseum*; Tosilos refuses to fight; nothing happens after the tramplings by the bulls and the pigs; there is no conflict of any sort while in the company of Don Antonio Moreno.

One thing that does happen more often in part II is that Don Quijote talks with people. He not only delivers speeches as he did previously but also has actual conversations with a large number of individuals. In part I, Don Quijote had what might be considered extended conversations on only four occasions: with the goatherd Pedro (chap. 12); Vivaldo (chap. 13); the group of galley slaves (chap. 22); and the canon of Toledo (chaps. 49–50).[4] In part II, Don Quijote speaks with the priest and the barber (chap. 1); Sansón Carrasco and Sancho (chaps. 3 and 4); the niece and housekeeper (chap. 6); Don Diego de Miranda (chap. 16); Lorenzo de Miranda (chap. 18); the cousin and Sancho (chap. 23); the duke, duchess, priest, and Sancho (chap. 31); the duke and duchess (chap. 32); Doña Rodríguez (chap. 48); Don Juan, Don Jerónimo, and Sancho (chap. 59); the author in the printing press (chap. 62); and Alvaro Tarfe and Sancho (chap. 72).[5]

None of these elements that characterize Don Quijote in the second part of the novel is completely new. We saw all of them in part I, especially in the last half following the reentry of the priest and the barber. Don Quijote perceived reality quite fully with the captive, Zoraida, the judge, and so on, in the inn. The

---

4. Don Quijote also talks at length, of course, with Sancho Panza—especially in chapters 10, 15, 17, 18, 20, 21, 23, 25, and 31.

5. Notice that Sancho Panza, more prominent in part II, participates in several of these conversations. Don Quijote and Sancho also talk at length together in chapters 2, 7, 8, 9, 10, 28, 29, 42–43, 58, 67, and 71.

adventure of the Princess Micomicona and the enchantment of Don Quijote were staged by Dorotea, the priest, and the barber, and neither of these episodes ever involved any real action or was ever satisfactorily resolved. The major change in technique takes place in the second half of part I, not in part II.

Never in part II does Don Quijote even come close to displaying the degree of dedication to and enthusiasm for knight-errantry that was characteristic of his acts and his words in the first half of part I. After the humiliation and defeat that he suffered in I, 52, and after the accumulated physical and spiritual decline that he experienced throughout his second sally, Don Quijote no longer existed as the knight-errant he had chosen to become in I, 1. The heroes of the books he used to read—Amadís, Tirante, or Belianís, for example—were not defeated, laughed at, manipulated by others, or forced to conform to a conventional and mediocre reality. Don Quijote's capitulation to reality—the reality from which he so desperately needed to escape when he was Alonso Quijano—not only marks the termination of his world of chivalry but also symbolizes the victory of conformity and oppression over individuality and freedom.

But Don Quijote did share with Amadís and company one essential quality: fame. A wise enchanter wrote a history of Don Quijote's exploits, and this book was read and enjoyed by a very large number of people. These people, led by Sansón Carrasco, imposed the world of chivalry on Alonso Quijano and turned him once more into Don Quijote. Trapped in a role that he no longer chooses to play, Don Quijote is thrust on the stage by Sansón Carrasco, who has read his history, assisted by the priest and the barber, who so enjoy laughing at their friend, and by Sancho Panza, who really likes being a squire-errant.

From the start of part II, Don Quijote fails to act as he did when the role of knight-errant was of his own choosing. He plays the part reluctantly and badly: he fails to deliver his lines properly and ignores or walks out on key scenes. When the consummate stage managers—the duke and duchess—take charge, Don Quijote loses the last bit of spirit remaining in him. The Don Quijote of all of part II is pathetic and sad, but after arriving at the ducal palace and definitively surrendering his will and his freedom, the pathos and sadness become even greater. The defeat that Don Quijote suffers at the hands of the vindictive Sansón Carrasco marks no turning point in the career of an already broken knight. As shown in Figure 5.1, Don Quijote's chivalric trajectory in part II is from little to less. Thus, the complete chivalric career of Don Quijote, outlined as simply as possible in Figure 5.2, is one of great decline in part I and virtually no change in part II.

5.2 Sancho Panza: Triumph

Chapter 5 of part II, the marvelous comic conversation that takes place between Sancho Panza and his wife Teresa, is often singled out as evidence of Sancho's new and growing sophistication in the second part of the novel. Cervantes himself is responsible for this opinion as he begins the chapter with a cau-

Figure 5.1.   Don Quijote's Career as a Knight-Errant (Part II)

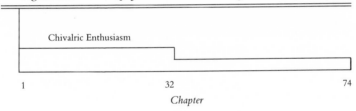

Figure 5.2.   A Simplified Version of Don Quijote's Career as a
Knight-Errant (Parts I and II)

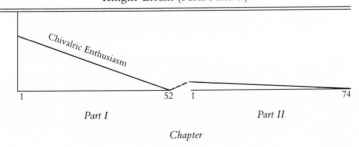

tionary paragraph in which he records his translator's misgivings[6] concerning the character's speech.

> Llegando a escribir el traductor desta historia este quinto capítulo, dice que le tiene por apócrifo, porque en él habla Sancho Panza con otro estilo del que se podía prometer de su corto ingenio, y dice cosas tan sutiles, que no tiene por posible que él las supiese; pero que no quiso dejar de traducirlo, por cumplir con lo que a su oficio debía, y así, prosiguió diciendo. (p. 611)

> (The translator of this history, when he comes to write this fifth chapter, says that he considers it apocryphal, because in it Sancho Panza speaks in a style unlike that which might have been expected from his limited intelligence and says things so subtle that he does not think it possible Sancho could have conceived them. However, desirous of doing what the task called for, he was unwilling to leave it untranslated, and therefore, he went on as follows.) (p. 448)

Twice more during the chapter the scene is interrupted in order to record the translator's concern (p. 614): "Por este modo de hablar, y por lo que más abajo dice Sancho, dijo el traductor desta historia que tenía por apócrifo este capítulo" ("It is this sort of talk, and what Sancho says below, that made the translator of the history say he considered this chapter apocryphal," p. 450); and (p. 616) "Todas estas razones que aquí va diciendo Sancho son las segundas por quien dice el tradutor que tiene por apócrifo este capítulo, que exceden a la capacidad de Sancho" ("These observations which Sancho makes here are the other ones on account of which the translator says he regards this chapter as apocryphal, inasmuch as they are beyond Sancho's capacity," p. 451).

6. Later, in section 5.4, I discuss the following narrative scheme: the deeds of Don Quijote and Sancho—written in Arabic by Cide Hamete Benengeli, translated into Spanish by a *morisco*, and edited and written for us by Miguel de Cervantes. The editor Cervantes, however, is sometimes careless with his terms, and it is possible that when he says *traductor* he is referring to himself. It makes little substantial difference whether the opinions expressed are the *morisco*'s or Cervantes's, but I have elected to read the passage literally and to assume that the editor is transmitting to the reader the opinion of his translator and collaborator.

A close examination of exactly what Sancho says and the way in which he says it, however, leads us to question the judgment of the translator. Immediately preceding the first statement just quoted, Sancho says:

> Mira, Teresa: siempre he oído decir a mis mayores que el que no sabe gozar de la ventura cuando le viene, que no se debe quejar si se le pasa. Y no sería bien que ahora, que está llamando a nuestra puerta, se la cerremos; dejémonos llevar deste viento favorable que nos sopla. (pp. 613–14)

> (Look, Teresa, I have always heard my elders say that he who does not know how to take advantage of luck when it comes to him has no right to complain if it passes him by. Now that it is knocking at our door, it will not do to shut it out. Let us go with the favoring breeze that blows upon us.) (p. 450)

Then, just before the second statement, he says:

> Mira, Teresa . . . , y escucha lo que agora quiero decirte; quizá no lo habrás oído en todos los días de tu vida, y yo agora no hablo de mío; que todo lo que pienso decir son sentencias del padre predicador que la cuaresma pasada predicó en este pueblo, el cual, si mal no me acuerdo, dijo que todas las cosas presentes que los ojos están mirando se presentan, están y asisten en nuestra memoria mucho mejor y con más vehemencia que las cosas pasadas. (p. 616)

> (Look here, Teresa, . . . and listen to what I am now going to say to you. Maybe you never heard it in your life, and I do not give my own notions; but what I am about to say are the opinions of his reverence the preacher who preached in this town last Lent and who said, if I remember rightly, that all things present that our eyes behold bring themselves before us and remain and fix themselves on our memory much better and more forcibly than things past.) (p. 451)

There is, certainly, a considerable intellectual sophistication in Sancho's statements on fortune and memory, and the imagery he uses is more erudite than popular, but in both cases he attributes his material to a reasonable source: "mis mayores" ("my elders") and, more specifically, "el padre predicador . . . la cuaresma pasada" ("his reverence the preacher . . . last Lent"). Several times previous to this chapter, often when he is about to say something unusual, Sancho has cited his sources, which tend to be precisely those referred to here: general wisdom—"dicen que" ("they say that"); "he oído que" ("I have heard that"); and so on—and the words of a priest, usually Pero Pérez, often taken from a sermon. Sancho's other main source is his master Don Quijote.[7] Throughout the rest of the novel, Sancho refers dozens of times to these sources.[8]

Perhaps at the time of redaction of this chapter, the translator was not yet accustomed to this characteristic trait of Sancho's and did not recognize that what struck him as unusual was thoroughly in character. At any rate, this error in judgment on the part of the translator, which the editor faithfully passes on to the reader (straightforwardly and in full accord, or with a wry and knowing smile?), has caused literal readers of the novel to believe, mistakenly, that Sancho Panza has spoken in a unique and extraordinary manner in this chapter.[9]

Sancho's speech in I, 20 (discussed in section 2.5)—given its early occurrence, the circumstances, its rhetorical devices, its ar-

7. For Sancho's previous appeals to general wisdom (to which he also refers implicitly whenever he cites a proverb), see I, 15, 150; I, 25, 264; I, 47, 515, 516; I, 49, 529; and I, 50, 540. For his ecclesiastical sources, see I, 20, 195, and I, 31, 341. For references from Don Quijote, see I, 15, 153; II, 2, 593; and II, 4, 608.

8. Again he refers to general wisdom, although at times he is more specific, citing "una agüela mía" ("a grandmother of mine"), "un romance antiguo" ("an old ballad"), "un boticario toledano" ("a Toledo apothecary"), "mi barbero" ("my barber"), or "una mi agüela" ("my grandmother"): II, 7, 626; 8, 637; 10, 644; 13, 670; 19, 721; 21, 733; 30, 811; 33, 838; 34, 845; 36, 861; 37, 865, 866; 39, 875; 43, 904; 65, 1083; 66, 1086, 1088; and 68, 1098. Don Quijote: II, 25, 744; 31, 814; 33, 841, 842; 36, 861; 37, 867; 51, 970; 72, 1126; and 73, 1127. The priest: II, 7, 626; 21, 734; and 73, 1127. On one occasion, Don Quijote registers the following opinion (II, 22, 747): "Esa pregunta y respuesta no es tuya, Sancho: a alguno las has oído decir" ("Sancho, that question and answer are not your own. You heard them from someone else," p. 547). Once more it is recorded in narration (II, 45, 921) that "él había oído contar otro caso como aquél al cura de su lugar" ("he had himself heard the curate of his village mention just such another case," p. 673).

9. Helmut A. Hatzfeld, for example, cites several aspects of what he considers falsifications in Sancho's speech, including ones not objected to by the translator, in order to justify the latter's objections to Sancho's style; *Explicación de textos literarios*, p. 70.

chaism, and the shifts in style—is his most interesting and revealing utterance in the entire novel. His speech on numerous
occasions is at least as intellectual, sophisticated, subtle, and erudite as is his conversation with Teresa. Ironically, a speech that
he delivers to Don Quijote and Sansón Carrasco just before this
chapter, near the end of II, 4, which begins (pp. 608–9) "Deso
es lo que yo reniego" ("That's the part I hate," p. 446), is one of
his longest and most complex. After Don Quijote states his decision to depart on a third sally, Sancho talks at some length,
mixing popular imagery—"como un muchacho goloso a media
docena de badeas" ("as a greedy boy would a half dozen mel-
ons"); popular exclamations—"¡Cuerpo del mundo!" ("God
help us!"); and proverbs—"Cuando te dieren la vaquilla, corre
con la soguilla" ("When they offer you a heifer, run with a hal-
ter")—with sententious statements—"tiempos hay de acometer
y tiempos de retirar" ("there is a time to attack and a time to
retreat"); a citation of his master's words—"que yo he oído decir, y creo que a mi señor mismo, si mal no me acuerdo, que")
("I have heard it said (and I think by my master himself, if I
remember rightly) that . . . "); and an eloquent statement of his
own very nonmaterialistic goal—"no pienso granjear fama de
valiente, sino del mejor y más leal escudero que jamás sirvió a
caballero andante" ("I don't set myself up to be a fighting man,
but only the best and most loyal squire that ever served knight-
errant"); all accompanied by a reasonably complicated and logical sentence structure.[10] Significantly, when Sancho finishes this

10. This speech runs some thirty-six lines. The only times that Sancho speaks at greater length are thirty-eight lines when he talks with
the duchess (II, 33, 837–38) and forty lines when he discusses his experiences as a governor with his master and the duke and duchess (II,
55, 1004–5). It is worth noting that after the latter, which is the longest
single speech that Sancho ever pronounces, the narration calls attention
to its length, adding, "Con esto dio fin a su larga plática Sancho"
("Here Sancho brought his long speech to an end," p. 733). As would
be expected, Sancho speaks not only more often but also at greater
length in part II than he did in part I. His other long speeches are
twenty-four lines in II, 7, 628–29; thirty-one and twenty-five lines in
II, 10, 644–45 and 645–46; twenty-four lines in II, 14, 672–73; twenty
lines in II, 27, 793–94; thirty-two lines in II, 28, 796–97; thirty-one
lines in II, 35, 855–56; twenty lines in II, 47, 933; twenty-five lines in
II, 53, 988; and thirty-three lines in II, 55, 999–1000.

speech, Sansón Carrasco comments (p. 609) that he has "hablado como un catedrático" ("spoken like a professor," p. 446).

Throughout his conversation with his wife, Sancho adopts a rude and condescending attitude (p. 612)—"Basta que me entienda Dios, mujer" ("It is enough that God understands me, wife," p. 448); "Calla, boba" (p. 613) ("Hush, you silly woman," p. 449); and so on—which recalls his briefer conversation with Teresa (I, 52, 556)—"No es la miel para la boca del asno" ("Honey is not for the mouth of the ass"); "No te acucies, Juana" (p. 557) ("Don't be in such a hurry to know all this," p. 401); and so forth. In general, Sancho's intellectually superior stance, defense of the chivalric quest, use of insults, criticism of his wife's association of ideas, correction of her pronunciation, and so on, all mirror Don Quijote's manner when dealing with his squire: Sancho is to Teresa as Don Quijote is to Sancho. But all this is an extension of what Sancho observed and did in part I. The great comic scene in II, 5, with its psychological realism and its ironic narrative structure, is of unquestioned genius, but it represents no inconsistency or falsification of character and is in no way innovative.

If Sancho's discussion with his wife in II, 5, is often cited as indicative of his new status in the second part, the enchantment of Dulcinea in II, 10, is the classic scene where his trajectory is considered to chart a new course (see section 3.6). This chapter has already been examined (in section 4.3) from the point of view of Don Quijote; it is equally crucial to Sancho Panza. Don Quijote cannot afford to confront the reality of the nonexistence of Dulcinea any more than Sancho can afford to allow such a confrontation to take place. Knight and squire proceed to El Toboso at the start of the third sally because that is the way the script is written, but while Don Quijote suggests one scenario to his squire, Sancho provides a very different one.

So many events prefigure Sancho's conduct in II, 10, that his scheme to present his master with an enchanted Dulcinea is almost inevitable. The importance of his tying the feet of Rocinante in I, 20, to keep Don Quijote from undertaking the adventure of the fulling mills can hardly be stressed enough. This early version of an enchantment in order to promote his own interests (see section 2.5) is Sancho's overt act in part I that anticipates and helps make possible his actions in II, 10.

The concept of a noble lady's being reduced to a peasant woman has been presented to Sancho in a variety of ways. First of all, it should be recalled that Sancho maintained for some while the belief that his master really was in love with some sort of princess or, at least, a high-born lady. It was a serious mistake on Don Quijote's part to reveal to his squire the reality of Aldonza Lorenzo in I, 25 (see section 2.6). This reality provided Sancho with the material he needed to invent his version of the interview that he was supposed to have had with Dulcinea in I, 31 (see section 3.1). A short while later at the inn (I, 37), Sancho saw this process of reduction in status in very real terms when the Princess Micomicona turned out to be no more than a "dama particular" ("private lady"), Dorotea, in love with Fernando (see section 3.3). Finally, in a key scene in which Don Quijote undermines the scenario that he will soon propose, Sancho hears his master relate the events of their earlier conversation about Sancho's supposed visit with Dulcinea (II, 8, 632) to "la envidia que algún mal encantador debe de tener a mis cosas, todas las que me han de dar gusto trueca y vuelve en diferentes figuras que ellas tienen" ("the spite some wicked enchanter seems to have against everything concerning me [which] changes all those things that give me pleasure and turns them into shapes unlike their own," p. 464).

The opposite process, that of elevating a woman of low stature to the status of a princess, has also taken place: in I, 16, when Maritornes, the innkeeper's daughter, became, for Don Quijote, the daughter of the lord of the castle.[11] As Sancho realizes, this is the same process by which the rustic Aldonza Lorenzo became Dulcinea del Toboso in the first place.

Thus Sancho has discussed the principle of reducing a princess to an ordinary woman and vice versa and has seen these processes in action. His master has suggested that this can be done by enchantment, as it was before. Sancho himself has previously presented Don Quijote with a deception in order to manipulate

11. See Rosales, *Libertad*, 2:134, note 153.

his actions; Sancho's decision to present a peasant woman as an enchanted Dulcinea seems perfectly logical.[12]

The technique that Sancho uses to convince Don Quijote that he is actually seeing Dulcinea is one of substitution. Sancho announces (II, 10, 647) the arrival of "la señora Dulcinea del Toboso, que con otras dos doncellas suyas viene a ver a vuesa merced. . . . y, sobre todo, vienen a caballo sobre tres cananeas remendadas" ("the lady Dulcinea del Toboso, who with two of her maids is coming to see your worship. . . . Moreover, they are mounted on three painted palfries," p. 474). Don Quijote's perception is quite different (p. 648): "yo no veo, Sancho . . . , sino a tres labradoras sobre tres borricos" ("I see nothing, Sancho, but three country girls on three jackasses," p. 475). The animals being ridden, rather than the riders, become the issue that Don Quijote and Sancho debate. Don Quijote's capitulation on this matter prepares the terrain for his acceptance of the peasant as Dulcinea. While it is true that this substitution answers the psychological need of both characters to avoid the subject of Dulcinea directly,[13] it is also true that Sancho uses the same technique that his master employed in I, 21. Sancho was skeptical when Don Quijote announced that he was about to win Mambrino's magic helmet, previously discussed by the two. The exchange between knight and squire is the mirror opposite of what happens in II, 10 (p. 208).

> DON QUIJOTE: "Dime, ¿no ves aquel caballero que hacia nosotros viene, sobre un caballo rucio rodado, que trae puesto en la cabeza un yelmo de oro?" ("Tell me, do you not see yonder knight coming towards us on a dappled grey steed, with a helmet of gold upon his head?")
>
> SANCHO PANZA: "Lo que yo veo y columbro . . . no es sino un hombre sobre un asno, pardo como el mío, que trae sobre la cabeza una cosa que relumbra" ("What I see and make

12. For further antecedents for Sancho's presentation of the peasant girl as Dulcinea, see Ronnie H. Terpening, "Creation and Deformation in the Episode of Dulcinea: Sancho Panza as Author," pp. 4–5.

13. Carroll B. Johnson, "A Second Look at Dulcinea's Ass: *Don Quijote*, II.10," p. 197. See also Gonzalo Torrente Ballester, *El "Quijote" como juego*, p. 176.

out . . . is only a man on a grey ass like my own, with something shining on his head," p. 142).[14]

This very scene may be in Sancho's mind, at least subconsciously, when he recalls Don Quijote's earlier tendency to transform reality (p. 646): "de locura que las más veces toma unas cosas por otras, y juzga lo blanco por negro y lo negro por blanco" ("with a madness that mostly takes one thing for another, white for black and black for white," p. 473).

In ever-increasing spirals of irony, Sancho will eventually be made to believe that he was a mere pawn of the enchanters who actually did cast a spell on a real Dulcinea (II, 33, 839–40); will have to effect her disenchantment by lashing himself thirty-three hundred times (II, 35, 853); is eventually paid by Don Quijote to complete the task (II, 71, 1116–17); but deceives his master again by whipping the trees (p. 1119).

None of these comments is intended to imply that Sancho Panza does not continue to grow spiritually and intellectually in part II; rather they are meant to stress that his actions in the second part are the logical extension of what happened in part I. Sancho is far more subject to sudden ups and downs than is his master (a single example: in II, 60, Sancho defeats Don Quijote in hand-to-hand combat and then a moment later tearfully calls to his master for help when he is frightened by human feet he feels dangling from some trees), and a detailed graph of his progression—which might be more complicated than that of Don Quijote—would be extremely difficult, if not impossible, to trace. In general, however, Sancho's trajectory, when traced in its most general outline, shows a steady rise in the first part

14. In a delightful and insightful reversal of positions, Sancho, anxious to profit from the knight's victory (pp. 211–12), asks "qué haremos deste caballo rucio rodado, que parece asno pardo, que dejó aquí desamparado aquel Martino [one of Sancho's variants for Mambrino] que vuestra merced derribó" ("what are we to do with this dapple-grey steed that looks like a grey ass, left by that Martino that your worship knocked off"), which forces an equivocation from Don Quijote: "Así que, Sancho, deja ese caballo, o asno, o lo que tú quisieres que sea" ("Therefore, Sancho, leave this horse, or ass, or whatever you will have it to be," p. 145).

(with a possible hiatus during the stay in the inn) and a continuation of the upward movement in part II (see Figure 5.3).

Many factors contribute to a profile of Sancho's character in part II. It would be beyond the limits of my intentions to do more than briefly indicate some of them. There is no question that with the experience of part I behind him, Sancho is throughout the second part a more confident, self-reliant, and assertive person. As observed earlier, he speaks more frequently, at greater length, and more articulately than previously. He offers opinions, gives advice, or interrupts the conversation of others far more often than he did in the first part. Everything he does and says indicates a greater intellectual maturity and subtlety than before.

Sancho Panza's idealism, nonmaterialistic motivation, and even occasional quixotism are characteristic throughout the second part. His concern for his image in Cide Hamete Benengeli's book and his ambition to win fame as a loyal squire are also typical. His willingness to turn down the duke's proffered governorship and his eventual renunciation of the position illustrate his modesty and his self-knowledge. His tenure as governor is rightly perceived as the triumphant culmination of his career in his unprecedented display of wisdom, maturity, self-restraint, and self-sacrifice.[15]

Figure 5.3.   Sancho Panza's Psychological Growth (Parts I and II)

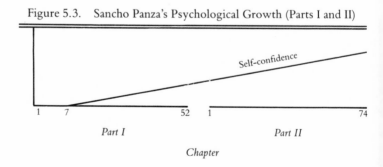

15. Arthur Efron's dismissal of Sancho's achievements ("his mediocre record") is unjust; *Don Quixote and the Dulcineated World*, p. 85.

Sancho fully assimilates his master's chivalric world in part II of the novel. Not only does he advise Alonso Quijano to make a third sally in II, 4, but the last time he speaks, in II, 74, it is to urge his master to leave his bed and sally forth as a shepherd-errant. While a governor, Sancho states his goals in terms that clearly echo the form of Don Quijote's statements of his chivalric mission (II, 49, 948): "Pienso favorecer a los labradores, guardar sus preeminencias a los hidalgos, premiar los virtuosos, y, sobre todo, tener respeto a la religión y a la honra de los religiosos" ("I mean to protect the peasants, to preserve the gentlemen's privileges, to reward the virtuous, and above all to respect religion and honor its ministers," p. 692). Sancho uses chivalric archaism more often than his master in part II and in fact uses the last archaism in the novel (II, 72, 1123).[16] Similarly, he is the last character to cite the positive example of the romances of chivalry (II, 74, 1136). Don Quijote may greet his defeat at the hands of the Caballero de la Blanca Luna with relief, but Sancho is described as (II, 64, 1080) "todo triste, todo apesarado, no sabía qué decirse ni qué hacerse: parecíale que todo aquel suceso pasaba en sueños y que toda aquella máquina era cosa de encantamento" ("wholly dejected and woebegone, . . . not [knowing] what to say or do. He thought it was all a dream, that the whole business was a piece of enchantment," p. 787).

Throughout part II, Sancho rises to the defense of Don Quijote, but he is most eloquent in response to questions by the duchess.

> Pero ésta fue mi suerte, y ésta mi malandanza; no puedo más; seguirle tengo: somos de un mismo lugar, he comido su pan, quiérole bien, es agradecido, diome sus pollinos y, sobre todo, yo soy fiel; y así, es imposible que nos pueda apartar otro suceso que el de la pala y azadón. (II, 33, 837)

> (But this was my fate, this was my bad luck, I can't help it; I must follow him. We're from the same village, I've eaten his

16. Salvador de Madariaga (*Don Quixote: An Introductory Essay in Psychology*, p. 193) points out that it is a sanchified Don Quijote who states the last proverb in the novel, but, because Madariaga pays no attention to the function of chivalric archaism in the novel, he does not notice that a quixotized Sancho uses the last archaism.

bread, I'm fond of him, I'm grateful, he gave me his ass-colts, and above all I'm faithful. So it's quite impossible for anything to separate us, except the pick and shovel.) (p. 612)

Sancho Panza may have been introduced reluctantly and hesitatingly into Don Quijote's world of chivalry, but he eventually assimilated it and mastered it, becoming its eloquent defender and living proof of its positive influence.

5.3 Sansón Carrasco et al.

The second part of Cervantes's novel contains many more characters than the first. In addition to the knight and his squire, more than 135 characters speak at least once.[17] The most prominent of these are listed in Table 5.1.

Sansón Carrasco replaces the priest and the barber in the role of Don Quijote's friend from his own village who undertakes the task of making the mad *hidalgo* turned knight-errant come back to his home and to sanity. The reader, who grew accustomed throughout part I to such characters, knows immediately what to expect from Sansón when he is described (II, 3, 597) as "no muy grande de cuerpo, aunque muy gran socarrón; . . . señales todas de ser de condición maliciosa y amigo de donaires y de burlas" ("not very big, but a great joker . . . all indications of a mischievous disposition and a love of fun and jokes"). Throughout chapters 3 to 7, Sansón lives up to this description, enjoying the antics of both Don Quijote and Sancho as they discuss Cide Hamete Benengeli's history and make plans for the third sally. Just as the priest in part I could not conceive of any way to make his friend return home except by inventing a charade in keeping with the latter's chivalric fantasy, Sansón Carrasco—influenced by his reading of part I and in consultation with the priest—can only use the questionable tactic of taking on the guise of a knight-errant himself in order to achieve his

17. The actual number of people who speak is more difficult to determine in part II than in part I. There are many scenes in which words are spoken by *labradores* ("farmers"), *circunstantes* ("bystanders"), *molineros* ("millers"), *lacayos* ("lackeys"), *criados* ("servants"), *corchetes* ("constables"), *peregrinos* ("pilgrims"), *zagales* ("shepherdesses"), *bandoleros* ("bandits"), *muchachos* ("boys"), and others.

Table 5.1.   Frequency of Speech among Secondary Characters
(Part II)

Character	Number of Speeches
Sansón Carrasco	66
The duchess	52
The duke	37
The duke's majordomo (also Merlin and the Countess Trifaldi)	36
Tomé Cecial	29
Teresa Panza	26
Maese Pedro	25
Doña Rodríguez	24
Pero Pérez, the priest	19
Ricote	16
Don Diego de Miranda	15
Don Antonio Moreno	15
Don Lorenzo de Miranda	14
The scholar/cousin who accompanies Don Quijote to the cave of Montesinos	14
Sanchica	14
Altisidora	13
Roque Guinart	11
Don Quijote's housekeeper	10
The unnamed pseudofarmer from Miguel Turra	10
The unnamed youth Sancho meets during the tour of his *ínsula*	10
The unnamed nephew of Don Antonio Moreno who speaks for the enchanted head	10

stated objective of making Don Quijote stop considering himself a knight-errant.

On his first sally, Sansón obviously enjoys his role, preparing an elaborate story complete with comic details (the giantess Giralda of Seville, his claim of having defeated Don Quijote de la Mancha, the name of Casildea de Vandalia, and so forth). His one oversight, the failure to provide himself with a good horse, puts an abrupt end to his enjoyable game and reveals his true

nature. When his squire Tomé Cecial (II, 15, 686), "hombre alegre y de lucios cascos" ("a lively jolly fellow," p. 502),[18] states his
intention to return home, Sansón replies (pp. 686–87): "pensar
que yo he de volver a la mía hasta haber molido a palos a don
Quijote es pensar en lo escusado; y no me llevará ahora a bus-
carle el deseo de que cobre su juicio, sino el de la venganza" ("to
suppose that I am going home until I have given Don Quixote
a thrashing is absurd. What urges me on now is not any wish he
may recover his senses but the desire for vengeance," p. 503).

On his second sally, Sansón Carrasco prepares no elaborate
scenario. He merely appears, challenges Don Quijote to defend
Dulcinea against his own lady (II, 64, 1077)—"sea quien fuere"
("let her be who she may," p. 785)—and proceeds with the combat. When Don Antonio Moreno follows him after his victory
in order to inquire about his identity and motives, Sansón lies—
or at least exaggerates grossly—when he responds (II, 65, 1081)
that Don Quijote's "locura y sandez mueve a que le tengamos
lástima todos cuantos le conocemos, y entre los que más se la
han tenido he sido yo" ("madness and folly make all of us who
know him feel pity for him, and I am one of those who have felt
it most," p. 788). He repeats the same self-serving lie to the duke
(II, 70, 1110), saying that the hope of curing Don Quijote's madness "era la intención que le había movido a hacer aquellas trans-
formaciones, por ser cosa de lástima que un hidalgo tan bien
entendido como don Quijote fuese loco" ("was the object that
had led him to adopt those disguises, as it was a sad thing for so
well-informed a gentleman as Don Quixote to be crazy," p.
809).

Sansón Carrasco, as hypocritical as the priest, the barber, and
the other staunch defenders of society's norms, never enjoys the

18. These epithets are of dubious accuracy. In his conversation with
Sansón Carrasco, Tomé Cecial demonstrates that he, like his fellow
peasant Sancho Panza, is quite clever. Talking with his master after
Sansón's defeat by Don Quijote, and after he had literally saved the
pseudoknight's life, Tomé asks the very meaningful and perceptive
question (p. 686), "¿cuál es más loco: el que lo es por no poder menos,
o el que lo es por su voluntad?" ("which is the madder, the man who is
mad because he cannot help it, or the man mad of his own free will?,"
p. 503).

reader's sympathy as did Pero Pérez in the first half of part I
when Don Quijote's comic fantasy evoked laughter.[19] In general,
throughout the second part, Don Quijote is morally superior to
his antagonists; in comparison with the Don Quijote of the latter
part of part I and all of part II, the other characters who manipulate and deceive him are perceived as less attractive and less sympathetic than the knight-errant.

Nowhere is the comparative superiority of Don Quijote more
evident than during his stay at the palace of the duke and duchess, who are aided by their staff, headed by the clever majordomo, the page, and the tiresome Altisidora. No other characters in the book can match these nobles in wealth, power, or
obnoxiousness. When they take in Don Quijote, they reduce his
stature and humiliate him as often and thoroughly as ever before
(see section 4.4). Sancho Panza is made into the duchess's personal court clown but ultimately emerges victorious through his
exemplary conduct as a governor. The duke and duchess, supposedly the embodiment of society's highest values, are never
motivated by anything more noble than a desire to enjoy as
many laughs as possible, no matter what the cost to others.[20]
The duke enjoys wielding his great power: his motto is that it is
(II, 42, 896) "dulcísima cosa el mandar y ser obedecido" ("so
sweet to command and be obeyed," p. 654).

The character of the duke is best revealed in the Doña
Rodríguez affair. In order not to offend a wealthy business as-
sociate, he allows the daughter of the *dueña* to remain dishon-
ored. When Doña Rodríguez exposes the duke's infamy by revealing the case to Don Quijote, the duke does not act to right
the wrong but prepares a new charade with the aim of having

19. John J. Allen, *Don Quixote: Hero or Fool?*, 1:42–43.
20. "One of the most unattractive aspects of the pranks of the Duke
and Duchess is that they use their noble station, which should carry
with it a sense of serious responsibility and concern for others, to deceive Don Quixote, Sancho, and Teresa into accepting their jokes at
face value. Instead of following the precept of 'noblesse oblige,' the
Duke and Duchess practice deception based on an inner sense of their
own superiority and their right to exploit others for their own pleasure"; Margaret Church, *Don Quixote: The Knight of La Mancha*, p. 138.
Another characteristic of the ducal pair is their idleness; see Luis Pérez,
"La ociosidad-muerte en el *Quijote*," p. 359.

Don Quijote defeated on the field of battle. The duke's fun is spoiled by the lackey Tosilos, who actually falls in love with and offers to marry the attractive daughter, and by the latter, who declares (II, 56, 1010) that she would rather be the "mujer legítima de un lacayo que no amiga y burlada de un caballero" ("lawful wife of a lackey than the jilted lover of a gentleman," p. 737). The duke, doubly angry because his entertainment has been ruined and he has been disobeyed, prevents the marriage from taking place. The girl takes the veil while her mother, after many years of service to the duchess, is either dismissed or resigns in protest and returns to Castile. Tosilos is placated by being assigned further responsibilities in the service of the duke; he is last seen delivering mail for his master, apparently not too distraught at what has happened (II, 67, 1090).[21]

While destroying the lives of those who are genuinely wronged and in distress, the miserable duke rises to the defense of a pseudo–*doncella menesterosa*, defending Altisidora's claim of theft against Don Quijote (and showing that he is still resentful of Tosilos's actions) by challenging him (II, 58, 1014): "Volvedle las ligas; si no, yo os desafío a mortal batalla, sin tener temor que malandrines encantadores me vuelvan ni muden el rostro, como han hecho en el de Tosilos mi lacayo, el que entró con vos en batalla" ("Return her garters, or else I defy you to mortal combat, for I am not afraid of wicked enchanters changing or altering my features as they changed those of my lackey Tosilos, who did battle with you," p. 740). This ironic juxtaposition provides the best single illustration of the duke's hypocrisy, meanness, and human insensitivity. When he and the duchess have

---

21. Rosales's reaction to the plight of those whose lives are ruined by the duke is interesting. He says (*Libertad*, 2:336–39) that he does not understand the reintroduction of Tosilos in II, 67, that this is disconcerting to the reader, that it would have been more in keeping with the character of the duke and his wife (see next note) to have treated Doña Rodríguez and her daughter in a better way, and that their lives should not have turned out so tragically. It is easier to sustain one's critical prejudice by citing Cervantes's shortcomings (Miguel de Unamuno is, of course, the ultimate example of this, but see also Carlos Varo in Chapter 3, note 19, and Chapter 4, note 38) than to accept the validity of the text as written and to reevaluate the moral stature of the characters.

Don Quijote and Sancho brought back to their palace for more fun with Altisidora, they become even more repugnant to the reader.

Echoing the words of the majordomo who admires Sancho's deeds as governor (II, 49, 949)—"Cada día se veen cosas nuevas en el mundo: las burlas se vuelven en veras y los burladores se hallan burlados" ("Every day we see something new in this world; jokes become realities, and the jokers find the tables turned on them," p. 692)—Cide Hamete Benengeli, while expressing his feelings in his own inadequate terms of *tontos* ("fools") and *locos* ("crazy people"), is critical of the ducal pair (II, 70, 1110): "Y dice más Cide Hamete: que tiene para sí ser tan locos los burladores como los burlados, y que no estaban los duques dos dedos de parecer tontos, pues tanto ahínco ponían en burlarse de dos tontos" ("And Cide Hamete says, moreover, that personally he considers the concocters of the joke as crazy as the victims of it, and that the duke and duchess came very close to looking like fools themselves when they took such pains to make fun of a pair of fools," p. 810). Though the judgment of the Arabic historian is, as we have seen repeatedly, by no means always reliable, in this case he seems to be essentially correct.[22]

----

22. The most eloquent dissenter to this opinion has been Rosales, who credits the duke and duchess with a generous and quixotic effort to create for Don Quijote a "comedia de la felicidad" ("comedy of happiness"), that is, a situation in which the knight's fondest dreams become reality. See the section "Somos de la madera de los sueños" in *Libertad*, 2:9–90. For Rosales, what the duke and duchess do to Don Quijote is hardly different from what Fernando, Cardenio, the priest, the barber, and others did previously and what Don Antonio Moreno and others will do later; he concludes (p. 81): "Así, pues, todos los personajes de la novela burlan, traban, golpean a Don Quijote. Este es su sino y su destino. No sé por qué razón hay que arrojar a los Duques del paraíso de la crítica y mantener en él a los demás" ("Therefore, all the characters of the novel mock, shackle, beat Don Quijote. This is his fate and his destiny. I do not know why it is necessary to expel the duke and duchess from the paradise of criticism and to keep the rest in it"). As I have attempted to demonstrate throughout, these characters deserve the same condemnation that has been traditionally accorded the duke and duchess. For a review of critical opinion concerning the ducal pair, see Rosales, *Libertad*, 2:13–16.

The problem with the duke and duchess, with Sansón Carrasco and with most of the other characters in part II is that
they are not responding to the reality of Don Quijote in the
second part, but to the original Don Quijote of part I, or, more
specifically, of the first half of part I. Had the Don Quijote of
the earliest adventures encountered a knight like the ones played
by Sansón, or had he been presented with the opportunity to act
out the roles assigned to him at the duke's palace, he would not
have had to expend so much energy transforming reality and
defending his transformations. But by the time that reality begins to conform to his original concept of a world governed by
chivalry, a process that begins with the priest and Dorotea in
Sierra Morena (see section 3.1), Don Quijote himself no longer
sustains that vision. In part II, the world of chivalry is thrust
back at Don Quijote again and again in spite of his inability to
respond with any real vigor. The use of that hallmark of Don
Quijote's chivalric world, archaism, illustrates the point with
clarity. In part II, Don Quijote uses archaism only six times,
while other characters use it fourteen times: Sancho Panza, seven
times; Sansón Carrasco, twice; and the duke, the Countess Trifaldi, Altisidora, Doña Rodríguez, and the duchess, once each
(see Appendix B).

The most important secondary characters of part II share with
the critics discussed in I, 20, the inability to see the Don Quijote
who stands before them; they continue to react to the Don Quijote of the early chapters of part I. The windmill principle applies to the fictional readers of the novel as well as it does to the
real ones. Cervantes has managed to merge reality and fiction
on still another level.

It is unfortunate that the characters of Cervantes's part II have
to meet the real Don Quijote rather than the apocryphal one of
Alonso Fernández de Avellaneda. It is the latter figure who most
conforms to the Don Quijote whom everyone recalls from part
I.[23] Avellaneda's protagonist is a raving madman who changes
his own identity, transforms reality, talks constantly in archaism,

23. Anthony Close observes that Alonso Fernández de Avellaneda's
Don Quijote presents a "case of arrested development: Don Quixote's
psychology arrested at the point which Cervantes reached in Part I,
Chapter 5"; *The Romantic Approach to "Don Quixote,"* p. 25.

and, in general, recalls the Don Quijote of I, 1–10.[24] As a whole, seventeenth-century readers—Avellaneda, Sansón Carrasco, the duke, and the duchess—were incapable of perceiving more than the grossest comic elements that were dominant in the earliest chapters of the novel. When Don Quijote asks Sansón Carrasco (II, 3, 598) which of his exploits are "las que más se ponderan" ("made the most of," p. 439) in Cide Hamete's history, Sansón responds with a list consisting of the windmills (I, 8); the fulling mills (I, 20); the armies of sheep (I, 18); the dead body (I, 19); the galley slaves (I, 22); the friars (I, 8); and the Biscayan (I, 8–9). It is by no means without relevance that all these adventures take place in the first—and most comic—half of part I.[25]

24. These elements are precisely those stressed by Martín de Riquer, in his introduction to the apocryphal part II, as being characteristic of Avellaneda's protagonist; see *Don Quijote*, pp. lxxxviii–xcvii and lvii–lix. In Avellaneda's part II, Don Quijote uses over one hundred archaisms in some twenty speeches, at times in ridiculous concentration (for example, I, 50–51, 99–101; II, 221–22, 232). Although there is a marked decrease in frequency of archaic speech in Avellaneda's character, there is no accompanying reconciliation with reality as the work progresses.

25. The novelists of eighteenth-century England who were inspired by Cervantes also looked relatively little past the first half of part I. Henry Fielding's two Cervantine novels, *Joseph Andrews* (1742) and *Tom Jones* (1749), draw particularly on the inn scenes of I, 16–17, and on minor characters such as Maritornes as well as on the figures of Don Quijote, Sancho Panza, and Rocinante. Parson Adams in *Joseph Andrews* is one of the most consciously quixotic characters in literature, even though he appears simplistic and mechanical (most reminiscent of the earliest Don Quijote) in comparison with Cervantes's protagonist. When Tobias Smollett's Sir Launcelot Greaves tries to explain to another character why he is unlike Don Quijote, he says, "I have not yet encountered a windmill for a giant; nor mistaken the public house for a magnificent castle: neither do I believe this gentleman to be the constable; nor that worthy practitioner to be master Elizabat, the surgeon recorded in Amadis de Gaul; nor you to be the enchanter Alquife, nor any other sage of history or romance.—I see and distinguish objects as they are discerned and described by other men"; *Sir Launcelot Greaves*, ed. David Evans (London: Oxford University Press, 1973), pp. 12–13. Note that these adventures and characters appear in the first half of part I of *Don Quijote*. In his novel *The Spiritual Quixote*, a satire on Methodism, Richard Graves includes an "Essay on Quixotism" in which he states that Don Quijote "not only mistook wind-mills for giants, and

Most of these generalizations also apply to other secondary characters in the second part of the novel, especially to Don Antonio Moreno. Don Quijote's urban host is a second-rate copy of the duke who laments to Sansón Carrasco (II, 65, 1082) that the latter has erred "en querer volver cuerdo al más gracioso loco que hay" ("in trying to bring the most amusing madman . . . back to his senses"), seeing in Don Quijote not his humanity but only "el gusto que da con sus desvaríos" ("the enjoyment his delusions give," p. 789).

Doña Rodríguez is an interesting and singular case. Her comic role as defender of the institution of *dueñas* aside, she is not the most intelligent or perceptive person in the novel. Somehow, in spite of all she sees going on around her, she manages to believe that Don Quijote is an authentic knight-errant, a true righter of wrongs, and comes to him with the bold proposition that he attempt to restore her daughter's honor. This is only the second time in the work that a woman in genuine need has appealed to him as a knight-errant,[26] and again Don Quijote fails to respond properly, ignoring her request as he prepares to leave the palace. Only her dramatic appeal in the presence of the duke and duchess, carefully rehearsed and couched in the classic terms of the knight's chivalric mission (II, 52, 977)—"enderezándole el tuerto que le tienen *fecho*" ("right the wrong that has been done to her," p. 713)—and stated in abundant archaism (*fecha, fija, habedes, fecho, queredes*),[27] forces Don Quijote to take some action.

---

an harmless flock of sheep for an army of Pagans; but challenged an honest farmer to mortal combat for correcting his own servant, and set at liberty some prisoners who by legal authority had been condemned to the galleys"; *The Spiritual Quixote*, ed. Clarence Tracy (London: Oxford University Press, 1967), p. 39. Again, all these adventures occur between I, 8, and I, 22, of Cervantes's novel. Although the direct and profound influence of Cervantes on eighteenth-century novelists is universally recognized and frequently written about, a comprehensive, detailed, scholarly study of the exact nature of that influence has not yet been written.

26. The other time was in I, 44, when Juan Palomeque's wife and daughter called on him to help the besieged innkeeper (see section 3.3).

27. Doña Rodríguez undercuts the stylistic effectiveness of the first part of her chivalric speech by descending in the second half into linguistic comedy with the accumulation of five words accented on the

As already described, Doña Rodríguez's desperate attempt to achieve justice for her daughter ends in absolute failure and in the dissolution of her family. Nowhere else in the novel does Don Quijote have the opportunity to do so much good for such obviously deserving people. His failure and the triumph of the duke make an eloquent comment on social reality: the needs of institutionalized power are served before justice is done. When the idealist who defends beauty or truth meets the powerful, rich, vacuous representatives of society's respectable standards (the merchants of Toledo in part I, the duke in part II), there is seldom any question of who will win.

I have accepted throughout that the priest and the barber, Sansón Carrasco and the duke, and all the others who manipulate and laugh at Don Quijote do indeed represent the societal norm. I also take note of the syllogism set up by Oscar Mandel ("That Don Quixote stands in some kind of opposition to the norm, all critics agree. It follows that if Don Quixote is the hero—if his departure from the norm is laudable—the norm must be presented as shabby")[28] in order to affirm that Don Quijote is in fact more laudable, or, at least, less objectionable, than the characters who represent the norm. Without directly addressing the question of intentional fallacy, I would add that Cervantes himself would seem to share, at least to some extent, this criticism of the norm. It seems significant that the terms used to describe the priest and Sansón Carrasco are "gran tracista" ("very clever") and "de condición maliciosa y amigo de donaires y de burlas" ("of a mischievous disposition and a love of fun and jokes," p. 438), while Sancho Panza is accurately described by his master (II, 43, 906) as possessing a "buen natural" ("good natural instincts," p. 661), a key phrase appearing frequently in Cervantes's works to indicate positive qualities. In Avellaneda's *Don Quijote*, those who perpetrate the practical jokes on the knight tend to be men of "buen gusto" ("good taste") and obviously—for Avellaneda—enlightened and admi-

---

antepenultimate syllable: *escurriésedes, desafiásedes, rústico, indómito, hiciésedes.*

28. Oscar Mandel, "The Function of the Norm in *Don Quixote*," p. 158.

rable representatives of the best society has to offer.[29] If we again refer to the concept of comparative characterization, we perceive that the final balance is in favor of Don Quijote and Sancho Panza over the priest, Sansón Carrasco, and the others. Unlike his rival Avellaneda, Cervantes seems to share this perception.

5.4 Miguel de Cervantes versus Cide Hamete Benengeli

The narrative structure of most of part I of *Don Quijote* appears to be relatively straightforward and uncomplicated.

1. After I, 8, the Moorish historian Cide Hamete Benengeli records the events in the lives of Don Quijote and Sancho Panza.
2. The historian's Arabic manuscript is then translated into Spanish by an unnamed *morisco*.
3. The Spanish version is edited for the reader by Miguel de Cervantes.

That the editor is in fact Cervantes is frequently questioned by many of the best readers of the book, who would have the final editor be the unnamed and never identified "segundo autor" mentioned in 8, 97, or perhaps an even more obscure "ultimate author."[30] I find no alternative, however, to agreeing with Edward C. Riley that "for practical purposes," the author of the final, edited text that we read is Miguel de Cervantes.[31] No one, to my knowledge, doubts that the *yo* of the prologue who relates himself to the character and text by claiming to be not the "padre" ("father," that is, the original author) but the "padrastre" ("stepfather," that is, the editor), and who tells the story of being visited by a friend while pondering the problem of writing a prologue for his book is anyone other than the person referred to on the title page where it says "compuesto por [com-

29. On this last point, see Stephen Gilman, *Cervantes y Avellaneda*, pp. 131–32.
30. See Ruth S. El Saffar, *Distance and Control in "Don Quixote." A Study in Narrative Technique*, pp. 30–31. See also George Haley, "The Narrator in *Don Quijote*: Maese Pedro's Puppet Show," pp. 146–48; and F. W. Locke, "*El sabio encantador*: The Author of *Don Quixote*," pp. 47–50.
31. Edward C. Riley, "Three Versions of Don Quixote," p. 808.

posed by] Miguel de Cervantes Saavedra." Since there is no evidence to indicate an alternative, the first-person editor who appears occasionally in part I and very prominently in his search for Cide Hamete's manuscript in chapter 9 should be considered the same person who narrated the prologue. The only passage that most seriously clouds the issue is the previously cited final paragraph in chapter 8 where the "autor" interrupts his narration because he has depleted his source material, although the "segundo autor" refuses to believe that no more material is available. The passage is somewhat confusing because both *autor* and *segundo autor* could conceivably refer to the writer of the text that we are reading,[32] but surely the latter term is in this context little more than a euphemism for *yo*, the *yo* who is so prominent in the following chapter.[33]

32. The same ambiguity and uncertainty of attribution is found in I, 20, 203, when the "autor desta historia" ("author of this history") who concludes that Sancho Panza is an Old Christian could be either the author or the editor, and in I, 22, 587, where the "autor desta historia" most logically seems to refer to the author of the final text, that is, the "editor," Miguel de Cervantes. The same problem exists in the final narrative paragraphs of I, 52, 557, 558, where the references to "el autor desta historia" and "el fidedigno autor desta nueva y jamás vista historia" ("trustworthy author of this new and unparalleled history," p. 402) probably refer to the editor rather than to the original author. Riley discusses Cervantes's casual use of various terms to refer to his own narrative presence in the novel in *Cervantes' Theory of the Novel*, p. 207.

33. It is the nature of the first-person fictional narrator to reveal his identity. When the narrator is not a character in the work or an identified fictional editor, he is assumed to be the person whose name is on the book's cover. This does not, of course, mean that it is a literal truth that Cervantes had a friend with whom he carried on the conversation recorded in the prologue (pp. 12–18) or that he literally searched through the streets of Toledo for the book's original manuscript (I, 9, 100–102). The Cervantes who edits and narrates *Don Quijote* may be fictionalized, but he most certainly is Cervantes; see Allen, *Hero or Fool*, 1:11–12. The historian–translator/editor device is, of course, common to the romances of chivalry; see Daniel Eisenberg, "The Pseudo-historicity of the Romances of Chivalry," pp. 253–59. Many modern novels also use this type of narrative framework. One that particularly recalls Cervantes is Alessandro Manzoni's *I promessi sposi* (Florence: Adriano Salani, 1909), which does not have the intermediary "translator" but does on a small scale evoke the ironic and complex tone of *Don Quijote*. The *io* who discusses his manuscript sources in the author's introduc-

There are a few noteworthy indications in the text that there could exist a fourth level of narration. The most significant is a reference (II, 44, 906) to "el propio original desta historia" ("the true original of this history," p. 661), which gives rise to the theory of F. W. Locke that there must have been an even more remote source for Cide Hamete Benengeli's manuscript.[34] This passage and others that can be read to make the Moorish writer a nonomniscient reporter[35] are provocative, but the possible multiplication of layers of narration does not alter the basic thrust of my presentation. While the narrative structure of *Don Quijote* is not always consistent or clear, the trilevel author–translator–editor relationship remains the basis for a discussion of Cervantes's narrative technique.

There are only a few hints of the editor's tampering with his material, the best example of which is the statement (I, 9, 102) that Don Quijote's squire is called both Panza and Zancas, "que con estos dos sobrenombres le llama algunas veces la historia" ("for by these two surnames the history several times calls him," p. 67), after which he is only called Panza, all citations of "Zancas" having presumably been regularized by the editor.[36] In the same passage, Cervantes notes that there were "otras algunas

tion (p. 6)—"Ma, quando io avrò durata l'eroica fatica di trascriver questa storia da questo dilavato e graffiato autografo, e l'avrò data, come si suol dire, alla luce, si troverà poi chi duri la fatica di leggerla?" ("But when I've had the heroic patience to transcribe this story from this scratched and faded manuscript, and brought it to light, as the saying goes, will there be anyone found then with enough patience to read it?"; *The Betrothed*, trans. Archibald Colquhoun [London: Dent, 1956], p. xxiv)—and who interrupts the narration on dozens of occasions in order to stress the work's historicity, comment on his sources, and so on (p. 11)—"il nome di questa, nè il casato del personaggio, non si trovan nel manoscritto, nè a questo luogo nè altrove" ("the manuscript does not give the name of the village or the surname of our character, here or later," p. 2)—is not considered by any critic with whom I am familiar as anyone other than Manzoni. It is not surprising that this device should be most readily found in historical novels.

34. Locke, "*El sabio encantador,*" p. 54.

35. Colbert I. Nepaulsingh, "La aventura de los narradores del *Quijote,*" pp. 515–16.

36. See Robert Alter, *Partial Magic: The Novel as a Self-conscious Genre,* p. 9.

menudencias . . . de poca importancia y que no hacen al caso a la verdadera relación de la historia" ("some other trifling particulars . . . of slight importance and have nothing to do with the faithful telling of the story") and which he has presumably edited out.

Cervantes intervenes occasionally to comment on his work and on the author. Most of the references to Cide Hamete are complimentary; he is described (I, 16, 158) as "muy curioso y muy puntual" ("of great scrupulousness and accuracy," p. 107) and (I, 27, 297) as "sabio y atentado" ("sage and sagacious," p. 207), and his text is regularly praised for its veracity, attention to detail, and historicity. But from the start, Cervantes also begins to exploit some of the comic possibilities that accompany his author. When he first discovers the manuscript (I, 9, 102), he laments that the author is Arabic, "siendo muy propio de los de aquella nación ser mentirosos" ("since lying is very common among those of that nation," p. 67). Then, after noting (p. 103) that historians should be "puntuales, verdaderos y no nada apasionados" ("exact, truthful, and wholly free from passion")— essentially the qualities praised in Cide Hamete—he eschews responsibility for any error in the story: "y si algo bueno en ella faltare, para mí tengo que fue por culpa del galgo de su autor" ("if any quality is lacking, I maintain it is the fault of its hound of an author," p. 68). But if the editor first undercuts his historian's authority and reliability by describing him as a lying dog of a Moor, he further subtly reduces his stature when he suppresses a passage by Cide Hamete in I, 16, on the grounds that hearsay evidence has it that the supposedly illustrious historian is in some fashion related to the brutish muleteer from Arévalo with whom Don Quijote fights in that chapter (p. 158): "y aun quieren decir que era algo pariente suyo" ("and they even say was in some degree a relation of his," p. 107), a comment that the editor recalls shortly afterward (I, 22, 220) when he describes Cide Hamete as an "autor arábigo y manchego" ("Arab and Manchegan author," p. 151).

The longest passage in which it is clearly the editor and not the historian who is speaking is contained in the opening paragraph of I, 28, where (p. 298) the praise for the protagonist and the defensive commentary on the "verdadera historia" and the "cuentos y episodios della" ("tales and episodes contained in it," p. 209) are not contained in the original Arabic manuscript but are remarks made by the editor. The shift back to the translation of the historical text is signaled by the phrase "la . . . historia . . . cuenta que" ("the . . . history . . . relates that"), which is in fact a variant of a standard formula (significantly, of Arabic origin) for appealing to an authority by citing or paraphrasing that authority's words.[37]

The form of this passage, as will be seen in more detail later, is crucial. It cannot be the author who refers to "la historia" or who says "dice la historia." Cide Hamete Benengeli, as author of "la historia" cannot logically cite his own words. Only the translator or the editor, who stand apart from the text and follow it chronologically, can refer to it or to its author. The formulaic expression "dice la historia que" provides our best clue in the effort to separate the narrative voices of the author and the editor.

After the slightly confusing and conflicting evidence sometimes presented in the earliest chapters when Cervantes has to rely for his information on various sources, from I, 9, until the end of the first part, the author, Cide Hamete Benengeli, presents a relatively straightforward and reliable account of events. The *morisco* translator is presumably reasonably accurate. The editor, Cervantes, once or twice casts doubt on his author but more often praises him and his work. The distinct impression left with the reader at the end of I, 52, when Cervantes, inspired by the rumor of a third sally but unaware of what is yet to come, sets out in search of more manuscript material, is one of confidence in the book's narrative framework.

Cide Hamete Benengeli's expanded role in part II of *Don Quijote* should be readily apparent to the reader; his name alone appears over six times more frequently in the second part.[38] But it

37. Raymond S. Willis, Jr., *The Phantom Chapters of the "Quijote,"* pp. 100–102.
38. In the index to Riquer's edition of *Don Quijote* (p. 1154), Cide Hamete Benengeli's name is listed as appearing only five times in part I and thirty-three times in part II. El Saffar estimates that he "appears at least a hundred times" in part II and that this increased presence is due

is the quality, not the quantity, of his appearance in the work that is important. The Moor is a far more unreliable narrator— even to the point of lying—while, at the same time, he is oblivious to changes in his characters, especially Don Quijote. His editor, Cervantes, is quite aware of these shortcomings on the part of the author and reacts by making Cide Hamete an object of ridicule.

John J. Allen first discussed the implications of the dialectic established between Cide Hamete Benengeli and Cervantes.[39] Helena Percas de Ponseti has recognized the importance of Allen's study,[40] but James A. Parr and Ruth S. El Saffar have expressed serious objection to the idea of separating the author and the editor.[41] El Saffar specifically laments that Allen "does not show us how to distinguish Cide Hamete's voice from Cervantes'."[42] I suggest that the main fault with Allen's article is that it does not go far enough. A reader's perception of an author can be directly determined by an editor. The editor can ignore, mask, eliminate, or otherwise soften any possible errors or inconsistencies on the part of the author, but he or she can also call attention to and comment on them. Cervantes does the latter.[43]

---

to "the need for distancing and clarification"; *Distance and Control*, p. 83.

39. John J. Allen, "The Narrators, the Reader and Don Quijote," pp. 201–12, subsequently incorporated into *Hero or Fool*, 2:3–15.

40. Helena Percas de Ponseti, "Sobre el enigma de 'los dos Cervantes,'" p. 10.

41. James A. Parr, "Aesthetic Distance in the *Quixote*," pp. 191–97; and Ruth S. El Saffar, "Concerning Change, Continuity, and Other Critical Matters: A Reading of John J. Allen's *Don Quixote: Hero or Fool? Part II*," pp. 241–46.

42. El Saffar, "Concerning Change," p. 243.

43. Riley has noted some of Cide Hamete's shortcomings and then has added this proviso ("Three Versions," p. 809): "But our principal doubts about Benengeli's reliability as a historian are planted in us by what Cervantes says about him on certain occasions." Mia I. Gerhardt, generally a careful and discerning reader of Cervantes's novel, completely fails to see the irony in certain statements by and about Cide Hamete Benengeli in part II. She says, for example, that he is presented (*Don Quijote, la vie et les livres*, p. 27) "comme un historien très scrupuleux" ("as a very scrupulous historian") and that after Don Quijote's comment about lying Moors in II, 3, Cide Hamete (p. 33) "N'est plus déprécié nulle part" ("is no longer deprecated anywhere").

In the remainder of this section, I discuss Cide Hamete's increased role in part II, point out many of his lies and errors of judgment, show how Cervantes directs the reader to laugh at him, and comment on how the historian's new role is related to the reader's perception of Don Quijote.

In part I, the only direct commentary on the story that can be attributed to Cide Hamete Benengeli is the marginal note on Dulcinea that causes the *morisco*'s laughter and reveals to Cervantes that he has discovered the manuscript for which he has been searching (9, 101). In part II, his interruptions and concurrent involvement with the work and the characters are found throughout: he praises Allah as Don Quijote's third sally is begun (8, 630); he would prefer not to narrate the protagonist's unbelievable madness when he sees the peasant girl whom Sancho calls Dulcinea (10, 642–43); he discusses his dilemma in properly describing Don Quijote's adventure with the lion (17, 702–3); he comments on the events Don Quijote claimed took place in the cave of Montesinos (24, 761–62); he takes an oath like a Christian (27, 788); he comments on the structure of his work as he is about to separate knight and squire (44, 906–7); he digresses on the subject of poverty (44, 911–12); he promises to relate an adventure in a later chapter (47, 937); and he makes a parenthetical aside during the Doña Rodríguez adventure (45, 941). In addition to these primarily comic appearances (most of which are discussed in more detail later), on dozens of occasions Cervantes calls attention to Cide Hamete simply by mentioning his name or by referring explicitly to "la historia" (particularly by using the formulaic "dice la historia que").

In the first part of the novel, Cide Hamete Benengeli commits only one judgmental error, a relatively minor inconsistency, when he makes two conflicting statements about Don Quijote's status after drinking the balm of Fierabrás (I, 17, 168, 171; see section 2.4). In part II, there are at least ten times when the increasingly unreliable historian either lies,[44] makes conflicting and inconsistent statements, or clearly misjudges his characters.

44. Recall that in part I Cervantes was worried about the fact that the historian on whom he had to depend was a lying Moor (I, 9, 102–3). In part II, the characters take up the same refrain: Don Quijote is disconsolate over the idea that his historian is Moorish and therefore a

1. After defeating Sansón Carrasco dressed as the Caballero de los Espejos, Don Quijote is twice described as proud and haughty (15, 685; 16, 687), but his actions and statements readily demonstrate the inappropriateness of these epithets (see section 4.3).

2. Cide Hamete Benengeli's altisonant statements in preparation for the encounter between Don Quijote and the lion (17, 702–3) are clearly inconsistent with the "niñerías" and "bravatas" ("silly bravado," p. 515) that follow.[45]

3. After the knight's descent into the cave of Montesinos, Cide Hamete suggests that the scene described by the protagonist must either be the truth or a conscious lie (24, 762), but the reader knows that the whole thing was a dream.

4. Perhaps the historian's most spectacular lie is his statement (31, 813) that when Don Quijote entered the duke's palace "aquél fue el primer día que de todo en todo conoció y creyó ser caballero andante verdadero, y no fantástico" ("this was the first time that he thoroughly felt and believed himself to be a real knight-errant and not an imaginary one," p. 595). The knight's chivalric trajectory as traced throughout this work, as well as the scene that immediately follows this statement, leave the reader no choice but to reject Cide Hamete's observation (see section 4.4).

5. One of the most obvious of the Moor's deceptions appears when he discusses the name of the Countess Trifaldi (38, 868): "y así dice Benengeli que fue verdad, y que de su propio apellido se llama *la condesa Lobuna*" ("And Benengeli says it was so, and that by her right name she was called the Countess Lobuna," p. 534). The whole Trifaldi adventure is no more than an elaborate sham in which the duke's majordomo plays the part of the countess.

6. In exactly the same category is the supposed farmer from Miguel Turra who is described in narration (47, 934) as "de muy buena presencia, . . . bueno y buena alma" ("a nice-looking man . . . an honest fellow and a good soul," p. 682), and who turns out to be a "bellacón" ("rogue") playing a role in order to make Sancho Panza look ridiculous (p. 937).

7. When Don Quijote departs from the duke's castle (58,

congenital liar (3, 597); Don Quijote and Sancho Panza specifically criticize the work of Cide Hamete (3, 602, and 4, 606, respectively).

45. See Allen, *Hero or Fool*, 2:9–11, for relevant observations concerning items 2, 3, 5, 6, and 10 in this list.

1015), it is stated that "los espíritus se le renovaban para proseguir de nuevo el asumpto de sus caballerías" ("he felt ready
to take up the pursuit of chivalry once more with renewed
vigor," p. 741), but it is clear from his conduct and statements
during the encounter with the four chivalric religious statues
that this is not true (see section 4.5).

8. Don Quijote is described as "hueco y pomposo"
("puffed-up and conceited") during the dinner in his honor in
Barcelona (62, 1054), but this is inconsistent with the presentation of the character (see section 4.5).

9. Cide Hamete's claim that Don Quijote is plagued more
than ever (67, 1091) by "pensamientos" ("reflections," p. 796)
after his defeat in Barcelona is not borne out either by the
knight's actions or by the historian's own pattern of statements about thoughts throughout part II (see section 4.5).

10. Demonstrably untrue is Cide Hamete's claim (71, 1119)
that the reason why Don Quijote sees an inn and not a castle
on the way back to the village is that "después que le vencie-
ron, con más juicio en todas las cosas discurría" ("ever since
he had been vanquished, he talked more rationally about
everything," p. 816). Don Quijote has never taken an inn for
a castle in part II, a fact that the historian himself noted on
two previous occasions (24, 768, and 59, 1029).

In part II, Cide Hamete lies and purposefully misleads the
reader. He also makes a series of observations about the characters, particularly Don Quijote, that are inconsistent with other
facts in the narration.[46] As stated earlier (section 4.3), Cide Hamete is a better historian than psychologist. Cervantes is inferentially aware of the increasing unreliability of his narrator and,

46. Allen also notes examples of the historian's "insensitivity" toward Don Quijote; *Hero or Fool*, 2:11. To Allen's observations I would
add the statement in II, 72, when knight and squire are on their way
home (pp. 1125–26), that they traveled for a day and night "sin suce-
derles cosa digna de contarse, si no fue que en ella acabó Sancho su
tarea" ("nor did anything worth mentioning happen to them, unless it
was that in the course of the night Sancho finished up his task," p. 821),
that is, that Sancho finally completed his lashes and thus fulfilled the
conditions for disenchanting Dulcinea. To pass off the accomplishment
of the task that has most preoccupied Don Quijote since II, 10, as a
mere afterthought is, to say the least, "insensitive."

although he continues to praise the veracity and accuracy of the narration, he offers a long series of comments on the Moor that ironically praise him and his work, subtly reduce his stature, or criticize and ridicule him outright.

The most frequent and obvious way in which Cervantes draws critical attention to Cide Hamete is by pointing out what the historian fails to say or what he omits:

1. "fundándose no sé si en astrología judiciaria que él se sabía, puesto que la historia no lo declara" (II, 8, 631) ("building, perhaps, upon some judicial astrology that he may have known, though the history says nothing about it," p. 463).

2. "venían tres labradoras sobre tres pollinos, o pollinas, que el autor no lo declara" (II, 10, 646) ("coming . . . three peasant girls on three colts or fillies; the author does not make the point clear," p. 474).[47]

3. "con cinco calderos, o seis, de agua, que en la cantidad de los calderos hay alguna diferencia" (II, 18, 709) ("with five or six buckets of water (for as to the number of buckets there is some dispute)," p. 520).[48]

4. "le tomó la noche entre unas espesas encinas o alcornoques; que en esto no guarda la puntualidad Cide Hamete que en otras cosas suele" (II, 60, 1037) ("he was overtaken by night in a thicket of oak or cork trees; for on this point Cide Hamete is not as precise as he usually is on other matters," p. 756).

5. "arrimado a un tronco de una haya o de un alcornoque—que Cide Hamete Benengeli no distingue el árbol que era—" (II, 68, 1100) ("propped up against the trunk of a beech or a cork tree—for Cide Hamete does not specify what kind of tree it was—," p. 802).

Other lengthier and more noteworthy editorial commentary

47. The manner in which the identity of the animals ridden by the three women is handled not only casts doubt on the reliability of the historian but also impugns that of the editor (see section 4.3).

48. In this passage, it appears as though Cervantes is comparing Cide Hamete's text against others and notes the discrepancy in numbers. But whether the editor's comment is read so as to blame the inconsistency on Cide Hamete or to indicate that the latter's opinion is merely one of several possibilities, the effect is essentially the same as that produced by the other passages cited in this list.

on the Moorish historian's work can also be found throughout part II. In a long aside in chapter 12, Cervantes appeals to extra-textual evidence to support a passing reference by Cide Hamete to the friendship between Rocinante and Sancho's donkey (p. 662): "que hay fama, por tradición de padres a hijos, que el autor desta verdadera historia hizo particulares capítulos della . . . Digo que dicen que dejó el autor escrito que" ("that it is handed down by tradition from father to son. The author of this true history devoted some special chapters to it . . . I may add that they say the author left it on record," pp. 484–85). His defense of the historian's use of human analogies (p. 663)—"Y no le parezca a alguno que anduvo el autor algo fuera camino" ("Let no one fancy that the author was at all astray," p. 485)—only underscores the burlesque tone of the whole passage.

Comparable in tone, but considerably reduced in scope, is the paragraph in II, 18, in which the *morisco* translator omits Cide Hamete's lengthy description of the home of Don Diego de Miranda (p. 708) "porque no venían bien con el propósito principal de la historia" ("as they were not in harmony with the main purpose of the story"), to which is appended the editorial judgment that the history "más tiene su fuerza en la verdad que en las frías digresiones" ("the strong point of which is truth rather than dull digressions," p. 519). Thus translator and editor concur in criticizing the historian's methodology, implying somehow that there is a lack of truth in the excised descriptive passage.

In the same spirit as the passages just discussed is a series of eight very important comic chapter introductions in which Cervantes engages in entertaining commentary on Cide Hamete Benengeli and his narration. In these, as much as in all other previously discussed passages combined, Cervantes brilliantly exploits the comic possibilities inherent in his historian/narrator. The structure of the passages is always identical: the opening paragraph of the chapter contains some sort of comic editorial commentary that lessens the stature of Cide Hamete Benengeli; the end of the critical passage is signaled by the use of the formulaic expression "cuenta la historia" or some variant of that phrase; narration is then resumed with no discernible carry-over of the comic tone.[49] This structure was used once in the first part (28, 298, cited earlier), but none of the mild humor in the paragraph was directed at the Moorish historian.

There are eight chapters of part II in which the technique of opposing Cervantes and Cide Hamete Benengeli is used.

1. Chapter 5 begins with the translator's complaint that Sancho speaks (p. 611) "con otro estilo del que se podía prometer de su corto ingenio" ("in a style unlike that which might have been expected from his limited intelligence," p. 447). This comment is dutifully passed on by the editor in a literally parenthetical introductory statement that ends with the words "y así, prosiguió diciendo" ("he went off as follows," p. 448). Thus the *morisco* directly and Cervantes inferentially (both here and in the subsequent parenthetical remarks on pp. 614 and 616) put into doubt the veracity of Cide Hamete's historical narrative. The irony is that Sancho's speech (and, therefore, also the author's narration) is perfectly appropriate; it is the translator's judgment that is questionable (see section 5.2).

2. The first words of chapter 8 (p. 630) are Cide Hamete's enthusiastic "¡Bendito sea el poderoso Alá!" ("Blessed be Allah the all-powerful!," p. 462), which, we are told, is repeated three times, along with an exhortation to enjoy the new exploits of Don Quijote. The final words of the paragraph signal

---

49. Throughout the *Espejo de príncipes y cavalleros*, the "translator/ editor," that is, the author Diego Ortúñez de Calahorra, occasionally comments in the first person on the "history" written by the wizard Artimidoro (assisted by the wizard Lirgandeo). This type of commentary is sometimes found in the opening section of a chapter and generally ends with some variant of "dice la historia que," in a form very similar (except for the general absence of intentional humor) to that used by Cervantes. Particularly noteworthy is the long introductory passage to chapter 38 of book III (*Espejo*, 6:88–92), to which Daniel Eisenberg calls attention as resembling Cervantes's practice in *Don Quijote*; see "*Don Quijote* and the Romances of Chivalry: The Need for a Reexamination," p. 520. While annotating this passage (*Espejo*, 6:89, note 8), Eisenberg notes that a scholarly study of the "traductor independiente" ("independent translator") who comments on the text would be a valuable contribution to our understanding of the romances of chivalry as well as of *Don Quijote*.

the editor's return to the narration: "y así prosigue diciendo" ("he goes on to relate that").

3. At the beginning of chapter 10 (pp. 642–43), it is stated that the author would prefer not to have to record the potentially unbelievable antics of Don Quijote, but he fulfills his duty to record the facts in detail, "sin añadir ni quitar a la historia un átomo de la verdad" ("without adding to the truth of the story or leaving out a jot," p. 471). Cervantes concurs— "y tuvo razón" ("he was right")—and then returns to his text in the first words of the second paragraph: "Y así, prosiguiendo su historia, dice que" ("So, going on with his story, he says that"). In retrospect, after reading the chapter, the reader could object in two ways to the historian's concern. First, Don Quijote's actions are not nearly as unbelievable as was stated: he merely sees the reality of the three peasant women but eventually rejects this evidence in favor of the convincing interpretation of his faithful squire (see section 4.3). Second, the "atoms of truth" alluded to obviously do not include such details as the type and gender of the animals that the three women ride.[50]

4. Chapter 24 opens with the translator's faithful transcription of Cide Hamete's marginal note about what Don Quijote claimed to have seen in the cave of Montesinos (pp. 761–62) before continuing with the narration: "Y luego prosigue, diciendo" ("And then he goes on to say," p. 558). As discussed earlier, the historian's suggestion that Don Quijote is either telling the truth about what literally happened or is consciously telling a lie is unacceptable in the face of evidence that the experience was a dream. Furthermore, the statement about what Don Quijote might have said about the episode on his deathbed dissolves into ambiguous hearsay—"puesto que se tiene por cierto que . . . dicen que se retrató della" ("some maintain, however, that . . . [they] say that he retracted")—and is absurdly meaningless.[51]

5. Cide Hamete Benengeli enters into chapter 27 with the

50. See Howard Mancing, "Dulcinea's Ass: A Note on *Don Quijote*, Part II, Chapter 10," pp. 73–77.

51. Allen has shown that no English translation of the novel has captured all the nuances in this passage; "Cide Hamete's English Translators," pp. 366–67. Ormsby's version is as close as anyone's, but I have had to modify it in order to make it more accurate.

words (p. 788) "Juro como católico cristiano" ("I swear as a Catholic Christian," p. 576). The translator speculates that the Moor does this in order to underscore the truth of what he has to say about Maese Pedro. But the thoughtful reader will realize that such a tacit admission of the superiority of Christianity over the historian's own Muslim beliefs is incongruous. An equally, or more, plausible interpretation of these words is that the Moor is being consciously facetious in employing them; after all, for Muslims, Christians are lying dogs, and to swear like a Christian is to invalidate the oath. But no matter what the oath "means," the passage is both comic and absurd. The first words of the second paragraph are "Dice, pues, que" ("Cide Hamete says, then, that"), and the narration is resumed.

6. Cervantes begins chapter 40 with lavish, though (by this point in the novel) heavily ironic, praise for Cide Hamete (p. 878): "Pinta los pensamientos, descubre las imaginaciones, responde a las tácitas, aclara las dudas, resuelve los argumentos; finalmente, los átomos del más curioso deseo manifiesta" ("He portrays the thoughts, he reveals the fancies, he answers implied questions, clears up doubts, sets objections at rest, and, in a word, makes plain the smallest points the most inquisitive can desire to know," p. 641). Then he addresses a series of ecstatic apostrophes to the four major characters (for by now Cide Hamete Benengeli has acquired the status and personality of a literary character): "¡Oh autor celibérrimo! ¡Oh don Quijote dichoso! "¡Oh Dulcinea famosa! ¡Oh Sancho Panza gracioso! Todos juntos y cada uno de por sí viváis siglos infinitos, para gusto y general pasatiempo de los vivientes" ("O renowned author! O happy Don Quixote! O famous Dulcinea! O witty Sancho Panza! All and each, may you live countless ages for the delight and amusement of the dwellers on earth!"). After this highly comic, mock-emotional outburst, Cervantes signals the return to a translation of the manuscript with the words "Dice, pues, la historia que" ("The history goes on to say that").

7. The first words of chapter 44 represent a brilliantly paradoxical *reductio ad absurdum* in the process of ridiculing the narrative structure of *Don Quijote* (p. 906): "Dicen que en el propio original desta historia se lee que llegando Cide Hamete a escribir este capítulo, no le tradujo su intérprete como él le había escrito" ("They say that in the true original of this his-

tory, as Cide Hamete wrote this chapter—which his interpreter did not translate as he wrote it," pp. 661–62). That Cervantes the editor, who theoretically has the manuscript before
him as he writes, should have to rely on hearsay evidence
("Dicen que") in order to report that while composing this
chapter Cide Hamete wrote that his translator mistranslated
it; that Cervantes would not consult with the translator, presumably working with him all the while, in order to correct
any possible errors; or that the editor and/or translator would
not either affirm or deny the validity of Cide Hamete's complaint all combine to destroy any shred of truthfulness, reliability, or historicity remaining in the presentation of the story.
The remainder of this long paragraph consists of the editor's
sympathetic recounting of the author's sad lament concerning
the frustrating restrictions imposed by his material, which is
also (as was the case in I, 28, 298) a defense against the inevitable criticism of his not following a rectilinear narrative account. The next paragraph opens with a standard formulaic
return to the story: "Y luego prosigue la historia diciendo
que" ("And so he goes on with his story saying that," p.
662).[52]

   8. Chapter 53 begins with a sententious observation by
Cide Hamete on the inevitable march of time, the seriousness
of which is undercut when the historian reverses the order of
the seasons of the year (p. 984): "la primavera sigue al verano,
el verano el estío, el estío al otoño, y el otoño al invierno, y el

52. The reaction of Diego Clemencín to this chapter opening provides a classic example of how literal-minded readers can completely
fail to understand, let alone appreciate, this sort of ironic narrative device (*Don Quijote*, pp. 1765–66, note 1): "Todo esto del principio del
capítulo es una algarabía que no se entiende. Porque ¿cómo podía leerse
en el propio original de la historia que no lo había traducido fielmente
su intérprete? Ni ¿qué tiene que ver esto con la queja que tuvo el moro
de sí mismo por haber tomado entre manos asunto tan seco y estéril?
. . . Resulta de todo, que pudiera muy bien haberse excusado este largo
y difuso preámbulo hasta donde vuelve a tomarse el hilo de la narra-
ción" ("All this from the beginning of the chapter is a gibberish that
cannot be understood. Because, how could it be read in the true original of the history that its interpreter had not faithfully translated it?
Now, what does this have to do with the complaint that the Moor had
about himself for having taken up such a dry and sterile topic? . . . As
a result, this long and diffuse preamble could very easily have been
eliminated, up to the point where the thread of narration is picked up
again").

invierno a la primavera" ("The spring goes looking for summer, the summer the fall, the fall the autumn, the autumn the winter, and the winter the spring," p. 718). Although editors of the novel often cite Covarrubias as proof that *seguir* can sometimes be used in the sense of *perseguir*, "to search for" (note that this meaning is used in the Ormsby translation), it is obvious from the beginning of the next sentence, "Esto dice Cide Hamete, filósofo mahomético," that *seguir* is to be used in its standard meaning of "to follow." That Cide Hamete Benengeli is now a Mohammedan philosopher and that he has everything backward can be considered a synthesis of his role in part II of *Don Quijote*. After his commentary on the author's statement, Cervantes, for the only time, simply returns to the narration of events without using "dice la historia."[53]

Very similar in effect to these chapter openings are the titles, presumably written by Cide Hamete Benengeli, of many of the chapters. Whereas in part I chapter titles are generally quite straightforward and accurately descriptive,[54] in part II there are several that are untrue or, at least, misleading. In the title of II, 6 (p. 617), it is stated that it is "uno de los importantes capítulos de toda la historia" ("one of the most important chapters in the whole history, p. 452), while the chapter, though interesting, is not important by any standards. In the title of II, 23, Cide Hamete anticipates his subsequent comment on Don Quijote's version of what happened in the cave of Montesinos by stating (p. 750) that the "imposibilidad y grandeza" ("impossibility and

53. I have not included in this list the beginning of II, 50 (p. 958): "Dice Cide Hamete, puntualísimo escudriñador de los átomos desta verdadera historia, que" ("Cide Hamete, the very painstaking investigator of the minute points of this true history, says that," p. 699). The praise in the editor's brief remark is humorous enough, for any reference to the "atoms" of the story is by this time bound to evoke at least an indulgent smile on the reader's lips, and the formulaic reference to the text is present, but the extreme brevity of the passage sets it apart from the others discussed together.

54. The only real problem with chapter titles in part I concerns those that seem to be misplaced. The title of I, 10, refers to the adventure with the Biscayan, which took place in the previous chapter, and to the encounter with the Yanguesans, which occupies I, 15. The titles of I, 29, and I, 30, are reversed. The battle that Don Quijote has with the wineskins in I, 35, is announced in the title of the following chapter.

magnitude") of the knight's story necessitates that it be considered apocryphal, an ambiguous suggestion of the existence of conflicting extratextual material. In II, 34 (p. 843), the Moor's description in the title of Merlin's prophesy as "una de las aventuras más famosas deste libro" ("one of the most famous adventures in this book," p. 616) is at least a gross exaggeration. His statement in the title of II, 64 (p. 1076), that Don Quijote's defeat in Barcelona is the adventure "que más pesadumbre dio a don Quijote" ("that gave Don Quixote more unhappiness," p. 784) is, as already observed, not consistent with the text. The historian reveals himself as not very perceptive of the differences between the two parts of the work when he uses the word *aventura* (a problematic term in part II, as discussed in section 5.1) almost twice as often in the chapter titles in the second part (twenty-five times) as in the titles of the first part (thirteen times). It is also worth noting that it is only in the second part that Cide Hamete includes several chapter titles that are completely frivolous.

II, 9, 638: Donde se cuenta lo que en él se verá ("Wherein is related what will be seen there," p. 468).

II, 28, 795: De las cosas que dice Benengeli que las sabrá quien le leyere, si las lee con atención ("On matters that Benengeli says he who reads them will know, if he reads them with attention," p. 582).[55]

II, 31, 812: Que trata de muchas y grandes cosas ("Which treats of many and great matters," p. 594).

II, 40, 878: De las cosas que atañen y tocan a esta aventura y a esta memorable historia ("On matters relating and belonging to this adventure and to this memorable history," p. 641).

II, 54, 990: Que trata de cosas tocantes a esta historia, y no a otra alguna ("Which deals with matters relating to this history and no other," p. 772).

II, 66, 1086: Que trata de lo que verá el que lo leyere, o lo oirá el que lo escuchare leer ("Which treats of what he who reads will see, or what he who has it read to him will hear," p. 792).

55. The phrase "dice Benengeli que" ("Benengeli says that") is obviously the editor's addition to the historian's chapter title.

II, 70, 1108: Que sigue al de sesenta y nueve, y trata de cosas no escusadas para la claridad desta historia ("Which follows sixty-nine and deals with matters indispensable for the clear comprehension of the history," p. 808).

Allen has clearly perceived that it is Cide Hamete Benengeli's "perspective on Don Quijote which is unreliable, because it does not change as the character changes, and so Cervantes contrives to alienate the reader from him."[56] I would go further and suggest that, in the second part of the novel, Cervantes, in his role as editor, establishes a clear opposition between himself (and the reader), on the one hand, and the author, Cide Hamete Benengeli, on the other. Cervantes, who most directly influences the reader's perceptions of all the characters (including Cide Hamete), implicitly stands relatively close to his protagonist and draws attention to the increasing distance between his own position and that of the insensitive, unperceptive, lying author. Directly and indirectly, subtly and openly, Cervantes mocks Cide Hamete and makes him an object of the reader's laughter; in fact, Cide Hamete Benengeli emerges as the most consistently comic character in part II of the novel.

The reader laughed heartily at Don Quijote throughout the first half of part I when the knight's chivalric madness was at its height. As Don Quijote reached his sad accommodation with reality later in part I, this laughter decreased. A reluctant and ineffective Don Quijote inspires more pity than laughter in part II. In order to maintain a humorous tone and to avoid establishing a dominant note of pathos over his work, Cervantes makes Cide Hamete turn on the protagonist and reveal his own comic shortcomings.

The reader of part II of *Don Quijote* continues to laugh at a supremely comic work of art. What is generally not realized is that the butt of this laughter is now less the comic antics of the mad knight-errant and more the absurdities of the historian/author and the narrative structure of the work. The main role of Cide Hamete Benengeli, "filósofo mahomético," in part II is to replace—or at least rival—Don Quijote as an object of laughter.

56. Allen, *Hero or Fool*, 2:5.

5.5 The Death of Alonso Quijano el Bueno

The conversion of Don Quijote back to Alonso Quijano in the final chapter completes the circular structure of the novel. The brief appearances of Alonso Quijano in I, 1, and II, 74, provide the framework within which the story of the chivalric career of Don Quijote is presented. Just as a close examination of the words and deeds of both the protagonist and his friends in I, 52, was crucial to an understanding of part I (see section 3.4), a careful reading of the book's last chapter proves to be essential to the understanding of part II and of the work as a whole.

After sleeping for some six hours, Don Quijote awakens and exclaims (II, 74, 1133), "¡Bendito sea el poderoso Dios, que tanto bien me ha hecho! En fin, sus misericordias no tienen límite, ni las abrevian ni impiden los pecados de los hombres" ("Blessed be Almighty God, who has shown me such goodness. In truth his mercies are boundless, and the sins of men can neither limit them nor keep them back!," p. 826). Only the niece is present at this first expression of her uncle's new born-again status, and she cannot understand what has taken place. She asks, "¿Qué es lo que vuestra merced dice, señor? ¿Tenemos algo de nuevo?" ("What are you saying, señor? Has anything happened?"). Her uncle responds by again praising God's mercy, calling the books of chivalry detestable, indicating that he is now in a state of "desengaño" ("revelation"), and claiming that he wants to repent of his sins and madness. He requests that she call "a mis buenos amigos: el cura, al bachiller Sansón Carrasco y a maese Nicolás el barbero" ("my good friends the priest, the bachelor Sansón Carrasco, and Master Nicolás the barber"). As these three enter, he exclaims:

> Dadme albricias, buenos señores, de que ya yo no soy don Quijote de la Mancha, sino Alonso Quijano, a quien mis costumbres me dieron renombre de *Bueno*. Ya soy enemigo de Amadís de Gaula y de toda la infinita caterva de su linaje; ya me son odiosas todas las historias profanas del andante caballería; ya conozco mi necedad y el peligro en que me pusieron haberlas leído; ya, por misericordia de Dios, escarmentando en cabeza propia, las abomino. (pp. 1133–34)

(Good news for you, good sirs: I am no longer Don Quixote of La Mancha, but Alonso Quixano, whose way of life won for him the name of Good. Now am I the enemy of Amadís of Gaul and of the whole countless troop of his descendants; odious to me now are all the profane stories of knight-errantry; now I perceive my folly, and the peril into which reading them brought me; now, by God's mercy, in my right senses, I loathe them.) (p. 826)

In this speech, as in his previous words to his niece, Alonso Quijano states his total capitulation: he now accepts without reservation the view originally proposed by his friends; the victory of Pero Pérez et al. is absolute. But although they have now achieved the exact results for which they have supposedly been working throughout the novel, the friends of Alonso Quijano seem to prefer to reject their own success, believing that (p. 1134) "alguna nueva locura le había tomado" ("some new madness had taken possession of him," p. 827). Sansón Carrasco again calls his friend "señor don Quijote," speaks of the disenchanted Dulcinea, and ends by stating, "Calle por su vida, vuelva en sí, y déjese de cuentos" ("Hush, for heaven's sake, be rational, and let's have no more tales"). There can be little doubt that his friends would rather continue to laugh at the comic exploits of Don Quijote than deal seriously with the illness and death of Alonso Quijano.

How do critical readers react to the death of Alonso Quijano? One interesting reaction is simply to see his renunciation of his life as Don Quijote and his uncompromising condemnation of the romances of chivalry as new, ironic, and comic twists to his madness.[57] But the great majority of readers, including many of the very best, hold that Alonso Quijano achieves a unique clarity of vision, a sublime goodness, a state of baroque *desengaño*, a victory over himself, a state of lucidity and knowledge, a sense of fulfillment, a supreme self-sacrifice, and an exemplary Chris-

57. This reading is best sustained by Leland H. Chambers, who states that the character's "recovered lucidity merely leads him out of one mania into another"; "Irony in the Final Chapter of the *Quijote*," p. 22. See also Michel Foucault, *Madness and Civilization: A History of Insanity in the Age of Reason*, pp. 31–32.

tian death.[58] An inevitable corollary, implicit or explicit, to this exalted view of Alonso Quijano's death is a devaluation of Don Quijote's life. No one makes this point as clearly as Carlos Varo.

> Don Quijote, pese a su grandeza, no era más que la caricatura de Alonso Quijano el Bueno, de él se nutría, en él tenía su cimiento. Don Quijote de la Mancha cumplió su mayor gloria haciéndonos conocer . . . la persona de Alonso Quijano el Bueno. . . . Don Quijote de la Mancha no fue para nosotros sino el guía para caminar hacia Alonso Quijano.[59]

> (Don Quijote, despite his grandeur, was only the caricature of Alonso Quijano the Good, he was nourished from him, he had his foundation in him. Don Quijote of La Mancha fulfilled his greatest glory letting us know . . . the person of Alonso Quijano the Good. . . . Don Quijote of La Mancha was for us but the guide to lead us to Alonso Quijano.)

It is clear that in the course of his chivalric career Don Quijote evolves away from an originally ludicrous and absurd figure

58. The following list of supporters of some variant of this opinion is by no means exhaustive: Miguel de Unamuno, *Our Lord Don Quixote: The Life of Don Quixote and Sancho with Related Essays*, pp. 310–11; Américo Castro, *El pensamiento de Cervantes*, p. 133; René Girard, *Deceit, Desire and the Novel: Self and Other in Literary Structure*, pp. 291–93; Carlos Varo, *Génesis y evolución del "Quijote,"* p. 561; Otis H. Green, *Spain and the Western Tradition*, 4:61–62; Allen, *Hero or Fool*, 1:89–90; Ruth S. El Saffar, *Novel to Romance: A Study of Cervantes's "Novelas ejemplares,"* pp. 8–11; Juan Bautista Avalle-Arce, *Don Quijote como forma de vida*, p. 213; Ciriaco Morón Arroyo, *Nuevas meditaciones del "Quijote,"* pp. 214–15. Thomas Mann's criticism of this reaction, although itself subjective and impressionistic, is well taken ("Voyage with Don Quixote," p. 461–62): "The death-bed chapter itself expresses this reversion. For Don Quixote is changed before he dies. The dying man wins—oh, joy!—his sane reason back. He has a long sleep, six hours long, and when he wakes he is by God's mercy mentally healed. His mind is free of the fog that had invaded it by the much reading of those dreadful books of knight-errantry; he sees their senselessness and depravity and will be no longer Don Quixote de la Mancha, knight of the doleful countenance, knight of the lions, but Alonzo Quixano, a reasonable man, a man like other men. That should rejoice us. But it rejoices us strikingly little, it leaves us cold, and to some extent we regret it." See also Theodore Holmes, "Don Quixote and Modern Man," pp. 58–59.

59. Varo, *Génesis y evolución*, pp. 541, 561.

(whose frequent comic statements and deeds fully earn him much—but not all—of the laughter and ridicule he evokes) and finally reaches the point where Sancho Panza is probably justified in saying (II, 72, 1126) that his master returns home "vencedor de sí mismo" ("victorious over himself," p. 821). But it is Don Quijote, not Alonso Quijano, who goes through the evolutionary process.[60]

The life of Don Quijote is of enormous interest and value. Many of the things he does result in destruction of property, a worsening of unpleasant situations, or even serious physical harm for innocent persons. But at other times his influence, though perhaps indirectly and/or unknowingly, is positive, and there can be no question that, without his long and intimate association with Don Quijote, Sancho Panza could never have risen above the "hombre de muy poca sal en la mollera" ("man with little grey matter in his skull"), as he was conceived by himself and others, to defend his master at the end of part I, to become a model governor in part II, and to finally return home a supremely self-confident man. Sancho fully achieves the goal recommended to him by his master at the duke's palace (II, 42, 898): "has de poner los ojos en quien eres, procurando conocerte a ti mismo, que es el más difícil conocimiento que puede imaginarse" ("you must keep in view that you are striving to know yourself, the most difficult thing to know that the mind can imagine," p. 655). The "education of Sancho Panza" may be a

60. Allen, the best proponent of the "victor over himself" reading of the novel, concedes the fact: "Don Quixote is a victor over himself *before* he renounces chivalry"; *Hero or Fool*, 1:89. The serious problem that I have with this position is based on the inescapable fact that Alonso Quijano el Bueno on his deathbed is a man in complete harmony with his "friends" and with his restrictive world. If it is the dying Alonso Quijano—and not Don Quijote—who wins a victory over himself, I am afraid that it can only be the same victory won by Winston Smith in George Orwell's *1984* (New York: Signet Classic, 1961): "He gazed up at the enormous face. Forty years it had taken him to learn what kind of smile was hidden beneath the dark mustache. O cruel, needless misunderstanding! O stubborn, self-willed exile from the loving breast! Two gin-scented tears trickled down the sides of his nose. But it was all right, everything was all right, the struggle was finished. He had won the victory over himself. He loved Big Brother" (p. 245).

cliché, but that such a process takes place and that it is one of the most significant and most positive aspects of the work are undeniable.[61] Still another important way in which the life of Don Quijote is a positive factor is seen in the area of comparative characterization (see section 3.2). It is Don Quijote who exposes to the reader the envy, pettiness, and insensitivity of the priest and the barber, the frivolousness and vindictiveness of Sansón Carrasco, and the moral bankruptcy of the idle rich ducal pair.

Alonso Quijano could never have done any of the things that characterize the life of Don Quijote. The Alonso Quijanos of the world stay at home, read their books, enjoy the company of people like Pero Pérez and Maese Nicolás, and do nothing at all of any value. Alonso Quijano is called "el Bueno" by his friends, but these friends are the people who in the course of the book most obviously prove their own mediocrity and meanness and who react to real, or potentially real, goodness by laughing at it and destroying it. In the entire novel, Alonso Quijano makes only two decisions: in I, 1, he rejects his empty and useless existence to become Don Quijote de la Mancha; then in II, 74, he categorically rejects his chivalric career in order to again assume the identity of Alonso Quijano el Bueno. The Alonso Quijano who dies at the work's end is the same person whose life at the beginning was so unbearable that he had to escape it. This life is neither exemplary nor interesting.[62]

61. It is an exaggeration to hold with Unamuno (see *Our Lord*, pp. 313–14) and other supersoft critics that Sancho Panza becomes fully quixotized and is capable of carrying on where his chivalric master leaves off. But to say that Sancho is not a far better human being for his association with Don Quijote would be even more absurd.

62. The statement (p. 1135) that "en tanto que don Quijote fue Alonso Quijano el Bueno, a secas, y en tanto que fue don Quijote de la Mancha, fue siempre de apacible condición y de agradable trato, y por esto no sólo era bien querido de los de su casa, sino de todos cuantos le conocían" ("whether as plain Alonso Quixano the Good or as Don Quixote of La Mancha, Don Quixote was always of a gentle disposition and kindly in all his ways, and hence he was beloved, not only by those of his own house, but by all who knew him," p. 827) is undoubtedly essentially true but does not even begin to break down the absolutely essential distinction that must be made between Alonso Quijano and Don Quijote. Rosales (*Libertad*, 2:258–59) insists that between "Alonso Quijano y Don Quijote no existe la menor contradicción.

Don Quijote's world is one of chivalry, and we cannot ignore his own concept of that chivalric world. As Don Quijote slowly abandons or compromises his principle of chivalric imitation, his consistent use of chivalric rhetoric, his willful transformation of reality in part I, he gains in humanity and shares increasingly in the everyday world of Sancho Panza and the rest of us. This evolutionary process, especially in its protracted final stage (all of part II), forms a meaningful process of disillusionment and increasing self-knowledge.

Alonso Quijano's world is one of repression and conformity, and we cannot ignore his own concept of this conformist world. The condition for accepting Alonso Quijano el Bueno is the total rejection of Don Quijote de la Mancha. The choice should not be difficult.[63]

As Juan Bautista Avalle-Arce has said (see section 1.1), the difference between Don Quijote and Alonso Quijano is the difference between the verbs *ser* ("to be," "to exist") and *valer* ("to be worthwhile"): Alonso Quijano *es* ("exists"); Don Quijote *vale* ("leads a worthwhile life"). The only meaningful thing that Alonso Quijano ever did was to become Don Quijote, and his final act is to renounce that part of his life. Don Quijote is superior to Alonso Quijano, and nothing proves it as much as the latter's death.

. . . Alonso Quijano y Don Quijote no son dos personajes distintos, ni aun dos etapas sucesivas de un mismo personaje, sino dos actitudes vitales simultáneas que constituyen su unidad" ("Alonso Quijano and Don Quijote there does not exist the slightest contradiction. . . . Alonso Quijano and Don Quijote are not two separate characters, nor even two successive phases of the same character, but rather two simultaneous and vital attitudes that constitute his unity") and that it is too simplistic to see Alonso Quijano as repenting of his madness on his deathbed (p. 266). I would insist that the distinction, far from being simplistic, is an absolute necessity.

63. Manuel Durán, who is also disturbed by Alonso Quijano's final recantation, summarizes the matter with admirable concision: "el lector se siente dominado y cautivado por la forma en que vive Don Quijote, no por la forma en que muere" ("the reader feels dominated and captivated by the way in which Don Quijote lives, not by the way in which he dies"); *La ambigüedad en el "Quijote,"* p. 204.

Appendix A: Chivalric Archaism

This appendix lists all the archaisms used by Don Quijote and the other major characters in the novel. As an aid to finding the relevant passages in *Don Quijote*, the first two words of each speech (and, when necessary, a character's name as well) are provided; a list of all the archaisms contained in each speech follows. Speeches are also identified, as they have been in the text, by part, chapter, and page numbers.

Don Quijote (Part I)

¡Oh princesa . . . : cautivo, habedes, fecho, afincamiento, la vuestra, fermosura, Plégaos, membraros, deste vuestro (I, 2, 42). No fuyan . . . : fuyan, las vuestras, desaguisado, ca, non, facerle (I, 2, 43–44). Bien parece . . . : fermosas, non, vos, acuitedes, mostredes, talante, non, ál (I, 2, 44). Nunca fuera . . . : fasta, fazañas, fechas, pro, las vuestras (I, 2, 45–46). No me . . . : fasta, la vuestra, pro (I, 3, 47–48). No esperaba . . . : pro, fazañas (I, 3, 48–49). ¡Oh señora . . . : fermosura, este tu, cautivo, atendiendo (I, 3, 52). Del sahumerio . . . : desfacedor (I, 4, 58–59). Bien te . . . : e, talante, rescibió, desfecho, infante (I, 4, 59–60). Non fuyáis . . . : Non, fuyáis, cautiva, atended (I, 4, 62). Ténganse todos . . . : malferido, cate, feridas (I, 5, 68). Ferido no . . . : Ferido (I, 7, 82–83). Non fuyades . . . :

Non, fuyades (I, 8, 89). La vuestra . . . : La vuestra, fermosura, facer, talante, este mi, cautivo, fecho (I, 8, 94). Si fueras . . . : cautiva (I, 8, 95). Ahora lo . . . : veredes (I, 8, 95). ¡Oh señora . . . : fermosura, este vuestro, la vuestra (I, 8, 96). Por cierto . . . : fermosas (I, 9, 104). Es un . . . : ferida (I, 10, 107). Yo hago . . . : folgar, desaguisado, fizo (I, 10, 108). ¿No han . . . : fazañas, fechos, fechos (I, 13, 127–28). Señor, eso . . . : fecho (I, 13, 130). Siempre deja . . . : feridas (I, 15, 152–53). Creedme, fermosa . . . : fermosa, este vuestro, habedes, fecho, pluguiera, fermosa (I, 16, 157). Quisiera hallarme . . . : fermosa, fermosura, habedes, fecho (I, 16, 160). Sea por . . . : fermosa, fermosura (I, 17, 164). Muchos y . . . : este vuestro, fecho, faceros (I, 17, 169). Quiérense mal . . . : fermosa (I, 18, 176). Deteneos, caballeros . . . : fecho, vos, fecho, desaguisado, fecistes, vos, ficieron (I, 19, 187). Desa suerte . . . : desfaciendo (I,

19, 189). Sancho amigo . . . : esta nuestra, fechos, cautivo (I, 20, 194–95). Defiéndete, cautiva . . . : cautiva (I, 21, 209). No dices . . . : fenestras, fermosas, fablar, furto, Levantarse han, tablas, fermosa, pro, talante, face, fablado, prometérselo ha (I, 21, 213–16). Pues desa . . . : desfacer (I, 22, 221). Contra cuerdos . . . : guisa, pro, fermosa (I, 25, 255–56). Soberana y . . . : ferido, fermosura, pro, afincamiento, maguer, asaz (I, 25, 268–69). No os . . . : fermosa, facienda, fasta (I, 29, 318). Yo vos . . . : vos (I, 29, 318). (None of the three major archaisms is present in this speech, but since the speech is a part of the dialogue between Don Quijote and Dorotea in which archaisms are abundant, the archaic sense of *vos* is obvious.) La vuestra . . . : La vuestra, fermosura (I, 29, 319). Y después . . . : talante, cautiva (I, 30, 330–31). Todo eso . . . : este su, cautivo (I, 31, 336). Seguramente puede . . . : fermosura, fermosa (I, 42, 467). ¡Oh mi . . . : fará, la tu, cautivo, este mi (I, 43, 478–79). Lástima os . . . : fermosa, hayades (I, 43, 479–80). Fermosa doncella . . . : Fermosa (I, 44, 488). Es común . . . : fermosa (I, 46, 503). No lloréis . . . : fermosas, desaguisado, fecho, habedes, fecho (I, 47, 512). A la . . . : sepades (I, 47, 514–15). Bueno está . . . : fadas, se cata, ferviente (I, 50, 537–40). Por cierto . . . : talente, fecho, desaguisado (I, 52, 550). Ahora, valerosa . . . : veredes, veredes (I, 52, 552). En una . . . : desaguisado, habedes, fecho, desfacer (I, 52, 553).

Don Quijote (Part II)

Anda, hijo . . . : fecho (II, 10, 643–44). Dios os . . . : mal ferido (II, 22,

749–50). Conocíla en . . . : deste su, cautivo (II, 23, 759–61). Corre, hijo . . . : fermosura (II, 30, 808). ¿Quién? ¿Quién . . . : fechos (II, 32, 828–29). Señora mía . . . : la vuestra, ferido, ferido (II, 32, 830–32).

Sancho Panza (Part I)

Querría, si . . . : feridas (I, 15, 148). Ni para . . . : fermosura (I, 17, 164–65). Paréceme, señor . . . : folgar (I, 19, 184–85). Señor, yo . . . : non, faga, desaguisado, fecho (I, 20, 195–96). Has de . . . : esta nuestra, fechos (I, 20, 204). También la . . . : ferido, ferir (I, 21, 211). Paréceme a . . . : ficieron (I, 25, 259). Así es . . . : ferido (I, 26, 278). Dichosa buscada . . . : desfaga (I, 29, 316–17). Pues mía . . . : fazaña (I, 30, 325). Pues si . . . : finojos (I, 31, 341).

Sancho Panza (Part II)

Sepamos agora . . . : desface (II, 10, 644–45). Reina y . . . : talente, cautivo (II, 10, 648–49). Hermosa señora . . . : fermosura, pro (II, 30, 808–9). De grandes . . . : la vuestra, fecho (II, 32, 834). No es . . . : desfaga (II, 44, 908). Aquello del . . . : fechorías (letter to Don Quijote) (II, 51, 975). Eso creo . . . : desfacedor (II, 72, 1123).

Archaism by Other Characters (Part I)

Juan Halduldo—Llamad, señor . . . : desfacedor, desface (I, 4, 59). Sobrina—Sepa, señor . . . : feridas (I, 5, 67). Pedro Alonso—Abran vuestras

. . . : mal ferido (I, 5, 68). Cura—Calle vuestra . . . : malferido (I, 7, 82). Cura—Esta hermosa . . . : desfaga, fecho (I, 29, 316). Dorotea—De aquí . . . : fasta, la vuestra, prez, lueñes (I, 29, 318). Cura—Eso no . . . : la vuestra, fazañas (I, 29, 321). Barbero—¡Oh Caballero . . . : afincamiento, yoguieren, faga, vegadas, fecho (I, 46, 508–9). Barbero—¿Quién ha . . . : desfacedor (I, 52, 550).

Archaism by Other Characters (Part II)

Sansón Carrasco—¡Oh la . . . : este tu, cautivo (II, 12, 665). Sansón Carrasco—Al buen . . . : fechos (II, 14, 676). Duque—¡Pasito mi . . . : fermosuras (II, 30, 811). Trifaldi—Ante estos . . . : fazañas (II, 38, 870). Altisidora—¡Oh, tu . . . : feridas (II, 44, 913–15). Doña Rodríguez—Días ha . . . : fecha, fija, habedes, fecho, queredes (II, 52, 977–78). Duquesa—Déosle Dios . . . : fechurías (II, 57, 1014–15).

Archaism in Narration (Part I)

Lleváronle luego . . . : Catándole, feridas, fallar (I, 5, 68). Y sin . . . : mal ferido (I, 8, 93–94). Dejamos en . . . : guisa, fendientes, fenderían (I, 9, 98–99). Por otra . . . : desfacer (I, 9, 100). Sucedió, pues . . . : facas, ál (I, 15, 147). Esta maravillosa . . . : furto (I, 16, 158–59). Pensando, pues . . . : fermosa, mal ferido (I, 16, 159–60). Llegó en . . . : malferido (I, 18, 180). Figurósele que . . . : mal ferido (I, 19, 187). Era la . . . : mal ferido (I, 19, 188). Sancho dijo . . . : desfacelle, fecho, facienda, fasta, fecho (I, 26, 280). En esto . . . : fermosura, fasta, hobiese, fecho, fazañas, ficiesen (I, 29, 315). Pero el . . . : fermosa (I, 29, 316). Tres cuartos . . . : fabló, guisa (I, 29, 318). A cuyas . . . : fermosa (I, 43, 479). Parecióle a . . . : ferida (I, 43, 480). Calló y . . . : fermosa (I, 46, 503).

Archaism in Narration (Part II)

Y así . . . : cautivo (II, 10, 643). Cuando el . . . : catarle, feridas (II, 28, 795). Sancho, con . . . : fermosura (II, 30, 809–10). Habiendo, pues . . . : fecho (II, 41, 892). Aquí dio . . . : malferida (II, 44, 915). Además estaba . . . : mal ferido (II, 48, 938). Miróla don . . . : fechuría (II, 48, 939). Aquí le . . . : desaguisado, fecho (II, 55, 1001).

Appendix B: Chivalric Motifs

This appendix lists all the passages and phrases that embody the six chivalric motifs used by Don Quijote and identified in the text (see section 1.4): fame, chivalric mission, strength, the order of chivalry, chivalric onomastics, and praise of Dulcinea. Each passage or phrase is identified, as in the text, by part, chapter, and page numbers.

Fame (Part I)

El jamás como se debe alabado caballero (I, 1, 39); mis famosos hechos (I, 2, 41); las famosas hazañas mías (I, 2, 42); un tan valiente y tan nombrado caballero (I, 4, 60); los más famosos hechos de caballerías que se han visto (I, 5, 66); ganado el prez en los tres días antecedentes (I, 7, 82); la más famosa aventura que se haya visto (I, 8, 92–93); obras que queden escritas en el libro de la Fama (I, 18, 175); se cobre nombre y fama tal (I, 21, 213); cobrado fama increíble por todo el universo (I, 21, 216–17); ganar perpetuo nombre y fama (I, 25, 256); de menor fama que la mía (I, 37, 412); en boca de la fama (I, 37, 418); hacerme famoso y conocido (I, 38, 423); famoso caballero andante (I, 47, 512); no de aquellos de cuyos nombres jamás la Fama se acordó (I, 47, 514).

Fame (Part II)

La fama que sus altas caballerías le tienen granjeada y adquerida (II, 14, 676); la fama que yo por ellas he ganado (II, 16, 688); por alcanzar gloriosa fama y duradera (II, 17, 706); impreso en historias, famoso en las armas (II, 59, 1028); conocido y famoso (II, 62, 1057); el mismo que dice la fama (II, 72, 1124).

Chivalric Mission (Part I)

Buscando las aventuras, en pro de los menesterosos (I, 3, 48); ha menester mi favor y ayuda (I, 4, 56); el desfacedor de agravios y sinrazones (I, 4, 58); hoy ha desfecho el mayor tuerto y agravio (I, 4, 60); es menester deshacer este tuerto (I, 8, 93); defender las doncellas, amparar las viudas . . . (I, 11, 115); en ayuda de los flacos y menesterosos (I, 13, 128); valer a los que poco pueden y vengar a a los que reciben tuertos, . . . (I, 17, 169); Favorecer y ayudar a los menesterosos y desvalidos (I, 18, 175–76); enderezando tuertos y desfaciendo agravios (I, 19, 189); desfacer fuerzas y socorrer y acudir a los miserables (I, 22, 221);

favorecer a los menesterosos y opresos de los mayores (I, 22, 228); volver por la honra de las mujeres (I, 25, 255); ayudarles como a menesterosos (I, 30, 325); desfagan los tuertos y agravios (I, 31, 342); dar libertad a los encadenados, soltar los presos, . . . (I, 45, 500); favorecer los huérfanos y menesterosos (I, 46, 503); el socorro que podría dar a muchos menesterosos y necesitados (I, 49, 529); favorecer a los desvalidos y menesterosos (I, 52, 550); desfacer semejantes agravios (I, 52, 553).

Chivalric Mission (Part II)

La defensa de reinos, el amparo de las doncellas, . . . (II, 1, 586); socorriendo viudas, amparando doncellas . . . (II, 16, 690); socorriendo a una viuda en algún despoblado (II, 17, 706); perdonar los sujetos, y supeditar y acocear los soberbios (II, 18, 716); dar favor y ayuda a los que huían (II, 26, 785); favorecer a los necesitados de favor y acudir a los menesterosos (II, 27, 791); Yo he satisfecho agravios, enderezado tuertos, . . . (II, 32, 822); el remedio de las cuitas, el socorro de las necesidades, . . . (II, 36, 865); perdonar a los humildes y castigar a los soberbois; . . . (II, 52, 978); favorecer y acorrer a los necesitados deste mundo, . . . (II, 55, 1002); socorrer y ayudar en sus necesidades a los vivos y a los muertos (II, 55, 1002).

Strength (Part I)

El valor de mi brazo (I, 2, 46); la bondad de mi espada (I, 8, 90); este mi fuerte brazo (I, 8, 90); ofrecer mi brazo y mi persona (I, 13, 128); el valor de

nuestros brazos y filos de nuestras espadas (I, 13, 129); el valor de este mi fuerte brazo (I, 15, 149); el valor de mi brazo (I, 18, 175); todo mi valor y esfuerzo (I, 19, 186); lo que mi brazo tiene bien merecido (I, 21, 217); el valor de mi brazo (I, 22, 229); el ayuda de Dios y la de mi brazo (I, 29, 319); el ayuda de Dios y de mi brazo (I, 30, 330); el valor que ella infunde en mi brazo (I, 30, 331); no hay ningún peligro en la tierra por quien no se abra camino mi espada (I, 37, 413); el valor de mi brazo y filos de mi espada (I, 38, 423); la fuerza del brazo que tal mano tiene (I, 43, 480); la fuerza de mi incansable brazo (I, 46, 503); el valor de mi brazo (I, 50, 539).

Strength (Part II)

Si Dios, si mi señora y mi brazo me valen (II, 14, 680); los filos de mi espada y el rigor de mi brazo (II, 16, 688); el valor de mi brazo (II, 29, 805); el favor de Dios y valor de mi brazo (II, 31, 816); la fuerza de mi brazo (II, 36, 865); la fuerza de mi brazo (II, 65, 1083).

The Order of Chivalry (Part I)

Como de ordinario les acontece a los caballeros andantes (I, 1, 38); ca a la orden de caballería que profeso non toca ni atañe facerle a ninguno (I, 2, 43–44); como está a cargo de la caballería y de los caballeros andantes (I, 3, 48–49); con que él me lo jure por la ley de caballería que ha recibido (I, 4, 58); ayer rescibió la orden de caballería (I, 4, 60); como pide la orden de caballería (I, 4, 61); costumbre muy usada de los caballeros andantes (I, 7, 86); no es dado a los caballeros andantes quejarse de herida alguna (I, 8, 90); por las leyes de caballería (I, 8, 92); ¿dónde has visto tú, o leído jamás, que caballero andante haya sido puesto ante la justicia . . . ? (I, 10, 106); es honra de los caballeros andantes no comer en un mes (I, 10, 110); de la caballería andante se puede decir . . . que todas las cosas iguala (I, 11, 112); los de mi profesión mejor parecen velando que durmiendo (I, 11, 118); La profesión de mi ejercicio no consiente ni permite que yo ande de otra manera (I, 13, 126); aquella famosa orden de caballería (I, 13, 127); los soldados y caballeros ponemos en ejecución lo que ellos piden (I, 13, 129); uso y costumbre en la caballería andantesca (I, 13, 130); no puede ser que haya caballero andante sin dama (I, 13, 130); a fe de caballero andante (I, 15, 148); en pena de haber pasado las leyes de la caballería (I, 15, 149); todas estas incomodidades son muy anejas al ejercicio de las armas (I, 15, 151); la vida de los caballeros andantes está sujeta a mil peligros y desventuras (I, 15, 151); por la orden de caballero que recibí (I, 17, 169); yo no puedo contravenir a la orden de los caballeros andantes (I, 17, 169); contravenir a las leyes de la caballería (I, 18, 173); De todo sabían y han de saber los caballeros andantes (I, 18, 183); los que profesamos la estrecha orden de la caballería (I, 18, 184); modos hay de composición en la orden de la caballería para todo (I, 19, 185); jamás he hallado que ningún escudero hablase tanto con su señor (I, 20, 206); ni es uso de caballería quitarles los caballos y dejarlos a pie (I, 21, 212); la orden de caballería que profeso (I, 22, 228); juro por la orden de caballería que recibí, . . . (I, 24,

245); está obligado cualquier caballero andante a volver por la honra de las mujeres (I, 25, 255); muy conforme a las reglas de caballería (I, 25, 256); sería contravenir a las órdenes de caballería (I, 25, 263); conforme a lo que profesado tengo (I, 29, 319); a los caballeros andantes no les toca ni atañe averiguar (I, 30, 325); es usada y antigua costumbre entre los caballeros y damas andantes (I, 31, 338); so pena que yo no sería buen caballero andante (I, 31, 339); fuérzame la ley de caballería a cumplir mi palabra antes que mi gusto (I, 31, 340); en este nuestro estilo de caballería es gran honra tener una dama muchos caballeros andantes que la sirvan (I, 31, 341); grandes e inauditas cosas ven los que profesan la orden de la andante caballería (I, 37, 418); no me es lícito poner mano a la espada contra gente escuderil (I, 44, 489); juro por la orden de caballería que profeso (I, 44, 492); son esentos de todo judicial fuero los caballeros andantes (I, 45, 500); jamás he leído . . . que a los caballeros encantados los lleven desta manera (I, 47, 510); todas estas desdichas son anexas a los que profesan lo que yo profeso (I, 47, 512); la manera de mi encantamento excede a cuantas yo he leído (I, 48, 527); las leyes de la caballería (I, 52, 550).

The Order of Chivalry (Part II)

Los innumerables trabajos que son anejos al andante caballería (II, 6, 622); la antigua usanza de la caballería andante (II, 7, 627); ninguna cosa desta vida hace más valientes a los caballeros andantes que verse favorecidos de sus damas (II, 8, 631); Por la fe de caballero andante (II, 11, 656); Yo no puedo ni debo sacar la espada . . . contra quien no fuere armado caballero (II, 11, 659); No hay ninguno de los andantes que no lo sea (II, 12, 664); cosas que no salgan de los límites de la caballería (II, 14, 681); no salen de los términos de la andante caballería (II, 14, 684); propio y natural oficio de caballeros andantes (II, 16, 690); en esto sigo la antigua usanza de los andantes caballeros (II, 17, 705); parece mejor un caballero andante, que . . . anda buscando peligrosas aventuras (II, 17, 706); Es una ciencia que encierra en sí todas o las más ciencias del mundo (II, 18, 710); dónde has visto tú, o leído, que ningún escudero de caballero andante se haya puesto con su señor (II, 28, 798–99); yo soy enamorado, no más de porque es forzoso que los caballeros andantes lo sean (II, 32, 822); el caballero andante sin dama es como el árbol sin hojas (II, 32, 829); la orden de la caballería andante que profeso (II, 48, 939); según la orden de la andante caballería, que profeso (II, 60, 1040–41).

Chivalric Onomastics (Part I)

Lanzarote (I, 2, 46); marqués de Mantua (I, 5, 64); Rodrigo de Narváez, Jarifa (I, 5, 66); Urganda (I, 5, 68); Turpín (I, 7, 82); Roldán, Reinaldos de Montalbán (I, 7, 83); Frestón (I, 7, 84); Frestón (I, 8, 89); Diego Pérez de Vargas (I, 8, 90); Agrajes (I, 8, 95); Fierabrás (I, 10, 107); marqués de Mantua, Valdovinos, Mambrino, Sacripante (I, 10, 108); Angélica la Bella (I, 10, 109); Arturo, Artús, Lanzarote del Lago, Ginebra, Quintañona, Amadís de Gaula, Felixmarte de Hircania, Tirante

el Blanco, Belianís de Grecia (I, 13, 127–28); Cervino, Orlando, Roldán (I, 13, 132); Amadís de Gaula, Arcalaus, Caballero del Febo (I, 15, 151); Amadís, Beltenebros, Oriana (I, 15, 153); Amadís, el Caballero de la Ardiente Espada (I, 18, 174); el de la Ardiente Espada, el del Unicornio, de las Doncellas, el del Ave Fénix, el Caballero del Grifo, el de la Muerte (I, 19, 191); al Cid Ruy Díaz, Rodrigo de Vivar (I, 19, 192); los Platires, los Tablantes, Olivantes, Tirantes, los Febos, Belianises (I, 20, 194); Gandalín, Amadís de Gaula, Gasabal, Galaor (I, 20, 206); Mambrino (twice; I, 21, 208); Amadís de Gaula, Rugel de Grecia, Daraida, Geraya, Darinel (I, 24, 251); Madásima (I, 24, 252); Madásima, Elisabat (I, 25, 255); Madásima, Elisabat (I, 25, 255–56); Amadís de Gaula, Belianís, Oriana, Beltenebros (I, 25, 257–58); Amadís, Roldán, Angélica la Bella, Medoro, Orlando, Rotolando (I, 25, 258); Mambrino (I, 25, 259); Mambrino, Roldán, Amadís (I, 25, 260); Astolfo, Bradamante (I, 25, 262); Amadís (I, 25, 265); Roldán, Bernardo del Carpio, Angélica, Medoro, Agramante, Amadís de Gaula, Oriana (I, 26, 272–73); Mambrino (I, 44, 492); Agramante, Sobrino (I, 45, 497); Amadises, de Gaula, de Grecia (I, 49, 533); Amadís, Floripes, Guy de Borgoña, Fierabrás, Carlomagno, Artús, Guarino Mezquino, Tristán, Iseo, Ginebra, Lanzarote, Quintañona, Pierres, Magalona, Roldán, Cid, Juan de Merlo, mosén Pierres, mosén Enrique de Remestán, Pedro Barba, Gutierre Quijada, conde de San Polo, Fernando de Guevara, micer Jorge, Suero de Quiñones, mosén Luis de Falces, Gonzalo de Guzmán (I, 49, 533–36); Amadís de Gaula (I, 50, 541).

Chivalric Onomastics (Part II)

Belianís, Amadís de Gaula (II, 1, 582); Amadís de Gaula, Palmerín de Inglaterra, Tirante el Blanco, Lisuarte de Grecia, Belianís, Perión de Gaula, Felixmarte de Hircania, Esplandián, Cirongilio de Tracia, Rodamonte, Sobrino, Reinaldos, Roldán, Rugero, Turpín (II, 1, 586–87); Amadís de Gaula (II, 1, 588); Morgante, Angélica (II, 1, 589); Sacripante, Roldán, Angélica (II, 1, 590); Galaor, Amadís de Gaula (II, 2, 595); Amadís (II, 6, 620); Ginebra, Lanzarote (II, 19, 719); Montesinos, Durandarte, Belerma, Guadiana, Ruidera (II, 22, 750); Montesinos, Durandarte, Belerma (II, 23, 752); Montesinos, Durandarte, Merlín, Belerma, Guadiana, Ruidera (II, 23, 753–56); Montesinos, Ginebra, Quintañona, Lanzarote (II, 23, 758); Montesinos, Belerma, Durandarte, marqués de Mantua, Baldovinos, Pedro de Portugal (II, 23, 759–61); Gaiferos (II, 26, 783); Gaiferos, Melisendra (II, 26, 784); Melisendra, Gaiferos, Marsilio, Carlomagno (II, 26, 785); Melisendra (II, 26, 786); Melisendra, Gaiferos (II, 26, 787); Diego Ordóñez de Lara, Vellido Dolfos (II, 27, 792); Roldán, Bernardo del Carpio (II, 32, 830); Magalona, Pierres (II, 41, 889); Montesinos (II, 41, 895); Merlín, Montesinos (II, 48, 938); Montesinos (II, 62, 1061); Merlín (II, 63, 1069); Roldán (II, 66, 1087).

Praise of Dulcinea (Part I)

Mi dulce señora (I, 1, 39); señora deste cautivo corazón (I, 2, 42); señora de la fermosura (I, 3, 52); sobre las bellas bella (I, 4, 59); no hay en el mundo todo doncella más hermosa que la em- peratriz de la Mancha (I, 4, 60); tamaña beldad como es la de mi señora (I, 4, 61); la linda (I, 5, 66); la sin par y hermosa (I, 8, 94); flor de la fermosura (I, 8, 96); la sin par (I, 9, 104); la dulce mi enemiga (I, 13, 131); aquella hermosa ingrata que digo entre mis dientes (I, 16, 157); la sin par (I, 16, 160); la fe que debo a mi señora (I, 17, 164); la incomparable señora mía (I, 20, 195); tanta fama de hermosa (I, 21, 211); la siempre señora mía (I, 25, 259); aquella ingrata y bella (I, 25, 261); la que merece ser señora de todo el Universo (I, 25, 265); tanto vale como la más alta princesa de la tierra (I, 25, 267); dulcísima (I, 25, 268); aquella que de mi corazón y libertad tiene la llave (I, 29, 318); aquella . . . , y no digo más (I, 30, 330); la sin par (I, 30, 331); aquella reina de la hermosura (I, 31, 336); Discreta señora (I, 31, 336); tan alta señora (I, 31, 337); aquella rosa entre espinas (I, 31, 337); Es liberal en estremo (I, 31, 338); es tan recatada (I, 31, 341); aquella por quien yo vivo (I, 35, 394); estremo de toda hermosura (I, 43, 478); aquella que, en el punto que sus ojos la vieron, la hizo señora absoluta de su alma (I, 43, 479); dulcísima (I, 52, 555).

Praise of Dulcinea (Part II)

La sin par (II, 8, 631); aquella jamás bastantemente alabada gentileza y hermosura (II, 8, 631); el sol de su belleza (II, 8, 632); la sin par (II, 9, 640); la sin par princesa (II, 9, 641); el sol de hermosura (II, 10, 643); estremo del valor que puede desearse (II, 10, 649); la hermosa (II, 14, 676); la sin par (II, 14, 683); la hermosura y gallardía de la sin par (II, 16, 688); la dulce prenda de mi mayor amargura (II, 18, 708); clarísima y sin par (II, 22, 748); La sin par (II, 23, 756); la sin par (II, 23, 758); único refugio de mis esperanzas (II, 29, 804); la hermosura de la sin par (II, 32, 827); hermosa sin tacha (II, 32, 829); la más bella del orbe (II, 32, 831); la sin par (II, 44, 915); la que tengo grabada y estampada en la mitad de mi corazón (II, 48, 938); la sin par belleza (II, 48, 940); la sin par (II, 59, 1031); la sin par (II, 62, 1058); la ilustre (II, 64, 1078); la más hermosa mujer del mundo (II, 64, 1079); el lugar que en mi alma tiene (II, 70, 1113); la sin par (II, 73, 1130).

Bibliography

Allen, John J. "Cide Hamete's English Translators." *Hispanic Review* 35 (1967): 366–67.

———. *Don Quixote: Hero or Fool?* 2 vols. University of Florida Monographs, Humanities, nos. 29 and 46. Gainesville: University of Florida Press, 1969, 1979.

———. "The Narrators, the Reader and Don Quijote." *Modern Language Notes* 91 (1976): 201–12.

Alonso, Dámaso. "El hidalgo Camilote y el hidalgo don Quijote." *Revista de Filología Española* 20 (1933): 391–97.

Alonso, Martín. *Enciclopedia del idioma.* 3 vols. Madrid: Aguilar, 1958.

Alter, Robert. *Partial Magic: The Novel as a Self-conscious Genre.* Berkeley: University of California Press, 1975.

Amadís de Gaula. Edited by Edwin B. Place. 4 vols. Madrid: C.S.I.C., 1959–1969.

Amadis of Gaul, Books I and II. Translated by Edwin B. Place and Herbert C. Behm. Lexington: The University Press of Kentucky, 1974.

Ansón, Luis María. Prólogo to *Guía del lector del "Quijote"* by Salvador de Madariaga. Selecciones Austral, no. 14. Madrid: Espasa-Calpe, 1976.

Auden, W. H. "The Ironic Hero: Some Reflections on Don Quixote." In *Cervantes: A Collection of Critical Essays,* edited by Lowry Nelson, Jr., pp. 73–81. Englewood Cliffs, N.J.: Prentice-Hall, 1969.

Auerbach, Erich. *Mimesis.* Translated by Willard Trask. Garden City, N.Y.: Doubleday/Anchor, 1957.

Avalle-Arce, Juan Bautista. *Don Quijote como forma de vida.* Madrid: Fundación Juan March/Editorial Castalia, 1976.

———. "Vital and Artistic Structures in the Life of Don Quixote." In *Medieval and Renaissance Studies: Proceedings of the Southeastern Institute of Medieval and Renaissance Studies, Summer, 1974,* edited by Dale J. B. Randall, pp. 104–21. Durham, N.C.: Duke University Press, 1976.

Avalle-Arce, Juan Bautista, and Edward C. Riley. "*Don Quijote.*" In *Suma cervantina,* edited by Avalle-Arce and Riley, pp. 47–79. London: Tamesis, 1973.

Avellaneda, Alonso Fernández de. *Don Quijote de la Mancha.* Edited by Martín de Riquer. 3 vols. Clásicos Castellanos, nos. 174–76. Madrid: Espasa-Calpe, 1972.

————. *Don Quixote de la Mancha (Part II)*. Translated by Alberta Wilson Server and John Esten Keller. Newark, Del.: Juan de la Cuesta, 1980.

Barrick, Mac E. "The Form and Function of Folktales in *Don Quijote*." *Journal of Medieval and Renaissance Studies* 6 (1976): 101–36.

Brantley, Franklin O. "Sancho's Ascent to the Spheres." *Hispania* 53 (1970): 37–45.

Brenan, Gerald. *The Literature of the Spanish People*. 2d ed. Cleveland: World Publishing Co., 1957.

Cannon, Carlota B. "Transformación y cambio de Don Quijote." *Revista de Estudios Hispánicos* 10 (1976): 193–202.

Casalduero, Joaquín. *Sentido y forma del "Quijote."* Madrid: Insula, 1949.

Castro, Américo. *Hacia Cervantes*. 3d ed. Madrid: Taurus, 1967.

————. *El pensamiento de Cervantes*. New ed. Edited by Julio Rodríguez-Puértolas. Barcelona and Madrid: Noguer, 1972.

Cejador y Frauca, Julio. *La lengua de Cervantes*. 2 vols. Madrid: J. Rates, 1905–1906.

Cervantes, Miguel de. *Don Quijote de la Mancha*. Edited by John J. Allen. 2 vols. Letras Hispánicas, nos. 100, 101. Madrid: Cátedra, 1977.

————. *Don Quijote de la Mancha*. Edited by Diego Clemencín. Madrid: Castilla, 1966.

————. *Don Quijote de la Mancha*. Edited by Martín de Riquer. Barcelona: Juventud, 1944.

————. *Don Quijote de la Mancha*. Edited by Martín de Riquer. Clásicos Planeta, no. 1. Barcelona: Planeta, 1962.

————. *Don Quijote de la Mancha*. Edited by Martín de Riquer. Hispánicos Planeta, no. 1. Barcelona: Planeta, 1975.

————. *Don Quixote*. Translated by John Ormsby. Edited by Joseph R. Jones and Kenneth Douglas. New York: W. W. Norton, 1980.

Chambers, Leland H. "Irony in the Final Chapter of the *Quijote*." *Romanic Review* 61 (1970): 14–22.

Chevalier, Maxime. *Lectura y lectores en la España de los siglos XVI y XVII*. Madrid: Turner, 1976.

Church, Margaret. *Don Quixote: The Knight of La Mancha*. New York: New York University Press, 1971.

Close, Anthony. "Don Quixote as a Burlesque Hero: A Re-constructed Eighteenth-Century View." *Forum for Modern Language Studies* 9 (1974): 365–78.

————. *The Romantic Approach to "Don Quixote."* Cambridge: Cambridge University Press, 1977.

Corominas, Juan. *Diccionario crítico etimológico de la lengua castellana*. 4 vols. Bern: Francke, 1954.

Covarrubias, Sebastián de. *Tesoro de la lengua castellana o española*. Edited by Martín de Riquer. Barcelona: Horta, 1943.

Cuervo, Rufino J. *Diccionario de construcción y régimen de la lengua castellana*. 2 vols. Bogotá: Instituto Caro y Cuervo, 1953–1954.

de Chasca, Edmund. "Algunos aspectos del ritmo y del movimiento narrativo del *Quijote.*" *Revista de Filología Española* 47 (1964): 287–307.

Díaz-Plaja, Fernando. *Nueva historia de la literatura española.* Barcelona: Plaza y Janes, 1974.

Díaz-Plaja, Guillermo. *En torno a Cervantes.* Pamplona: Eunsa, 1977.

Diccionario de Autoridades. 6 vols. Facsimile ed. in 3 vols. Madrid: Gredos, 1964.

Dunn, Peter N. "Una ironía estructural en el *Quijote.*" Paper read at I Congreso Internacional sobre Cervantes, 6 July 1978, Madrid.

Durán, Manuel. *La ambigüedad en el "Quijote."* Xalapa: Universidad Veracruzana, 1960.

Efron, Arthur. "Critics Attend Human Dogfight and Miss the Action—Headline 1977." Paper read at Fordham Cervantes Congress, 8 December 1977, New York City.

———. *Don Quixote and the Dulcineated World.* Austin: University of Texas Press, 1971.

Eisenberg, Daniel. "Cervantes' *Don Quijote* Once Again: An Answer to J. J. Allen." In *Estudios literarios de hispanistas norteamericanos dedicados a Helmut Hatzfeld con motivo de su 80 aniversario,* edited by Josep M. Sola-Solé, Alessandro Crisafulli, and Brunno Damiani, pp. 103–10. Barcelona: Hispam, 1974.

———. "*Don Quijote* and the Romances of Chivalry: The Need for a Reexamination." *Hispanic Review* 41 (1973): 511–23.

———. "Pero Pérez the Priest and His Comment on *Tirant lo Blanch.*" *Modern Language Notes* 83 (1973): 321–30.

———. "The Pseudo-historicity of the Romances of Chivalry." *Quaderni Ibero-Americani,* nos. 45–46 (1975), pp. 253–59.

El Saffar, Ruth S. "Cervantes and the Games of Illusion." In *Cervantes and the Renaissance,* edited by Michael D. McGaha, pp. 141–56. Newark, Del.: Juan de la Cuesta, 1980.

———. "Concerning Change, Continuity, and Other Critical Matters: A Reading of John J. Allen's *Don Quixote: Hero or Fool? Part II.*" *Journal of Hispanic Philology* 4 (1980): 237–54.

———. *Distance and Control in "Don Quixote." A Study in Narrative Technique.* North Carolina Studies in the Romance Languages and Literatures, no. 147. Chapel Hill: University of North Carolina Press, 1975.

———. *Novel to Romance: A Study of Cervantes's "Novelas ejemplares."* Baltimore: The Johns Hopkins University Press, 1974.

Entwistle, William J. *The Spanish Language.* London: Faber and Faber, 1936.

Ferrer Chivite, Manuel. "El cura y el barbero o Historia de dos resentidos." Paper read at I Congreso Internacional sobre Cervantes, 7 July 1978, Madrid.

Fjelsted, Ruth Naomi. "Archaisms in *Amadís de Gaula.*" Ph.D. dissertation, State University of Iowa, 1963.

Flores, R. M. *The Compositors of the First and Second Madrid Editions of*

"Don Quixote," Part I. London: The Modern Humanities Research Association, 1975.

Forcione, Alban K. *Cervantes, Aristotle, and the "Persiles."* Princeton, N.J.: Princeton University Press, 1970.

Foucault, Michel. *Madness and Civilization: A History of Insanity in the Age of Reason.* Translated by Richard Howard. New York: Pantheon Books, 1965.

———. *The Order of Things: An Archaeology of the Human Sciences.* New York: Pantheon Books, 1970.

García Díez, Víctor F. "La fabla en algunas comedias históricas del siglo de oro." Ph.D. dissertation, University of Iowa, 1967.

Gerhardt, Mia I. *Don Quijote, la vie et les livres.* Amsterdam: N. V. Noord-Hollandsche Uitgevers Maatschappij, 1955.

Gili y Gaya, Samuel. *Amadís de Gaula.* Barcelona: Facultad de Filosofía y Letras, 1956.

———. *Tesoro lexicográfico (1492–1726).* Madrid: C.S.I.C., 1960.

Gilman, Stephen. *Cervantes y Avellaneda.* Translated by Margit Frenk Alatorre. Mexico City: El Colegio de México, 1951.

Girard, René. *Deceit, Desire and the Novel: Self and Other in Literary Structure.* Translated by Yvonne Freccero. Baltimore: The Johns Hopkins University Press, 1965.

Green, Otis H. *Spain and the Western Tradition.* Vol. 4. Madison: University of Wisconsin Press, 1966.

Haley, George. "The Narrator in *Don Quijote*: Maese Pedro's Puppet Show." *Modern Language Notes* 80 (1965): 145–65.

Hanssen, Friedrich. *Gramática histórica de la lengua castellana.* Buenos Aires: El Ateneo, 1945.

Hart, Thomas R., and Steven Rendall. "Rhetoric and Characterization in Marcela's Address to the Shepherds." *Hispanic Review* 46 (1978): 287–98.

Harvey, L. P. "Oral Composition and the Performance of Novels of Chivalry in Spain." *Forum for Modern Language Studies* 10 (1974): 270–86.

Hatzfeld, Helmut A. *Explicación de textos literarios.* Supplement to vol. 1 of *Explicación de textos literarios.* Sacramento: California State University, 1973.

———. *El "Quijote" como obra de arte del lenguaje.* 2d ed. Madrid: C.S.I.C., 1966.

Holmes, Theodore. "Don Quixote and Modern Man." *Sewanee Review* 78 (1970): 40–59.

Huizinga, J. *The Waning of the Middle Ages.* Translated by F. Hopman. Garden City, N.Y.: Doubleday/Anchor, 1954.

Johnson, Carroll B. "A Second Look at Dulcinea's Ass: *Don Quijote*, II. 10." *Hispanic Review* 43 (1975): 191–98.

Jones, Harold G. "Grisóstomo and Don Quijote: Death and Imitation." *Revista Canadiense de Estudios Hispánicos* 4 (1979): 85–92.

Keniston, Hayward. *The Syntax of Castilian Prose: The Sixteenth Century*. Chicago: The University of Chicago Press, 1937.
Lapesa, Rafael. *Historia de la lengua española*. 5th ed. Madrid: Escelicer, 1959.
———. "El lenguaje del *Amadís* manuscrito." *Boletín de la Real Academia Española* 36 (1956): 219–25.
Lazarillo de Tormes. Edited by Alberto Blecua. Clásicos Castalia, no. 58. Madrid: Castalia, 1972.
Le Guin, Ursula K. *The Language of the Night*. Edited by Susan Wood. New York: G. P. Putnam's Sons, 1979.
Lloréns, Vicente. *Aspectos sociales de la literatura española*. Madrid: Castalia, 1974.
Locke, F. W. "*El sabio encantador*: The Author of *Don Quixote*." *Symposium* 23 (1969): 46–61.
López Landeira, Ricardo. "Los encantadores de Don Quijote y su crítica literaria." *Anales Cervantinos* 12 (1973): 115–28.
Mackey, Mary. "Rhetoric and Characterization in *Don Quijote*." *Hispanic Review* 42 (1974): 51–66.
Madariaga, Salvador de. *Don Quixote: An Introductory Essay in Psychology*. London: Oxford University Press, 1961.
———. *Guía del lector del "Quijote."* Prologue by Luis María Ansón. Selecciones Austral, no. 14. Madrid: Espasa-Calpe, 1976.
Mancing, Howard. "Alonso Quijano y sus amigos." Paper read at I Congreso Internacional sobre Cervantes, 7 July 1978, Madrid.
———. "Cervantes and the Tradition of Chivalric Parody." *Forum for Modern Language Studies* 11 (1975): 177–91.
———. "The Comic Function of Chivalric Names in *Don Quijote*." *Names* 21 (1973): 220–35.
———. "The Deceptiveness of *Lazarillo de Tormes*." *PMLA* 90 (1975): 426–32.
———. "Dulcinea's Ass: A Note on *Don Quijote*, Part II, Chapter 10." *Hispanic Review* 40 (1972): 73–77.
———. "A Note on the Formation of Character Image in the Classic Spanish Novel." *Philological Quarterly* 54 (1975): 528–31.
Mandel, Oscar. "The Function of the Norm in *Don Quixote*." *Modern Philology* 55 (1958): 154–63.
Mann, Thomas. "Voyage with Don Quixote." In *Essays of Three Decades*, translated by H. T. Lowe-Porter, pp. 429–64. New York: Alfred A. Knopf, 1957.
Maravall, José Antonio. *Utopía y contrautopía en el "Quijote."* Santiago de Compostela: Pico Sacro, 1976.
Márquez Villanueva, Francisco. "La locura emblemática en la segunda parte del *Quijote*." In *Cervantes and the Renaissance*, edited by Michael D. McGaha, pp. 87–112. Newark, Del.: Juan de la Cuesta, 1980.
Mendeloff, Henry. "The Maritornes Episode (*DQ*: I, 16): A Cervantine Bedroom Farce." *Romance Notes* 16 (1975): 753–59.
Menéndez Pidal, Ramón. "Un aspecto en la elaboración del *Quijote*."

In *De Cervantes y Lope de Vega*, pp. 9–60. Colección Austral, no. 120. Madrid: Espasa-Calpe, 1940.

———. *Manual de gramática histórica española*. 12th ed. Madrid: Espasa-Calpe, 1966.

———. *Romancero hispánico*. 2d ed. 2 vols. Madrid: Espasa-Calpe, 1968.

Meyer, Herman. *The Poetics of Quotation in the European Novel*. Translated by Theodore Ziolkowski and Yetta Ziolkowski. Princeton, N.J.: Princeton University Press, 1968.

Millé y Giménez, Juan. *Sobre la génesis del "Quijote."* Barcelona: Araluce, 1930.

Morales Oliver, Luis. *Sinópsis de "Don Quijote."* Madrid: Fundación Española, 1977.

Moreno Báez, Enrique. *Reflexiones sobre el "Quijote."* Madrid: Editorial Prensa Española, 1968.

Morón Arroyo, Ciriaco. *Nuevas meditaciones del "Quijote."* Madrid: Gredos, 1976.

Murillo, L. A. "*Don Quixote* as Renaissance Epic." In *Cervantes and the Renaissance*, edited by Michael D. McGaha, pp. 51–70. Newark, Del.: Juan de la Cuesta, 1980.

Nelson, Lowry, Jr. Introduction to *Cervantes: A Collection of Critical Essays*. Englewood Cliffs, N.J.: Prentice-Hall, 1969.

Nepaulsingh, Colbert I. "La aventura de los narradores del *Quijote*." In *Actas del Sexto Congreso Internacional de Hispanistas*, edited by Alan M. Gordon and Evelyn Rugg, pp. 515–18. Toronto: Department of Spanish and Portuguese of the University of Toronto, 1980.

———. "Cervantes, *Don Quijote*: The Unity of the Action." *Revista Canadiense de Estudios Hispánicos* 2 (1978): 239–57.

Neuschäfer, Hans Jörg. "Don Quijote como ser social. Nuevo aspecto de la dialéctica cervantina." In vol. 2 of *Studia Hispanica in Honorem R. Lapesa,* pp. 399–410. Madrid: Gredos, 1974.

Ortega y Gasset, José. *Meditations on "Quixote."* Translated by Evelyn Rugg and Diego Marín. New York: W. W. Norton, 1961.

Ortúñez de Calahorra, Diego. *Espejo de príncipes y cavalleros*. Edited by Daniel Eisenberg. 6 vols. Clásicos Castellanos, nos. 193–98. Madrid: Espasa-Calpe, 1975.

Palmerín de Olivia. Edited by Guiseppe di Stefano. *Studi sul "Palmerín de Olivia,"* vol. 1. Pisa: Università di Pisa, 1960.

Parker, Alexander A. "Fielding and the Structure of *Don Quixote*." *Bulletin of Hispanic Studies* 33 (1956): 1–16.

Parr, James A. "Aesthetic Distance in the *Quixote*." In *Studies in Honor of Gerald E. Wade*, edited by Sylvia Bowman et al., pp. 187–97. Madrid: Porrúa Turanzas, 1979.

Percas de Ponseti, Helena. *Cervantes y su concepto del arte*. 2 vols. Madrid: Gredos, 1975.

———. "Los consejos de Don Quixote a Sancho." In *Cervantes and the*

Renaissance, edited by Michael D. McGaha, pp. 194–236. Newark, Del.: Juan de la Cuesta, 1980.

———. "Sobre el enigma de 'los dos Cervantes.'" *The American Hispanist* 2, no. 16 (1977): 9–11.

Pérez, Luis. "La ociosidad-muerte en el *Quijote*." *Revista de Archivos, Bibliotecas y Museos* 21 (1964–1965): 355–62.

Pierce, Frank. *Amadís de Gaula*. TWAS, no. 372. New York: Twayne, 1976.

Plank, Robert. "Quixote's Mills." *Science-Fiction Studies* 1 (1973): 68–78.

Powys, John Cowper. *Enjoyment of Literature*. New York: Simon & Schuster, 1938.

Predmore, Richard L. *The World of Don Quixote*. Cambridge, Mass.: Harvard University Press, 1967.

Profeti, Maria Grazia. "'Afectación' e 'descuido' nella lingua del *Palmerín*." *Studi sul "Palmerín de Olivia*," vol. 3, *Saggi e ricerche*, pp. 45–73. Pisa: Università di Pisa, 1966.

Real Academia Española. *Diccionario histórico de la lengua española*. Madrid: Real Academia Española, 1972.

Riewald, J. G. "Parody as Criticism." *Neophilologus* 50 (1966): 125–48.

Riffaterre, Michael. "Criteria for Style Analysis." *Word* 15 (1959): 154–74.

Riley, Edward C. *Cervantes' Theory of the Novel*. Oxford: Clarendon Press, 1962.

———. "Don Quixote and the Imitation of Models." *Bulletin of Hispanic Studies* 31 (1954): 3–16.

———. "Three Versions of Don Quixote." *Modern Language Review* 68 (1973): 807–19.

Riquer, Martín de. *Aproximación al "Quijote."* Barcelona: Teide, 1967.

———. "Cervantes and the Romances of Chivalry." In *Don Quixote*, edited by Joseph R. Jones and Kenneth Douglas, pp. 895–913. Translated by Joseph R. Jones. New York: W. W. Norton, 1980.

———. "Cervantes y la caballeresca." In *Suma cervantina*, edited by Juan Bautista Avalle-Arce and Edward C. Riley, pp. 273–92. London: Tamesis, 1973.

———. "Don Quijote, caballero por escarnio." *Calvileño* 7, no. 41 (September–October 1965): 47–50.

———. "El *Quijote* y los libros." *Papeles de Son Armadans* 54, no. 160 (1969): 5–24.

Robert, Marthe. *The Old and the New: From Don Quixote to Kafka*. Translated by Carol Cosman. Berkeley: University of California Press, 1977.

Rodríguez-Moñino, Antonio. "El primer manuscrito del *Amadís de Gaula*." *Boletín de la Real Academia Española* 36 (1956): 199–216.

Rojas, Francisco de. *La Celestina*. Edited by Julio Cejador y Frauca. 2 vols. Clásicos Castellanos, nos. 20, 23. Madrid: Espasa-Calpe, 1963.

———. *The Spanish Bawd.* Translated by J. M. Cohen. Baltimore: Penguin, 1964.

Romero Flores, Hipólito R. *Biografía de Sancho Panza, filósofo de la sensatez.* 2d ed. Barcelona: Aedos, 1955.

Rosales, Luis. *Cervantes y la libertad.* 2 vols. Madrid: Sociedad de Estudios y Publicaciones, 1960.

———. "Pequeña historia de un mito." In *Lírica española*, pp. 143–93. Madrid: Editora Nacional, 1972.

Rosenblat, Angel. *La lengua del "Quijote."* Madrid: Gredos, 1971.

Ruiz-Fornells, Enrique. *Las concordancias de "El Ingenioso Hidalgo don Quijote de la Mancha."* Vol. 1. Madrid: Ediciones Cultura Hispánica, 1976.

Russell, P. E. "*Don Quixote* as a Funny Book." *Modern Language Review* 54 (1969): 312–26.

Schutz, Alfred. "Don Quixote and the Problem of Reality." In *Studies in Social Theory*, vol. 2 of his *Collected Papers*, edited by Avrid Brodersen, pp. 135–58. The Hague: Martinus Nijhoff, 1964.

Serrano-Plaja, Arturo. *"Magic" Realism in Cervantes: "Don Quixote" as Seen through "Tom Sawyer" and "The Idiot."* Translated by Robert S. Rudder. Berkeley: University of California Press, 1970.

Sobré, J. M. "Don Quijote, the Hero Upside-Down." *Hispanic Review* 44 (1976): 127–41.

Sorensen, Jorge E. "The Importance of Sierra Morena as a Point of Transition in *Don Quijote*." In *Studies in the Spanish Golden Age: Cervantes and Lope de Vega*, edited by Dana B. Drake and José A. Madrigal, pp. 46–52. Miami: Ediciones Universal, 1978.

Spaulding, Robert K. *How Spanish Grew.* Berkeley: University of California Press, 1943.

Stagg, Geoffrey. "Revision in *Don Quixote*, Part I." In *Hispanic Studies in Honour of J. González Llubera*, edited by Frank Pierce, pp. 347–66. Oxford: Dolphin Book Co., 1959.

Steele, Charles W. "Functions of the Grisóstomo–Marcela Episode in *Don Quijote*: Symbolism, Drama, Parody." *Revista de Estudios Hispánicos* 14 (1980): 3–17.

Terpening, Ronnie H. "Creation and Deformation in the Episode of Dulcinea: Sancho Panza as Author." *The American Hispanist* 3, no. 25 (1978): 4–5.

Torrente Ballester, Gonzalo. *El "Quijote" como juego.* Madrid: Guadarrama, 1975.

Two Spanish Picaresque Novels. Translated by Michael Alpert. London: Penguin, 1969.

Ullman, Pierre. "The Burlesque Poems Which Frame the *Quijote*." *Anales Cervantinos* 9 (1961–1962): 213–27.

———. "An Emblematic Interpretation of Sansón Carrasco's Disguises." In *Estudios literarios de hispanistas norteamericanos dedicados a Helmut Hatzfeld con motivo de su 80 aniversario*, edited by Joseph M.

Sola-Solé, Alessandro Crisafulli, and Brunno Damiani, pp. 223–38. Barcelona: Hispam, 1974.

Unamuno, Miguel de. *Our Lord Don Quixote: The Life of Don Quixote and Sancho with Related Essays.* Translated by Anthony Kerrigan. Bollingen Series no. 85.3. Princeton, N.J.: Princeton University Press, 1967.

Valdés, Juan de. *Diálogo de la lengua.* Edited by Juan M. Lope Blanch. Clásicos Castalia, no. 11. Madrid: Castalia, 1969.

Van Doren, Mark. *Don Quixote's Profession.* New York: Columbia University Press, 1958.

Varo, Carlos. *Génesis y evolución del "Quijote."* Madrid: Alcalá, 1968.

Wardropper, Bruce. "*Don Quixote*: Story or History?" *Modern Philology* 63 (1965): 1–11.

Weiger, John G. *The Individuated Self: Cervantes and the Emergence of the Individual.* Athens: Ohio University Press, 1979.

Weimann, Robert. "Past Significance and Present Meaning in Literary History." In *Preserve and Create: Essays in Marxist Literary Criticism,* edited by Gaylord C. LeRoy and Ursula Beitz, pp. 30–53. New York: Humanities Press, 1973.

Willis, Raymond S., Jr. *The Phantom Chapters of the "Quijote."* New York: Hispanic Institute, 1953.

Index

Actors, DQ's encounter with, 142–43, 168, 169

Adventures. *See* Pattern of adventure

Allen, John J.: on archaism, 16n, 20n, 27n, 30n, 69n, 131n; on Pero Pérez, 93n, 109n, 135n, 185n; on adventures, 112–13n; on DQ's chivalric trajectory, 122, 125; on DQ early in part II, 134n; on *Don Quijote, Part I,* 136n; on pigs and bulls, 164n; on Cide Hamete Benengeli, 197, 199n, 200n, 204n, 209; on death of Alonso Quijano, 213n

Alonso, Pedro, 44, 92, 111

Altisidora: DQ pinched by, 154, 160, 164; affair of, 164–65, 168, 169, 185, 187; frequency of speech, 183; defended by duke, 186–87; uses archaism, 188

Amadís de Gaula, 35, 63, 70, 95n, 170, 189n, 210; style model for DQ, 1, 15, 17n, 30; penance imitated by DQ, 14, 81–84

Amadís de Gaula, archaic style of, 22–24

Andrés: adventure of, 41–42, 83, 90, 92, 113, 114, 115; frequency of speech, 91

Archaism. *See* Chivalric archaism

Arms and letters, DQ's speech on, 98, 99, 161

Ass (Sancho's), 57, 59–60n, 142n, 202

Avalle-Arce, Juan Bautista: on Alonso Quijano, 11–12, 215; on romances of chivalry, 26; on DQ's penance, 83n; on reality, 113n; on windmill adventure, 116n; on DQ's chivalric trajectory, 121–22, 125; on lion adventure, 145n; on cave of Montesinos, 147; on death of Alonso Quijano, 212n

Avellaneda, Alonso Fernández de, 116n, 135n, 188–89, 191–92. *See also* Chivalric archaism

Barcelona, 3, 62n, 142n, 162–63, 200, 208

Basin: adventure of, 70, 93, 115, 169, 178–79; dispute about, 100–102, 114

Belianís de Grecia, 14, 35, 170

Belianís de Grecia, 11, 42n, 57n

Benengeli, Cide Hamete. *See* Cide Hamete Benengeli

Biscayan, adventure of, 48, 52–53, 79, 83, 92, 99, 114, 115, 168–69, 189, 207n

Books of chivalry. *See* Romances of chivalry

Braying episode, 151–52, 168, 169

Bulls episode, 161, 164–65, 168, 169

Caballero de la Blanca Luna. *See* Sansón Carrasco

Caballero de los Espejos. *See* Sansón Carrasco

Canon of Toledo, 138; frequency of speech, 91; with Pero Pérez, 103–4, 106–7; debates with DQ, 107, 169; watches DQ's fight with Eugenio, 108–9

Cardenio, 10, 138, 147n, 187n; fight with DQ, 81, 82, 97, 113n; penance in Sierra Morena, 82, 84; frequency of speech, 91; comparative characterization, 92; at the inn, 98, 102

Carrasco, Sansón, 10, 142n, 168; role early in part II, 3, 135–37, 139, 169, 175, 189; as Caballero de los Espejos, 3, 62n, 132, 143–44, 182–84, 199; role in part II, 4, 170, 182–85, 188–89; as Caballero de la Blanca

Luna, 162–64, 170, 181, 190; frequency of speech, 183; represents society's norm, 191; comparative characterization, 192, 214; at death of Alonso Quijano, 210–11

Cave of Montesinos, 107, 116, 132, 147–48, 168, 169, 198, 199, 204, 271

Cervantes, Miguel de, as editor of *Don Quijote*, 4, 129, 131n, 172n, 174, 192–209

Chivalric archaism: used by DQ, 1, 15–22, 25–26, 30, 38, 71, 138; used by other characters, 2, 44–45, 86, 94, 102, 188, 190; used by Sancho, 2, 64, 72–74, 77, 79, 82, 174–75, 181; not recognized by modern readers, 15–16, 20–22; major archaisms, 16–18; supplementary archaisms, 18–20; in the romances of chivalry, 18n, 22–26; frequency of use by DQ, 27–32, 50, 130–31, 138, 154, 188; used in Avellaneda's novel, 30n, 188, 189n; as a characteristic of quixotic adventures, 47, 114; relating to Rocinante, 57–58, 61

Chivalric mission: defined, 33–34; referred to by DQ, 34, 132; referred to by other characters, 40, 68, 91–93, 181, 190. See also Chivalric motifs

Chivalric motifs: used by DQ, 1, 3, 33–37, 71, 132; as a characteristic of quixotic adventures, 47, 114. See also Chivalric mission; Chivalric onomastics; Fame; Order of chivalry; Praise of Dulcinea; Strength

Chivalric onomastics: defined, 35–36; referred to by DQ, 36, 131–32. See also Chivalric motifs

Chivalric trajectory: of DQ, 1–3, 30, 32, 37, 62, 93, 96, 97, 109–11, 115, 117–22, 126, 129–30, 132–33, 137, 138, 143, 154, 160–61, 170–71, 188, 199, 209, 212–13, 215; of Sancho Panza, 2, 4, 81, 100–101, 111–12, 120n, 129–30, 176, 179–80, 213–14

Cide Hamete Benengeli: as a comic character, 1, 4–5, 201–9; as an unreliable narrator, 1, 65, 144–45, 155, 163–64, 187, 195–209; as author of *Don Quijote, Part I*, 3, 129, 135–37, 172n, 180, 182, 189, 192–

96; dialectic with Cervantes, 4, 131n, 192–209. See also Lies

Clemencín, Diego: on romances of chivalry, 18n, 25n, 35n, 40n, 41n, 42n, 59n, 63n, 66n, 86n, 124; on Vivaldo, 62n; on lies by DQ, 70n; on Pero Pérez, 109n

Comparative characterization: in part I, 2, 56, 84, 91–92, 98, 102–3, 109, 214; in part II, 4, 161, 185–86, 192, 214; defined, 91

Critics of *Don Quijote*: on chivalric trajectory, 118–22, 126; soft, 122–24, 213n; hard, 122–25. See also individual critics

Dead body, adventure of, 67–68, 80, 113, 115, 189. See also López, Alonso

Don Quijote, Part I: effect on DQ in part II, 135–37; read by other characters, 154, 170, 182, 188

Dorotea: role in part I, 2, 4, 90, 96, 117, 188; as the Princess Micomicona, 40n, 55n, 81, 84, 85–89, 94–95, 97, 99, 114, 115, 118, 138, 170, 177; frequency of speech, 91; at the inn, 97–98, 100–101, 102, 138–39, 177. See also Enchanters

Dubbing ceremony, 38, 40–41, 83, 86n, 92

Duchess, 55n, 169, 175n, 181; as DQ's hostess, 13, 130, 132, 153, 154, 157–58, 160, 168, 170, 185–90; frequency of speech, 154, 157n, 183; pinches DQ, 154, 160, 164; as a reader of *Don Quijote, Part I*, 154, 188–89; comparative characterization, 185, 214; uses archaism, 188

Duke, 55n, 169n, 175n; as DQ's host, 3, 130, 132, 153, 154, 157, 160, 168, 170, 180, 185–91; comparative characterization, 4, 185–87, 214; frequency of speech, 154, 157n, 183; as a reader of *Don Quijote, Part I*, 154, 188–89; uses archaism, 188; represents society's norm, 191

Dulcinea del Toboso, 42, 48, 59, 61n, 87, 92, 146n, 152n, 162, 184, 198, 205; invoked by DQ, 15, 39, 41, 42, 50, 98; invoked as part of quixotic adventures, 47, 113; discussed by DQ and Vivaldo, 55–56, 92; reality as Aldonza Lorenzo, 75n, 82–83, 88–89, 140, 177; DQ's letter to, 81, 83, 94; Sancho's supposed visit to, 88–89, 141, 177; Sancho's enchantment of, 116, 119–21, 132, 138–42, 157, 163, 169, 176–79, 198, 200n, 204, 211. *See also* Praise of Dulcinea

Efron, Arthur: on *Don Quijote* in translation, 26–27n; on DQ's pain, 53n; on Maritornes, 59n; on DQ's fight with Eugenio, 110n; on Pero Pérez, 110n; on DQ's advice to Sancho, 158n; on lies by DQ, 158n; on Sancho's governorship, 180n
Eisenberg, Daniel: on the romances of chivalry, 11n, 18n, 23–24n, 38n, 52n, 66n, 151n, 193n, 203n; on archaism, 24n, 131n; on the dubbing ceremony, 41n; on Pero Pérez, 93n; as a hard critic, 124
El Saffar, Ruth S.: on DQ's chivalric trajectory, 121n; on the puppet show, 149n; on DQ in part II, 154n; on Cide Hamete Benengeli, 192n, 196–97n, 197; on death of Alonso Quijano, 212n
Enchanted boat. *See* Water mills
Enchanters: Pero Pérez and others as, 2, 96, 101–7, 111; as DQ's excuse for failure, 45–46, 64, 67, 138, 153, 167, 169; as author of *Don Quijote*, *Part I*, 136, 170. *See also* Enchantment
Enchantment: as part of quixotic adventure, 47, 114; of Rocinante, 69, 77, 176; of DQ, 75n, 99–102, 103–7, 110, 170. *See also* Dulcinea del Toboso; Enchanters
Eugenio, 61n, 108–9, 113n, 117, 134

Fabla. See Chivalric archaism
Fame, 33, 132, 137, 157, 170. *See also* Chivalric motifs
Fernando, 147n, 187n; frequency of speech, 91; at the inn, 97–98, 100–102, 177
Fierabrás, balm of, 54, 64, 72–73, 198
First sally, 1–2, 37–45, 49–50, 111, 133
Frequency of speech: importance of, 27–28; in part I, 28–32, 72, 91; in part II, 130–31, 137n, 154, 183

Friars, adventure of, 48, 115, 189
Fulling mills, adventure of, 69, 73–77, 93, 114, 115, 146n, 176, 189

Galley slaves, adventure of, 71, 81, 87, 113, 114, 115, 134, 138, 169, 189
Goatherds: audience for DQ's Golden Age speech, 53, 54–56, 92, 138; in Sierra Morena, 82, 84
Golden Age, DQ's speech on, 27n, 54, 56, 78, 98, 161
Grisóstomo: burial of, 2, 54–57, 62, 78, 79, 146, 147n, 161; as a model for DQ's penance, 84; comparative characterization, 84, 92

Haldudo, Juan, 42, 83, 99, 113; comparative characterization, 92
Hatzfeld, Helmut A.: on chivalric motifs, 33, 36; on Sancho, 174n
Helmet. *See* Basin; Mambrino
Housekeeper, 9, 45–46, 169

Imitation: of style of romances of chivalry, 1, 13, 15, 25–26, 30n, 215; during penance in Sierra Morena, 13–15, 82–84
Inauthenticity of DQ as a knight-errant, 53, 56, 64–65, 71, 81, 84, 89–90, 97, 99, 107–8, 117, 143, 146–53, 160, 162, 170, 190. *See also* Chivalric trajectory; Knight-errant; Lies; Role playing

Knight-errant: as a theoretical ideal, 1, 13, 15, 30, 37–39, 45, 53n, 63, 66, 83, 87, 117, 132, 134–35, 155, 170; DQ's summary of typical life of, 71, 85, 154–55n. *See also* Chivalric trajectory; Inauthenticity; Role playing

Lies, 108; by DQ, 56, 62, 63, 65, 70, 81, 117, 158, 204; by Sancho, 79–80, 138; by Pero Pérez, 87; by Sansón Carrasco, 184; by Cide Hamete Benengeli, 195, 197, 198–200, 209
Lion, DQ's encounter with, 121, 142n, 145–46, 167n, 168, 169, 198, 199
López, Alonso, 68, 93, 113. *See also* Dead body

Lorenzo, Aldonza. *See* Dulcinea del Toboso
Luis, Don, 90n, 99, 101n, 102

Madariaga, Salvador de: on reality, 51n; on DQ's chivalric trajectory, 118–20, 125, 139n, 181n; on enchantment of Dulcinea, 138
Mambrino, helmet of, 70, 169, 178. *See also* Basin
Mancing, Howard: on archaism, 16n, 24–25n; on comparative characterization, 91; on the windmill principle, 117; on the enchantment of Dulcinea, 142n, 204n
Mandel, Oscar: on hard and soft critics, 122–23; as a hard critic, 124–25; on society's norms, 191
Marcela: as a pseudoshepherdess, 54–56, 58, 63; DQ's defense of, 56–57, 146; rhetorical speech of, 78
Maritornes, 79, 189n; adventure of, 58n, 59–60, 63–64, 85, 93, 114, 115, 177; ties DQ's hand, 61
Merchants, adventure of, 42–44, 52, 92, 114, 115, 161, 163n, 191
Micomicona, Princess. *See* Dorotea
Miranda, Don Diego de, 145, 168, 169, 202; frequency of speech, 183
Montalvo, Garci Rodríguez de, 22–24
Moreno, Don Antonio: as DQ's host, 4, 55n, 162, 169, 182, 184, 187n, 190; frequency of speech, 183
Morisco (translator of *Don Quijote*), 172–74, 192, 196, 198, 202, 203, 204, 206
Muleteers, adventure of, 41, 115

Nicolás, Maese: Alonso Quijano's friend, 1, 10, 12n, 45, 90, 93, 132, 210, 214; role in part I, 2, 81, 84, 93–96, 103, 111, 117, 138–39, 170; role in part II, 3, 133–35, 137, 143, 156n, 169–70, 182, 187n; frequency of speech, 91; at the inn, 102, 138–39; on the return home, 106–11; represents society's norm, 108, 109–10n, 124, 184–85, 191; comparative characterization, 109, 214
Niece, 9–10, 44, 45, 169, 210–11
Norms of society, 5, 106–8, 109–10n, 124, 185, 191–92

Order of chivalry: cited by DQ, 35, 43, 56, 63, 70, 82, 132, 150; parodied by others, 41, 42. *See also* Chivalric motifs
Orlando Furioso, as model for DQ's penance, 82–84

Pain. *See* Reality
Palomeque, Juan, el Zurdo, 58, 97, 99, 113, 148, 150, 154, 190n; frequency of speech, 91
Panza, Sancho, 48, 54, 56, 57, 58, 59–61n, 62, 67, 70, 94, 96, 142n, 146, 147, 148, 151, 156n, 157–58, 159n, 161, 169, 182, 184n, 189n, 193n, 194, 198n, 205, 213, 215; role in part I, 1–2, 17n, 49–54, 70, 93, 117; role in part II, 3, 130, 135–37, 170; chivalric trajectory, 4, 28, 79–81, 93, 119–21, 129, 179–82, 213–14; as governor, 4, 154, 157–59, 180n, 185n, 187, 199; frequency of speech, 28, 72, 75n, 82, 91, 131, 137n, 154, 160, 174n, 175n; recruited by DQ, 45, 78–79, 85, 90, 133; as Reality Instructor, 47, 48, 49, 51, 53–54, 66, 72, 82, 87, 104–8, 113, 138, 143, 152, 167, 168; blanketing of, 61n, 65–66, 73, 75n, 109, 152; desire to return home, 66, 82, 152; uses archaism, 69, 72, 77, 181n, 188; ties Rocinante's feet, 69, 77, 138, 176; rhetorical speech, 73–78, 104–5, 171–76, 203; at the inn, 81, 100–101, 102, 177; on the return home, 103–12; comparative characterization, 191–92. *See also* Dulcinea del Toboso
Panza, Teresa: conversation with Sancho, 171–76, 185n; frequency of speech, 183
Parody: of romances of chivalry, 20–22, 67n, 116n, 124, 131n; of DQ by others, 57–61, 69, 91–92
Pasamonte, Ginés de: as Maese Pedro, 61n, 147, 148–49, 168; frequency of speech, 91, 183
Pastoral themes, 2, 32, 54–57, 58–59n, 60, 161, 181
Pattern of adventure: chivalric adventure in part I, 2, 46–47, 110, 112–17; pseudoadventures in part II, 3,

137–38, 152–53, 167–70
Pedro, Maese. *See* Pasamonte, Ginés de
Penance: Cardenio's, 82, 84, 92; DQ's, 82–84, 89, 92, 97, 114, 116
Penitents, adventure of, 3, 108, 110–11, 115, 117, 160, 170
Percas de Ponseti, Helena: on Alonso Quijano, 9n; on Rocinante, 58n; on DQ's advice to Sancho, 158n; on Cide Hamete Benengeli, 197
Pérez, Pero, 27n, 75, 78, 87, 174; as Alonso Quijano's friend, 1, 4, 10, 12n, 45–46, 90, 93, 132, 210, 214; role in part I, 2, 4, 81, 84, 93–96, 117, 138–39, 170, 188; role in part II, 3, 133–35, 137, 143, 156n, 169–70, 182, 187n; comparative characterization, 4, 192, 214; on the return home, 75n, 103–11; frequency of speech, 91, 101n, 183; at the inn, 97, 101–2; represents society's norm, 108, 109–10n, 124, 184–85, 191–92
Pérez de Viedma, Ruy, 138, 169; frequency of speech, 91; at the inn, 98, 101; comparative characterization, 98, 102
Pigs episode, 164, 169
Praise of Dulcinea, 36, 132. *See also* Chivalric motifs; Dulcinea del Toboso
Predmore, Richard L.: on Sancho Panza, 89n; on adventures, 112–13n, 167n
Pseudoadventures. *See* Pattern of adventure
Puppet show, Maese Pedro's, 132, 148–50, 168

Quijano, Alonso: life of, 1, 9–13, 117; becomes DQ, 1, 11–13, 170; renounces romances of chivalry, 4, 210–11; forced to become DQ again, 133–37; death of, 210–15
Quixotic adventures. *See* Pattern of adventure

Reality, 12, 117, 124, 136n, 142n, 147, 168, 187n, 188, 191; of pain, 2, 50, 52–54, 71, 97, 110–11; DQ's concessions to, 2, 32, 64, 69–70, 71–72, 81, 84, 90, 117, 119, 170, 209,

215; DQ's transformation of, 39, 41, 47, 48, 59, 66, 70, 98, 113, 138, 148, 150–51, 152, 167, 179, 188, 215; stated in narration, 47, 110, 113, 152; DQ's perception of, 63, 71, 85, 138, 143, 145, 153n, 156, 167, 168n, 169. *See also* Dulcinea del Toboso
Reality Instructor. *See* Panza, Sancho
Rhetoric of chivalry. *See* Chivalric archaism; Chivalric motifs
Riley, Edward C.: on imitation, 13n; on DQ's penance, 83n; on reality, 113n; on Cervantes as editor, 192, 193n; on Cide Hamete Benengeli, 197n
Riquer, Martín de: on archaism, 16, 21, 38n, 131; on dubbing ceremony, 41n; on romances of chivalry, 67n; on windmills, 116n; on chivalric trajectory, 121n; as a hard critic, 124; on Pero Pérez, 135n; on Avellaneda, 189n
Robert, Marthe: on Alonso Quijano, 11n; on imitation, 13, 48n; fails to recognize archaism, 16–17n; ignores DQ's pain, 53n
Rocinante, 42, 43, 46, 49, 64, 143, 151, 169, 189n; parodies DQ, 2, 4, 61; role in part II, 3, 136–37; erotic adventures of, 57–61, 63, 79, 99; humanized, 58, 60–61n, 202; enchanted by Sancho, 69, 77, 138, 176
Rodríguez, Doña, 156, 169; appeals to DQ, 160, 185–86, 190–91, 198; frequency of speech, 183; uses archaism, 188
Role playing; forced on DQ, 4, 170; by DQ, 51, 56, 71, 155–56n; by Sancho, 72, 80; by other characters, 94–95, 105, 183. *See also* Inauthenticity; Knight-errant
Romances of chivalry, 40n, 48, 53, 86n, 87, 136, 145, 159n, 170, 193n, 203n; as inspiration for DQ, 1, 10–11, 15–16, 25–26, 38, 42–45, 59, 70, 75, 85, 104, 133; style of, 18n, 22–26; parodied, 20–21, 124, 131n; read by other characters, 55, 92, 95, 100, 154; cited by Sancho, 181. *See also* Quijano, Alonso
Rosales, Luis: on archaism, 16n, 50;

on Cardenio, 84n; on chivalric trajectory, 121n; on adventures, 168n; on enchantment of Dulcinea, 177n; on duke and duchess, 186n, 187n; on Alonso Quijano, 214–15n

Second sally, 2, 45–48, 50, 93, 111, 170

Sexual matters: in the romances of chivalry, 55–56n, 95; Rocinante, 57–61; DQ, 59–61, 83n; Dorotea, 95

Sheep, adventure of, 66, 85, 93, 97, 113, 115, 150–51, 189

Sierra Morena, 2, 13, 32, 72, 81, 84, 85, 89, 102, 116, 118, 188

Strength, 33, 34, 51, 63, 89, 132, 138. *See also* Chivalric motifs

Third sally, 133, 136–37, 139, 148, 149, 159n, 167, 175, 176, 181, 182, 198

Torrente Ballester, Gonzalo: on DQ's first sally, 45n; on enchanters, 46n; on Sancho Panza, 79n; on Sancho's supposed visit to Dulcinea, 89n; on Cide Hamete Benengeli, 156n; on the enchantment of Dulcinea, 178n

Tosilos, 167n, 168, 169, 186

Trifaldi, Countess, 157, 160, 168, 169, 183, 188, 199

Unamuno, Miguel de: on DQ's chivalric trajectory, 96–97; as a soft critic, 123; on death of Alonso Quijano, 212n; on Sancho Panza, 213n

Varo, Carlos: on role of Sancho, 49n, 51n; on pain, 53n; on humor in part I, 62; on DQ's fight with Eugenio, 110n; on pigs and bulls, 164n; on Alonso Quijano, 212

Vivaldo, 27n, 55–56n, 62, 89, 92, 107, 169

Water mills, adventure of, 116n, 152–53, 163

Windmill principle, 117, 126, 188

Windmills, adventure of, 46–48, 49, 52, 112, 115–17, 122, 153, 189

Wineskins, adventure of, 97, 100, 101, 113, 114, 115, 168

Yanguesans, adventure of, 57, 63, 72, 93, 113, 114, 115, 122, 138, 207n

Zoraida, 98, 138, 169